DATE DUE

MY 9'05			

DEMCO 38-296

INVENTORY CONTROL AND MANAGEMENT

INVENTORY CONTROL AND MANAGEMENT

C. D. J. WATERS
The University of Calgary

JOHN WILEY & SONS
Chichester · New York · Brisbane · Toronto · Singapore

Copyright © 1992 by John Wiley & Sons Ltd,
Baffins Lane. Chichester.

gland

!43) 779777
9777

uly 1997, September 1998, October 1999

:ans,
ge

without the written permission of the publisher.

Other Wiley Editorial Offices

John Wiley & Sons, Inc., 605 Third Avenue,
New York, NY 10158-0012, USA

Jacaranda Wiley Ltd, 33 Park Road, Milton,
Queensland 4064, Australia

John Wiley & Sons (Canada) Ltd, 22 Worcester Road,
Rexdale, Ontario M9W 1L1, Canada

John Wiley & Sons (SEA) Pte Ltd, 37 Jalan Pemimpin #05-04,
Block B, Union Industrial Building, Singapore 129809

Library of Congress Cataloging-in-Publication Data

Waters, C. Donald J
    Inventory control and management / C. Donald J. Waters.
      p. cm.
    Includes bibliographical references and index.
    ISBN 0–471–93081–4 (ppc)
    1. Inventory control.   I. Title
TS160.W38 1992
658.7´87—dc20   91–28942
                                                        CIP

British Library Cataloguing in Publication Data

A catalogue record for this book is available from the British Library

ISBN 0–471–93081–4

Typeset in 10/12pt Times from author's disks by Text Processing Department,
John Wiley & Sons Ltd, Chichester
Printed and bound in Great Britain by Biddles Ltd, Guildford and King's Lynn

To Jack

CONTENTS

PREFACE

INTRODUCTION

Every organisation holds stocks of some kind. As these stocks are expensive and need careful management, a fundamental question is, "Why do organisations hold stocks?". The main answer is they allow for variations and uncertainty in supply and demand: they provide a buffer between suppliers and customers.

As all organisations, from the largest down to the very smallest, hold stocks, problems of inventory control are almost universal. Over the past 70 years or so "scientific inventory control" has developed many approaches for tackling these problems. This book describes the main results of this work.

Holding stocks can be very expensive. A typical manufacturing company holds 20% of its production as stock, and this has annual holding costs of around 25% of value. It is not surprising that organisations have put a considerable amount of effort into minimising these costs, while maintaining the service offered to customers.

AUDIENCE

This book is an introductory text on inventory control. It is self-contained, and develops the subject from basic principles through to higher level material. No previous knowledge of inventory control is assumed, and anyone reading the book should develop understanding of the subject at a reasonable level. It is suitable for several groups of people including:

- students doing a general course in management, business, commerce, or some related field which includes a description of inventory control
- students doing a specialised course in operations management, management science, operational research, production, or some related field
- practising managers who want to learn about inventory control and how it can be applied to their work.

Because it is aimed at a wide audience, the level of mathematics is kept deliberately low. In particular, results are not derived by rigorous proofs, but principles are illustrated by worked examples. The aim is to explain the principles of inventory control without getting bogged down in mathematical manipulation.

CONTENTS

The book is divided into three sections:

- Section I gives a general introduction to inventory control. It describes the purpose of stock, costs involved, aims of stock control and so on.
- Section II looks at independent demand inventory systems. These are widely used approaches which are based on quantitative models and forecast demand.
- Section III looks at dependent demand systems, where demand for materials is found directly from production plans. This area has received a lot of attention recently, especially Just-in-Time systems.

Section I lays the foundations for the rest of the book. It introduces the objectives and methods of inventory control and in particular classifies methods of inventory control into dependent demand and independent demand systems.

Section II considers the more widely used independent demand systems. The first three chapters of this section describe models of inventory systems, while the last two chapters describe some of the information needed to support these models. In particular:

- Chapter 2 describes the economic order quantity analysis
- Chapter 3 describes other models with deterministic demand
- Chapter 4 describes models with probabilistic demand
- Chapter 5 looks at ways of forecasting demand
- Chapter 6 looks at other information needed by these models

Section III describes dependent demand inventory systems. The first two chapters describe specific methods, while the last chapter describes the planning needed to support these methods. In particular:

- Chapter 7 describes Material Requirements Planning
- Chapter 8 describes Just-in-Time systems
- Chapter 9 looks at methods of planning and scheduling.

The emphasis of the material is on methods of inventory control which have proved useful in practice. These are, however, based on sound theoretical principles, so the book draws a balance between theory and practice.

Each chapter starts with a synopsis of the material to be covered and a list of specific aims. The body of the chapter contains frequent summaries of important points and self-assessment questions to check understanding. At the end of each chapter is a list of the main material covered, further problems, and references for further reading. Solutions to the self-assessment questions are given in Appendix II at the back of the book.

SECTION I
INTRODUCTION

This book is divided into three sections. This, the first section, gives an introduction to inventories and their control. It describes why stocks are held, how they are controlled, what the costs are, how demand is forecast, how to cope with uncertainty, and so on.

Historically there have been many views of stocks, ranging from a measure of wealth which should be maximised, to an expensive waste of resources which should be eliminated. In recent years the predominant view has stocks as an expensive but necessary part of business. This theme is developed in the first section of this book. In particular, we suggest that stocks are kept to allow for variations and uncertainty in supply and demand. Then a primary aim of inventory control is to ensure that this allowance is made at minimum cost.

Inventory control is needed in every organisation. A typical manufacturing company holds 20% of its production as stock, and this has annual holding costs of around 25% of value. All organisations, not just manufacturers, hold stocks of some kind and these represent a major investment which should be managed efficiently. If stocks are not controlled properly the costs can become excessive and reduce an organisation's ability to compete. Efficient inventory control then becomes a real factor in an organisation's long-term survival.

There are basically two approaches to inventory control:

- independent demand systems, which use quantitative models to relate forecast demand, order size and costs.
- dependent demand systems, which use production plans directly to calculate stock requirements.

Section II of the book, comprising Chapters 2 to 6, looks at independent demand inventory systems. Section III, comprising Chapters 7 to 9, describes dependent demand inventory systems.

Individual organisations should try to minimise their own inventory costs. Stock levels are, however, very sensitive to changing conditions, and the resulting aggregate stock can give important information about the economy as a whole. In particular, it can be used to judge economic confidence and developments in the business cycle at a national level.

1
BACKGROUND TO INVENTORY CONTROL

SYNOPSIS

This chapter introduces the subject of inventory control. It starts by defining some of the terms used, and then asks the basic question, "Why are stocks held?". A number of reasons can be suggested, but the most important one is to provide a buffer between variable and uncertain supply and demand. A frequent aim of inventory control is to provide this buffer at minimum cost.

Inventory control often relies on a balance between conflicting costs. The cost of holding enough stock to give a specified level of customer service, for example, can be balanced by the cost of running out of stock and losing sales. The point at which these balances occur determines the answers to fundamental questions about what should be kept in stock, when should orders be placed, how much should be ordered, and so on.

Inventory control systems can be classified in a number of ways, but a particularly useful one differentiates:

- dependent demand systems, where demand for an item is generally forecast from historic figures;
- independent demand systems, where demand is found directly from production plans.

Both of these have associated costs which can be high.

Throughout most of this century the usual aim of inventory control has been to minimise the total costs of holding stock. One result of this has been a trend for organisations to hold smaller stocks. This trend can be seen on a national scale with aggregate stocks becoming smaller in relation to Gross National Product. Superimposed on this trend are short-term fluctuations which are responses to changing economic conditions. In particular, stock levels tend to decline during periods of recession and increase during periods of economic growth. In the last few years some organisations have adopted inventory control systems which aim at eliminating, or at least minimising, stocks. Such systems are explored in more detail in later chapters.

OBJECTIVES

After reading this chapter and completing the exercises you should be able to:

- define some terms associated with inventory control
- appreciate the reasons for holding stock
- list the fundamental questions of inventory control
- outline the differences between dependent and independent demand inventory systems
- list the costs associated with stock holdings
- outline some differing views of stocks
- describe the changing pattern of stocks at a national level
- discuss the way stocks change during business cycles

1.1   INTRODUCTION

1.1.1   Definition of Inventory Terms

We should start our discussion of inventory control by defining some of the terms used. We have already mentioned "stock" and "inventory", so we should be clear what these mean.

- *Stock* consists of all the goods and materials stored by an organisation. It is a supply of items which is kept for future use.
- *Inventory* is a list of the items held in stock.

An immediate problem here is that Americans use "inventory" to mean both the list of items in stock, and the stock itself. In recent years this convention has become more common and the terms are becoming increasingly interchangeable. We will stick to the formal definitions given above. This still allows us to use both "inventory control" and "stock control" to describe the means of controlling stocks. Another problem is that "stock" is used in the sense of "stocks and shares" to describe the capital raised by a company. Normally these ambiguities do not cause problems, but sometimes we must be careful to use the correct terms.

"Inventory control", or "stock control", consists of all the activities and procedures used to ensure the right amount of each item is held in stock.

While we are discussing definitions we should also make a clear distinction between "item" and "unit".

- *An item* is a single type of product which is kept in stock: it is one entry in the inventory.
- *A unit* is the standard size or quantity of a stock item.

When a shop stocks 500-gram tins of beans, the item is "500-gram tins of beans", and each tin of beans is a unit. Similarly, pint bottles of milk are an item on a shop's inventory, and each bottle is a unit; £1 stamps are an item in a post office, and each stamp is a unit; unleaded petrol is an item in a filling station, and each litre is a unit; portland cement is an item for a builders' merchant, and every sack of cement is a unit; and so on. Every product which has a unique stock number is an item. Some people use other terms, and one common alternative is SKU (stock keeping unit) instead of item.

Now we have defined the basic terms of inventory control, we can see how these are related to actual operations. Typically, stocks are held at an intermediate point between suppliers and customers. Then the usual operations follow a cycle which comprises:

- delivery of an item from a supplier
- this delivery is a relatively large quantity, so it is broken down into smaller units
- these units are kept in stock until needed
- over time customers submit demands for the item
- units are removed from stock to meet these demands
- at some appropriate time another delivery of the item is ordered

As we are describing general principles here, the details of items or storage arrangements are not important. Sometimes, however, it is easier to visualise a specific operation, so we might imagine the stocks in a supermarket. Here, lorries make relatively infrequent large deliveries. Boxes in which goods are delivered are opened in the supermarket, and individual units are put on storage shelves. These units are removed in small quantities to meet customer demand. The lorries replenish stocks, while the customers create demand which is met by depleting stock, as shown in Figure 1.1.

It is important to realise that every organisation holds stocks of some kind. Manufacturers hold stocks of raw materials, warehouses stock finished goods, offices have stationery stores, banks have reserves of money, households have stocks of food, and so on. Many organisations are faced by similar problems of inventory control, so when we describe one specific type of organisation this is usually done to illustrate a general theme. This is particularly relevant when we refer to a "product" or something having been "produced". A product can be any type of goods or service and does not refer exclusively to manufactured goods.

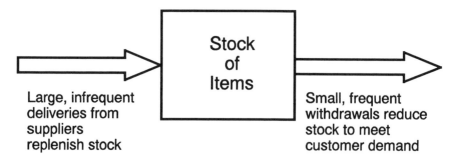

Figure 1.1 Function of stock

Similarly, when we talk about a "customer" we mean anyone or anything which is creating a demand to be met by removing units from stock. A "supplier" is anyone or anything which replenishes or adds to stock.

In Summary

Stocks of different kinds are held in every organisation. They form a buffer between suppliers and customers, and are replenished by deliveries from suppliers and reduced to meet demands from customers. The different items held in stock are listed on an inventory.

1.1.2   Reasons for Holding Stock

Every organisation holds stock of some kind. These stocks will clearly have associated costs to cover tied-up capital, warehouse operations, deterioration, and so on. An obvious question, then, is, "Why do organisations hold stock?". There are several answers to this, but the dominant one is, "To allow a buffer between supply and demand".

We can demonstrate this by considering the stock of bread at a bakery. If the bakery knew exactly when demands would occur, they could bake bread exactly as it is needed. This would eliminate stock, and have the advantages that:

- every customer would have fresh bread
- no bread would go stale and be wasted

In practice, however, bakers do not know exactly when customers will demand bread, so they keep a stock to allow for the uncertainty. There is another important factor in this example. The most efficient way of producing bread is to bake an oven-full at a time. Most customers only want a small quantity, so there is a mismatch between the supply rate and the demand rate.

Similar situations arise in many different circumstances. Consider, for example, two work stations in an assembly line. If the output from the first work station is transferred immediately it is finished to start work on the second work station, there are no stocks of work in progress. If, however, there is any delay before starting on the second, or if several units are transferred between work stations at the same time, there are effectively stocks of work in progress.

The main purpose of stocks, then, is to act as a buffer between supply and demand. They allow operations to continue smoothly when the supply rate does not exactly match the demand rate, and they allow a buffer against uncertainty in demand. We could also argue that there is inevitably some uncertainty in supply caused by delays to delivery vehicles, breakdown of equipment, disruptions to supplier's production, rejections of poor quality materials, and so on. Thus, stocks give a buffer between variable and uncertain supply, and variable and uncertain demand (see Figure 1.2).

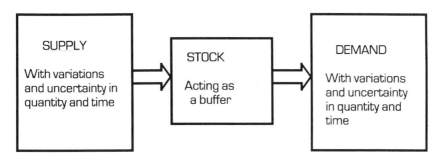

Figure 1.2 Stock as a buffer between uncertain and variable supply and demand

A fuller list of reasons for holding stock includes:

- to act as a buffer between different operations (i.e. to "decouple" operations")
- to allow for mismatches between supply and demand rates
- to allow for demands which are larger than expected, or at unexpected times
- to allow for deliveries which are delayed or too small
- to avoid delays in passing products to customers
- to take advantage of price discounts on large orders
- to buy items when the price is low and expected to rise
- to buy items which are going out of production or are difficult to find
- to make full loads and reduce transport costs
- to provide cover for emergencies
- to maintain stable levels of operation
- and so on

At first sight, one option for eliminating stocks of finished goods would be to guarantee deliveries within a specified time. This policy works if production lead times are short (so that products can be made to order) or someone else is prepared to hold stocks (perhaps a manufacturer, wholesaler, importer or main distributor). This approach can reduce stock holding costs, but the service, measured by delivery time, is inevitably reduced. The implication is that a balance is needed between service offered and costs of stock holding.

In Summary

The main purpose of stocks is to act as a buffer between supply and demand. Stocks allow smooth operations to continue through variations and uncertainty in supply and demand.

1.1.3 Classification of Stocks

Just about everything is held as stock somewhere, whether it is raw materials in a factory, finished goods in a shop or tins of baked beans in a pantry. One useful classification of stocks (see Figure 1.3) has:

- raw materials
- work in progress
- finished goods

This is a fairly arbitrary classification, as one organisation's finished goods is another organisation's raw materials. Some organisations (notably retailers and wholesalers) have stocks of finished goods only, while others (manufacturers, say) have all three types. On a national scale, around 30% of stocks are raw materials, 40% work in progress and 30% finished goods.

Some stock items do not fall easily into these categories, and two additional types can be defined as:

- spare parts (for machinery, equipment, etc.)
- consumables (oil, paper, etc.)

A less widely used classification of stock describes its overall purpose.

- *Cycle stocks* are the normal stocks formed by products arriving in large regular orders to meet smaller, more frequent customer demand.
- *Safety stocks* are a back-up supply of products which are held for use in an emergency.
- *Seasonal stocks* are the stocks which are held to maintain stable operations through seasonal variations in demand.
- *Pipeline stocks* are the products which are currently being moved from one location to another.
- *Other stock* consists of all products which are held for any other reason.

There are many valid reasons for organisations to hold stocks. Nonetheless, stocks form a substantial investment (as we shall see later in the chapter). Some form of control is needed to ensure this investment remains at an acceptable level, and methods for this are described in the following section.

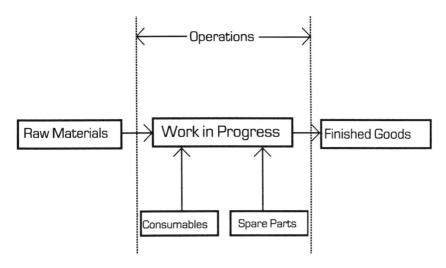

Figure 1.3 A classification of stocks

In Summary

Stocks can be classified in a number of ways, with the most useful having raw materials, work in progress, finished goods, spare parts and consumables.

SELF-ASSESSMENT QUESTIONS

1.1 What is the difference between stock and inventory?
1.2 If a stock item is *"Everyperson's Encyclopaedia"*, what is a unit?
1.3 What is the main reason for holding stock?
1.4 How can stock holdings be classified?

1.2   METHODS OF INVENTORY CONTROL

1.2.1   Background

Before we look in detail at methods of inventory control we should discuss what this control is trying to achieve. Essentially it is trying to make stock holdings as efficient as possible, but there are several ways in which this efficiency can be judged. Common measures concern the amount of stock held, the cost of holding this, how many times there are shortages when demand cannot be met, how frequently stock is turned over, and so on.

Perhaps the most common measure of performance describes the service level given to customers. The service level for an item is generally defined as the proportion of customer demand which is met from stock, and this depends directly on the amount of stock held. If small stocks of the item are kept, they will be insufficient to meet all demand and there will be shortages. Conversely, if high stocks are held there is less chance of a shortage, but stock holding costs are higher. The most common aim of inventory control is to achieve some specified customer service at minimum cost. Then a warehouse, for example, might have an objective of meeting 95% of demand at minimum cost.

Even when an organisation has clearly defined objectives for its inventory control system, there are a number of requirements which must be met before these can be achieved. These include:

- a desire to minimise costs associated with stock holding or achieve some other measurable objective
- the availability of models to identify optimal stock policies, and people who know how to use these models
- availability of accurate data for the models, which is available in time for the results to be implemented
- ability to control stocks to achieve the levels identified as optimal
- knowledge of environmental influences

In recent years the desire to minimise stock holding costs has become almost universal, as this is recognised as a key element in maintaining competitiveness. Appropriate models are also widely available and few organisations of any size will be unaware of them. The next two requirements have been more elusive. Until the late 1960s inventory plans were difficult to implement because of problems in collecting and analysing data. The difficulty was that stock control was done manually using complex systems of cards and hand-written records. These made it almost impossible to collect enough accurate data in time to do anything with it. This problem was solved with the introduction of computers in the 1960s.

Computers allowed information to be rapidly collected, processed and distributed. Decisions could now be made on the basis of accurate forecasts of demand, costs, supplier information, current stock levels, and so on. Later developments in computer systems allowed inventory control to move from batch processing in the 1960s, to on-line and interactive systems in the 1970s. By the 1980s separate business systems were integrated so that the control of inventories could be almost completely automated. When the efficiency of these systems is considered, it is not surprising that surveys suggest over 90% of industrial stocks are computerised.

In Summary

A frequent aim of inventory control is to achieve a specified customer service level at minimum cost. This control can only be achieved when a number of requirements are met, and this generally means that computers must be used.

1.2.2 Basic Questions of Inventory Control

At first sight inventory control systems seem rather complicated. There are, however, only a few basic questions to answer and the most important of these are:

- What items should be stocked?
- When should an order be placed?
- How much should be ordered?

Some aspects of these questions are discussed below.

What Items Should be Stocked?

Holding stock is expensive so controls are needed to ensure that stock levels remain as low as possible. This means:

- stocks of existing items are kept at reasonable levels
- no unnecessary items are added to the inventory
- all items which are no longer used are removed from the inventory

Unless tightly controlled, there is a tendency for stock holdings to drift upwards. In organisations which are not particularly short of money or storage space it is common to see stock levels rising quite rapidly. This is partly because stocks of existing items are allowed to rise, based on the argument "we are succeeding because we give good customer service which needs high stocks". At the same time new stock items are being continuously introduced. As a company's operations evolve, its requirements for stock items change, and new items are introduced to replace older ones which are no longer needed.

Unfortunately, this picture of replacing old items by new ones is somewhat idealised. New stock items are often introduced without much planning, while old items are simply left in stock in case they are needed again. This is particularly common with inventories of spare parts. When a new machine is bought to replace an older one the necessary spare parts are added to stock, but nobody remembers to remove the spares for the replaced machine. These remain in stock until someone notices them.

As more items are added, the inventory grows. Eventually this causes enough concern for stock levels to be reviewed, perhaps when supplies of space or money become scarcer. Unfortunately, these reviews often call for rapid stock reductions, and they might typically give the instruction "stock holdings must be reduced by 10%". The easiest way of achieving this is by not replacing items when they are issued. Consequently, fast-moving items which are used frequently have their stock levels reduced, while slow-moving items which are seldom, if ever, used are left on the shelves at their original levels.

This situation should never occur, as stocks should be controlled using rational policies to relate holdings to demand. Similarly, analyses should be done, before an item is added to the inventory, to compare the costs and benefits of holding it to those of not holding it. Checks should also be made on usage of items already in stock, and if it is cheaper to discontinue stocking them they should be removed as quickly as possible. Items which have no forecast demand should also be removed from stock, and those which have had no demand over some period (typically a few months) should be carefully reviewed.

When Should an Order be Placed?

There are three different approaches to this question. The first is a periodic review system, which places orders at regular intervals of time. Any variation in demand is then allowed for by changing the order size. This system is often used in supermarkets, where stocks are reviewed at the end of a day and any units sold are replaced.

The second system is a fixed order quantity system. In this the stocks are monitored, and when they decline to a specified level an order of fixed size is placed. Any variation in demand is allowed for by changing the time between orders.

The third system looks more directly at the demand and orders enough stock to meet known demand. Thus the time and quantity ordered depend directly on demand.

Whichever system is used, the question of when an order should be placed depends on a number of factors, including:

- details of the inventory control system used
- type of item (materials, finished goods, and so on)
- type of demand (high or low, constant or erratic, known exactly or estimated)
- value of the item and associated holding costs
- cost of placing an order
- lead time between placing an order and receiving it
- supplier (location, reliability, etc.)
- a range of other possible factors

Variations in stock levels over time using these three approaches are illustrated in Figure 1.4.

How Much Should be Ordered?

Every time an order is placed there are associated costs for administration, delivery, and so on. If large, infrequent orders are placed, the costs of ordering and delivery are kept low, but stock levels and average inventory value are high. If small frequent orders are placed, costs of ordering and delivery are high, but average stock level

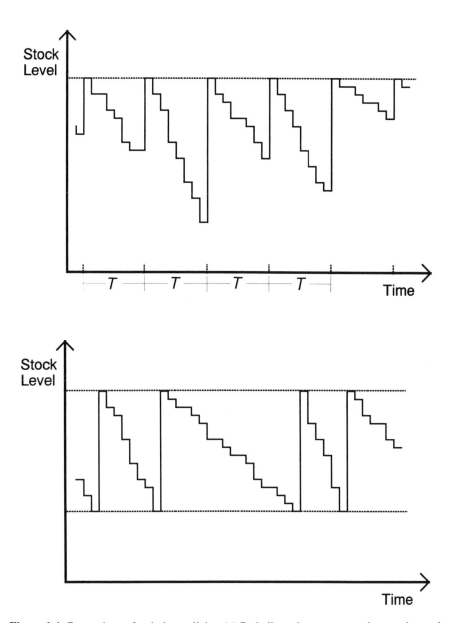

Figure 1.4 Comparison of ordering policies. (a) Periodic review system replaces units used in each period. (b) Fixed order quantity system varies the timing of orders

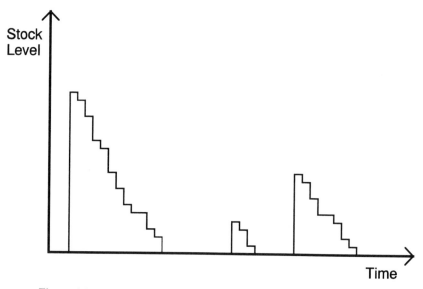

Figure 1.4 (continued) (c) Ordering enough to meet known demand

is low (see Figure 1.5). Several analyses look at these two extremes and find a compromise which minimises the overall total cost. Details of such calculations are described in Chapter 2, but we could suggest intuitively that the best order quantity would depend on:

- demand pattern
- price of the item, including discounts for larger orders, impending price rises, etc.
- cost of placing and receiving an order
- cost of holding stock
- cost of shortages
- delivery rates
- and so on

Other Questions

We have discussed three fundamental questions of inventory control, but it may seem that we have omitted several others such as:

- What should average stock levels be?
- How much will be invested in stock?
- What are the annual costs?
- What service level is being offered?
- How often will there be shortages?

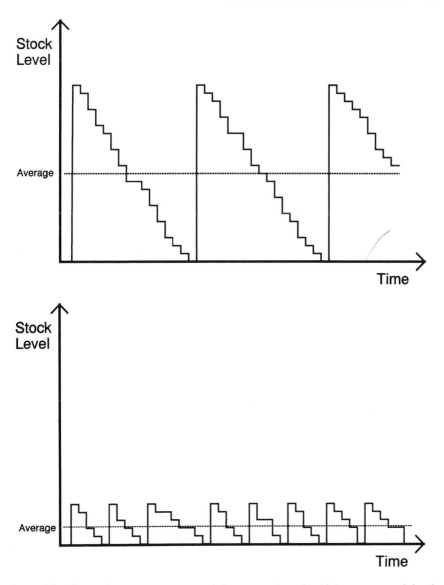

Figure 1.5 Effects of order size. (a) Large infrequent orders give high average stock level. (b) Small, frequent orders give low average stock level

In practice the answers to these questions come from the three fundamental questions above. Once a decision is made about the frequency and amount ordered, average stock levels and hence costs, service level and likelihood of shortage are automatically set. We could, of course, tackle the questions from another viewpoint and ask about an optimal investment in stock, which would then set the time and quantity of orders. This circular argument reinforces the principle that there are only a few variables which need to be calculated and then answers are automatically provided for a range of other questions.

In Summary

There are three fundamental questions in stock control. These ask about the items to stock, the timing of orders and the quantities ordered. Answers to these questions fix a range of other values.

SELF-ASSESSMENT QUESTIONS

1.5 What is the most common aim of inventory control?
1.6 Why has inventory control become more effective in recent years?
1.7 What are the most important questions to answer in inventory control?
1.8 What methods are used for timing orders?
1.9 Why is the average stock level not included as a fundamental question in inventory control?

1.2.3   Approaches to Inventory Control

In the last section we asked some fundamental questions of inventory control, and now we can look at different ways of answering these. There are two fundamentally different approaches which are based on the methods of assessing demand. We will call these "independent demand" and "dependent demand" systems (see Figure 1.6).

Independent Demand Systems

These assume that the demand for an item is independent of the demand for any other item. Then the aggregate demand for an item is made up of many independent demands from separate customers. In these circumstances the only reasonable approach to forecasting aggregate future demand is to project historic trends. Inventory control is then based on quantitative models which relate demand, costs and other variables, to find optimal values for order quantities, timing of orders, and so on.

Independent demand models can use either fixed order quantities or periodic reviews.

- Fixed order quantity systems place an order of fixed size whenever stock falls to a certain level. A central heating plant, for example, may order 25 000 litres of oil whenever the amount in the tank falls to 2500 litres. Such systems need continuous monitoring of stock levels and are better suited to low, irregular demand for relatively expensive items.
- Periodic review systems place orders of varying size at regular intervals to raise the stock level to a specified value. Supermarket shelves, for example,

may be refilled every evening to replace whatever was sold during the day. The operating cost of this system is lower and it is better suited to high, regular demand of low-value items.

Independent demand inventory systems are described in Section II of this book.

In practice, the supply and demand for different items is often related: fish is often sold with chips, 250-gram and 500-gram tins of beans are delivered at the same, demand for both domestic electricity and gas are linked through the weather, demand for all components of a product depend on the final demand for the product, and so on. In these situations, dependent demand systems can have advantages.

Dependent Demand System

These assume the demand for an item is directly related to the demand for other items. This is particularly clear when the demand for materials is related to the demand for finished products. Thus, in a car assembly plant the demand for doors and wheels are both directly related to the demand for finished cars.

Dependent demand systems generally use production plans to forecast demand for each item and then order enough units to satisfy this known demand. These methods are formalised into approaches such as "material requirements planning" and "just-in-time" which are described in Section III of this book.

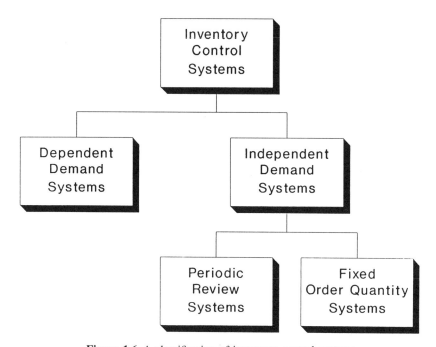

Figure 1.6 A classification of inventory control systems

Dependent demand and independent demand systems work best in different circumstances. Dependent demand systems are most useful for controlling the stocks of materials needed to support manufacturing. Unfortunately, such systems can be difficult to administer, and at present they have only proved beneficial in a narrow range of organisations. This means that most stocks are controlled by independent demand systems. In principle, though, we could suggest that:

- independent demand systems are most suited to stocks of finished goods and spare parts
- dependent demand systems are more suited to raw materials and work in progress

In Summary

Independent demand inventory systems assume demand for each item is independent. They use quantitative models and forecasts of demand to define optimal order quantities and times. Dependent demand inventory systems assume demand for an item depends on known demand for other items. Then the supply is matched closely to actual demand.

1.2.4   Costs of Carrying Stock

All stock holdings incur costs. These typically amount to 25% of value held a year, but most organisations view this as a necessary overhead which must be carried to ensure its continued smooth functioning. This gives a general view of stocks as expensive but unavoidable. It is not surprising, though, that organisations are keen to find ways of minimising their stock holding costs.

In some circumstances minimising stock holding costs is analogous to minimising stocks. Usually, however, this is not the case. Low stocks lead to shortages which can have very high costs, and overall costs could be reduced by increasing the amount of stock and reducing the number of shortages. Generally, stock holding costs are determined by a number of factors and an appropriate objective is to minimise total costs rather than total stock. To examine this objective more thoroughly we need to describe some details of the costs involved.

The usual classification of stock holding costs has:

- unit cost
- reorder cost
- holding cost
- shortage cost

These are discussed in more detail below.

Unit Cost

This is the price charged by suppliers for one unit of the item, or the cost to the organisation of acquiring one unit. In general it is fairly easy to find values for the unit cost by looking at quotations or recent invoices from suppliers. Sometimes this is more difficult if there are several suppliers offering alternative products or giving different purchasing conditions. If the company makes the item itself it may be difficult to set a reliable production cost or to calculate a valid transfer price.

Reorder Cost

This is the cost of placing a repeat order for the item and might include allowances for drawing up an order (with checking, getting authorisation, clearance, distribution and filing), computer time, correspondence and telephone costs, receiving (with unloading, checking and testing), supervision, use of equipment and follow-up. Sometimes costs such as quality control, transport, delivery, sorting and movement of received goods are included in the reorder cost.

The reorder cost should be the cost of repeat orders and not the cost of first-time purchases, which might have additional allowances for finding and checking suitable suppliers, assessing reliability and quality, requesting quotations, negotiations with alternative suppliers, and so on. In practice, the best estimate for a reorder cost might be found by dividing the total annual cost of the purchasing department (plus any other relevant costs) by the number of orders sent out.

A special case of the reorder cost occurs when an item is made within the company. Then the reorder cost is a batch setup cost which might include production documentation costs, production lost while resetting machines, idle time for operators, material spoilt in test runs, slowed production during familiarisation, time for specialist tool setters, and so on.

Holding Cost

This is the cost of holding one unit of an item in stock for one period of time. As the usual period for calculating stock costs is a year, a holding cost might be expressed as, say, £10 a unit a year.

The most obvious cost of holding stock is money tied up which either is borrowed (in which case interest is paid) or could be put to other use (in which case there are opportunity costs). Other holding costs are due to storage space (supplying a warehouse, rent, rates, heat, light, etc.), loss (due to damage, pilferage and obsolescence), handling (including all movement, special packaging, refrigeration, putting on pallets, etc.), administration (stock checks, computer updates, etc.) and insurance.

It is difficult to suggest typical annual values for these, but one view has percentages of unit cost, as:

	% of unit cost
cost of money	10–20
storage space	2-5
loss	4-6
handling	1-2
administration	1-2
insurance	1–5
Total	19-40

Shortage Cost

If there is demand for an item for which stocks have been exhausted and if replenishment takes a finite time, then there is a shortage which usually has some associated cost. In the simplest case a retailer might lose direct profit from a sale which is not made. The effects of shortages are usually wider than this and include allowances for loss of goodwill, loss of future sales, loss of reputation, and so on. Shortages of parts for a production process might cause considerable disruption and force rescheduling of production, retiming of maintenance period, laying-off of employees, and so on. Also included in shortage costs might be allowances for positive action to counteract the shortage, perhaps sending out emergency orders, paying for special deliveries, using alternative and more expensive suppliers or storing partly finished goods.

Unfortunately, many of these shortage costs are difficult to evaluate and are often little more than informed guesses. Costs of lost future sales, for example, might be estimated, but there is no reliable procedure for getting exact figures. It is often suggested that shortage costs are inherently inaccurate and misleading, and they should only be used with caution.

Despite the difficulty of evaluation, there is general agreement that shortage costs are often high. Then we can look again at the purpose of stocks and rephrase our earlier statement by saying, "the cost of shortages can be very high and to avoid them organisations are willing to incur the relatively lower costs of carrying stock".

Shortages can be avoided if the lead time (between placing an order and getting the units in stock and ready for use) is short. Often, however, the lead time is long, so planning must be done some time in advance. The lead time occurs because of:

- time for order preparation. When a decision is made to place an order, there is some delay before the order is ready to send to a supplier. With small items this can be short and involve a few administrative details. Larger orders need time for preparing invitations to tender, design of items, arranging finance, and so on.
- time to pass order to supplier. This is the total time needed to get the order from an organisation to a supplier. With orders placed by telephone, FAX or

computer this is negligible, but there may be several days' delay if the post is used.

- time at supplier. This is the time needed for a supplier to process the order and prepare it. This is highly variable and can be very short for small items already in stock, or very long, for items which have to be specially designed and then made.
- time to pass goods back from supplier. This is the time needed to deliver items. It is usually a few days for local suppliers, but can be several weeks for an international shipment or months for complex deliveries.
- time to process delivery. This is the time taken between receiving the delivery and getting the goods available in the stock. This might include time for checking, inspection, recording, cataloguing, movement, and so on.

In Summary

Holding stocks is expensive, with typical costs amounting to 25% of unit cost a year. The costs of holding stock can be classified as unit, reorder, holding or shortage.

1.2.5   Stock Turnover

A widely used measure of inventory performance is stock turnover. This is defined as the ratio of the cost of units sold to average stock. Here the cost of units sold is the total cost of buying or acquiring the units which were later sold to customers.

$$\text{stock turnover} = \frac{\text{cost of annual sales}}{\text{average value of stocks}}$$

This ratio varies considerably between industries. Car assembly plants and oil refineries achieve turnovers of around 50, so that most units are kept in stock for about a week. This level of turnover is a result of efficient operations, and most organisations work with far lower levels. Department stores and electrical suppliers, for example, will generally have stock turnovers below 5.

If the stock turnover can be increased without affecting customer service the costs to an organisation will decrease. Thus, turnover is a useful measure of performance. Unfortunately, differences in operations mean that comparisons cannot be made between different industries, but within any particular industry an organisation can make direct comparisons with its competitors. If its turnover is below the industry norm either there must be a good reason, or else their performance should be improved.

In Summary

Stock turnover is defined as the ratio:

$$\frac{\text{cost of goods sold}}{\text{stocks held}}$$

Higher values of this ratio indicate better organisational performance.

Worked Example 1.1

A wholesaler buys an item for £10 a unit and sells it for £15 a unit. Annual sales of the item are around 1000 units, with average stocks of 150 units. Each unit held in stock costs approximately 25% of cost a year.

(a) Describe the stock holdings.
(b) If average stocks of the item could be reduced to 100 units without affecting customer service, what would be the benefits?

Solution

(a) A number of measures can be calculated for the stock.
   - Stock turnover is:

$$\frac{\text{cost of goods sold}}{\text{value of average stock}} = \frac{1000 * 10}{150 * 10} = 6.67$$

   - Annual gross profit on the item is:

$$\text{sales} * (\text{selling price} - \text{unit cost}) = 1000 * (15 - 10)$$
$$= £5000 \text{ a year}$$

   - Average investment in stock is:

$$\text{number of units held} * \text{unit cost} = 150 * 10 = £1500$$

   - Annual stock holding cost is:

$$\text{average number of units in stock} * \text{cost of holding each unit}$$
$$= 150 * 0.25 * 10 = £375 \text{ a year}$$

   - Stock holding cost per unit sold is:

$$\frac{\text{stock holding cost}}{\text{number of units sold}} = \frac{375}{1000} = £0.38$$

(b) If the average stock could be reduced to 100 units without affecting customer service, the wholesaler would be operating more efficiently. In particular:

- stock turnover = $(1000 * 10)/(100 * 10) = 10$
- average investment in stock = $100 * 10 = £1000$
- annual stock holding cost = $100 * 0.25 * 10 = £250$
- stock holding cost per unit sold = $250/1000 = £0.25$
- additional profit = $375 - 250 = £125$ a year

SELF-ASSESSMENT QUESTIONS

1.10 How is demand for an item found in an independent demand inventory system?

1.11 List four types of cost associated with stock holdings.

1.12 Very roughly, what is the cost of storing a freezer full of food in a kitchen?

1.13 What is the largest cause of lead times?

1.14 Should organisations aim for a high stock turnover or a low one?

1.3   ALTERNATIVE VIEWS OF STOCKS

1.3.1   Historic Views

We suggested earlier that inventory control often tries to achieve a specified service level at minimum cost. This objective is relatively recent and has only developed properly since the 1920s. It is really a compromise between two extreme views. For most of history, stocks have been considered measures of wealth and were, therefore, beneficial. Within the past few years the opposite view has grown and many organisations now view stocks as a waste which should be eliminated.

Throughout most of history stock holdings have been considered beneficial: amassing physical goods at times when they were not needed has been a sign of personal or collective wealth. Informal approaches to inventory control began when stocks of food were kept to cover periods of famine: those who held large stocks had the highest chance of survival. When inventories became associated with physical goods, the aim was still to maximise holdings which were seen as a measure of personal wealth. A well known quotation from Pappillon (1677) suggests, "The stock of riches of a kingdom doth not only consist of our money, but also in our commodities and ships for trade and magazines furnished with all necessary material".

The prevailing climate in these times was to collect as much stock as possible. This was sensible in times when production and distribution of any commodity was uncertain. During the 19th century, however, production and distribution became more organised and, provided a stable monetary system was in place, third parties could hold stocks and moderate the tensions between variable supply and demand.

By the turn of the 20th century supplies of goods to industrialised countries could be more or less guaranteed. This removed the need to buy goods when they were available rather than when they were needed and the resulting stability allowed a change of view. This suggested that stock holdings were expensive and needed formal planning. Several methods were developed to help with this planning, and they had the common goal of minimising costs rather than minimising stocks. Sometimes this difference was not fully appreciated. During one period in the 1920s there were widespread difficulties when companies reduced stocks to levels which made it impossible to operate effectively.

"Scientific Inventory Control" has developed since the 1920s and is based on the observation that inventories can be controlled by setting "optimal" stock levels. There are, of course, different opinions about what "optimal" levels are. For some time, it was felt that a "fixed accelerator" might be used to define an optimal stock level as some fixed proportion of sales (see, for example, Abramovitz (1950)). This approach proved ineffective and a "flexible accelerator" was suggested to allow for differences between aims and actualities, time delays, and so on (see Lovell (1961, 1964). More recently, increasingly sophisticated models and mathematical analyses have suggested flexible approaches which allow stock levels to be based on individual circumstances. These include "just-in-time" systems which have very low stocks.

This brief review has shown how opinions on stocks have changed over time. Until the late 19th century stocks were generally maximised. For most of this century inventory control has aimed at minimising costs by achieving some optimal stock level. Unfortunately, this has not always been easy. Considerable efforts have been put into calculating or defining optimal stock levels, but it is only recently that computerised control procedures have given a reasonable chance of achieving them. Most recently there have been moves towards just-in-time systems which reduce stock to very low levels.

In Summary

For most of history stocks have been beneficial and have been maximised. For most of this century, the object has changed to minimising the total cost of holding stock. More recently, some developments have aimed at working with very low stocks.

1.3.2 Changing Patterns of Stock Holding

Whenever there is uncertainty in operations or lack of control, organisations will tend to be cautious and hold more stock than necessary. Only when an effective control mechanism is in place can they reduce stocks and remove the extra cushion of safety. We could hypothesise, then, that from the 1920s to the 1960s inventory control procedures would steadily improve and there would be a consistent reduction in stocks. By the 1960s, when computer systems became widely available, holdings would decline more quickly. Perhaps, there would be further reductions in the 1980s with the growth of just-in-time systems and other improved control systems.

It is difficult to discuss such changes in absolute terms, but we can relate aggregate national stock holdings to the Gross National Product. Then, we would expect to see inventory levels declining as a proportion of GNP. Figure 1.7 shows the ratio of total stock holdings to GNP for the past 40 years. Reliable figures before this are difficult to obtain and would be distorted by the world wars and the severe economic recession between.

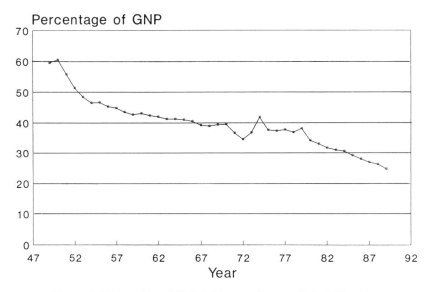

Figure 1.7 Proportion of GNP held as stock in the United Kingdom

Figure 1.7 supports our hypothesis that the amount of stock held has been declining. At the end of the 1940s and into the early 1950s there was a rapid decline in stocks which can be attributed to the economy returning to normal after the Second World War.

From the early 1950s to the early 1970s there was a further steady decline of the type suggested. Although the introduction of computers had a profound effect on inventories, the consequences were felt over many years rather than as a short burst of change. In the early 1970s there was a sudden pattern change, which was caused by the rapid increase in oil prices and the economic disruption which followed. Then the fall in stocks continued to the end of the 1970s, but the rate of decline seems to have accelerated in the 1980s.

In Summary

The total amount of stock held nationally shows a long-term decline as a proportion of Gross National Product. This is generally caused by better control, but there are some unexpected effects (such as recession in the early 1970s).

1.3.3   Effects of the Business Cycle

Stock holdings are clearly following underlying trends, but superimposed on these are shorter-term fluctuations. Many of these are caused by wider economic influences over which individual organisations have no control. The sudden increase in oil costs in 1973 had an obvious effect on manufacturers and, no matter how good their inventory policies were, they would have been disrupted by the scale of the changes. Oil price rises affected industrial output and many stock items became unobtainable or very expensive. This encouraged organisations to return to the system of grabbing items when they came available and holding on to them until they were actually needed.

There are other factors which have a less dramatic influence, including interest rates and inflation. These factors are often related to general business cycles. A traditional view of business cycles starts with industry being optimistic about the future. Sales are expected to rise, so production is increased to match perceived future demand. Then inventories build up as sales lag behind production, and at some point industry loses confidence and cuts back on production to deplete the excessive stocks. This causes a decline in the economy, which only picks up again when stocks are lower and production is not meeting expected demand.

A precise relationship between stock levels and business cycles has not yet been found, and there is a general belief that each business cycle is in some ways unique. Nonetheless, there is a widespread belief that long-term business cycles and stock level are closely related, and in particular that inventory levels, as one of the easiest factors to change, tend to fluctuate more than the business cycle itself (Figure 1.8).

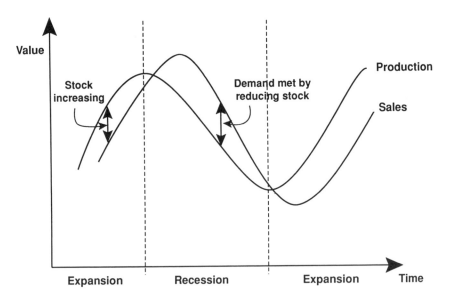

Figure 1.8 Stock levels in the business cycle

One view has fluctuations in inventories actually causing business cycles. Klein and Popkin (1961) suggested that if 75% of inventory variations had been controlled in the United States between the wars there would not have been any recessions. This kind of study encourages suggestions for prohibiting wide fluctuations in inventories by taxes or other means. Such measures have never been implemented, mainly because of difficulties in defining "excess" fluctuations (see Silver and Peterson (1985)).

Moving to specific economic factors, it is sometimes suggested that high interest rates should lead to low stock levels. This does, however, seem an unreasonable argument as stock holding costs are already high at 25% of value a year and small variations in interest rates should have no significant effect.

Another important influence on stock levels is inflation. The real cost of holding inventory can be discounted by an allowance for inflation, and during periods of high inflation we would expect stock levels to rise.

In Summary

On a national scale, stock levels are directly related to the business cycle. Although the details of this relationship are unclear, stocks tend to fall during recession and rise during growth.

SELF-ASSESSMENT QUESTIONS

1.15 Is the objective of minimising the costs of stock holding the same as minimising stock?
1.16 Minimising costs is always the objective of inventory control. Is this statement true or false?
1.17 Why do stocks tend to fall during periods of recession?
1.18 On a national scale, if variations in stock levels could be reduced, the severity of business cycles would also be reduced. Is this statement true or false?
1.19 Do interest rates affect stock holdings?

SUMMARY OF CHAPTER

This chapter has introduced the basic ideas of inventory control. It has laid the foundations on which later chapters build. In particular it has:

- defined some terms used in stock control
- discussed the reasons for holding stock
- listed the fundamental questions of inventory control
- outlined alternative systems for controlling stock

- described the costs associated with stocks
- discussed different views of stocks
- outlined the changing level of stocks and how these are related to general economic activity

REFERENCES FOR FURTHER READING

Abramovitz, M. (1950) *Inventories and Business Cycles*, The National Bureau of Economic Research, New York.

Brown, R.G. (1977) *Materials Management Systems*, John Wiley, New York.

Buffa, E.S. and Miller, J.G. (1979) *Production-Inventory Systems: Planning and Control*, Irwin, Homewood, IL.

Greene, J.H. (1970) *Production and Inventory Control Handbook*, McGraw-Hill, New York.

Hax, A.C. and Candea, D. (1984) *Production and Inventory Management*, Prentice Hall, Englewood Cliffs, NJ.

Klein, L.R. and Popkin, J. (1961) An Economic Analysis of the Post War Relationship between Inventory Fluctuation and Change in Aggregate Economic Activity, in *Inventory Fluctuation and Economic Stabilization*, The Joint Economic Committee, Washington, D.C.

Love, S.F. (1979) *Inventory Control*, McGraw-Hill, New York.

Lovell, M.C. (1961) Manufacturers' Inventories, Sales Expectations and the Accelerator Principle, *Econometrica*, **29**, 293–314.

Lovell, M.C. (1964) Determinants of Inventory Investment, in *Models of Income Distribution*, edited by I. Friend, Princeton University Press, Princeton, NJ.

Mack, R.P. (1967) *Information, Expectations and Inventory Fluctuations*, Columbia University Press.

Papillon, F. (1696) *A Treatise Concerning the East India Trade*, London (1677).

Plossl, G.W. and Welch, W.E. (1979) *The Role of Top Management in the Control of Inventory*, Reston Publishing, Reston, VA.

Plossl, G.W. and Wight, O. (1967) *Production and Inventory Control*, Prentice Hall, Englewood Cliffs, NJ.

Silver, E. and Peterson, R. (1985) *Decision Systems for Inventory Management and Production Planning* (2nd edn), John Wiley, New York.

Starr, M.K. and Miller, D.W. (1962) *Inventory Control: Theory and Practice*, Prentice Hall, Englewood Cliffs, NJ.

Vollman, T.E., Berry, W.L. and Whybark, D.C. (1988) *Manufacturing Planning and Control Systems*, Irwin, Homewood, IL

Wight, O.W. (1974) *Production and Inventory Management in the Computer Age*, Cahners Books, Boston, MA.

SECTION II
INDEPENDENT DEMAND
INVENTORY SYSTEMS

Section I looked at a number of important issues for inventory control. In particular it discussed the reasons why organisations hold stocks, the kind of goods held and the associated costs. We suggested that a typical manufacturing company holds 20% of its production as stock, with annual costs of about 25% of value. This is a large investment for any company, and it is not surprising that considerable efforts have been made to rationalise stock holdings and reduce the associated costs to a minimum.

There are basically two approaches to inventory control:

- independent demand systems, which use mathematical models to relate forecast demand, order size and costs
- dependent demand systems, which use production plans or operating schedules to calculate stock requirements.

Section II of this book, comprising Chapters 2 to 6, looks at independent demand systems. Section III, comprising Chapters 7 to 9, describes dependent demand systems.

Chapter 2 starts by describing the most important model of inventory control. This "classic analysis" builds a simplified model of an inventory system and develops an equation for the optimal order size. Although it is based on a number of assumptions, this analysis gives results which are widely applicable.

A next step is to extend the model developed in the classic analysis by removing some of the assumptions. Many extensions have been suggested and some of these are described in Chapter 3. In particular, deterministic models are described with discounts in the unit cost, finite replenishment rates, back-orders, lost sales and impending price rises. Chapter 4 introduces uncertainty to the models, emphasising variable demand and lead time. An approach to periodic review systems is also described.

Literally hundreds of models have been developed for independent demand inventory systems. It would be impossible to give an exhaustive description of these, so the aim of this section is to describe some of the more practical analyses and use these to demonstrate general principles.

The last two chapters in this section consider the information needed to support an independent demand inventory system. This information is divided into "forecasts of demand" and "other information". Then Chapter 5 discusses a number of forecasting methods, including judgemental, causal and projective methods. Chapter 6 discusses the other information needed for independent demand inventory systems, and describes links with other functions.

2
ECONOMIC ORDER QUANTITY MODEL

SYNOPSIS

This chapter describes some quantitative models which can be used for controlling inventories. The first model is the "classic analysis" which relates order size to demand for an item and associated costs. In particular, an optimal order size (the economic order quantity (EOQ)) is found to minimise total costs. A number of other calculations are based on this result.

The classic analysis is based on a number of assumptions. Some of these are removed in following chapters, but even the basic analysis is widely used. The robustness of the model is demonstrated by calculating the errors introduced when variables are only known approximately, or when the quantity ordered is adjusted to some convenient size.

Calculation of the economic order quantity answers the question, "How much should be ordered?" The final analysis in this chapter calculates a reorder level to answer the related question, "When should orders be placed?".

This chapter introduces ideas and methods which are developed more fully in later chapters. If you find the material straightforward you should be well-prepared to move on, but if you have any difficulties it would be sensible to reread the chapter and clear them up now.

Wherever possible ideas are introduced through examples rather than by rigorous mathematical proof. The amount of mathematical manipulation is reduced to a minimum and is included only to show how results are obtained or to make more general points.

OBJECTIVES

After reading this chapter and completing the exercises you should be able to:

- appreciate the background to the classic analysis of inventory control

- list the assumptions of the classic analysis
- derive and use an economic order quantity (EOQ)
- describe some limitations of the EOQ analysis
- calculate the effect of moving away from the EOQ
- calculate the effects of errors in costs and forecast demand
- calculate the costs implied by current operations
- decide when it is cheaper to round-up rather than round-down for orders of integer size
- calculate a reorder level (ROL) for finite lead time
- discuss some limitations of the ROL
- design a two-bin system

2.1   THE CLASSIC ANALYSIS OF INVENTORY CONTROL

The first analysis described in this chapter lays the foundation for all scientific inventory control. It was this analysis which first demonstrated that an optimal order size could be calculated to minimise associated costs. Its importance is often recognised by calling it the "classic analysis".

The classic analysis builds a model of an inventory system and calculates the order quantity which minimises total costs. Thus it finds an answer to the question, "How much should be ordered?". The answer is an optimal order size which is called the economic order quantity (EOQ).

The EOQ calculation is the most important analysis of inventory control, and arguably one of the most important results derived in any area of operations management. The first reference to the work is by Harris in 1915, but the result is often credited to Wilson who independently duplicated the work and marketed the results in the 1930s.

The classic analysis defines a relationship between order size, demand for an item and the associated costs. Then by minimising the total cost, an expression is found for the optimal order quantity.

2.1.1   Assumptions of the Analysis

The stock level of an item varies over time, with a typical pattern shown in Figure 2.1. At some point, A, a delivery arrives and raises the stock level. Then demands are met and the stock level declines. An order for replenishment is placed at B and this arrives at time C. This general pattern, with some short-term variations, is repeated as long as the item is kept in stock. Sometimes an unexpectedly heavy demand or delayed delivery will mean that stocks run out (as at point E) and then shortages can be represented by negative stock levels. At other times an unexpectedly low demand or fast delivery will mean that deliveries arrive when they are not really needed (as at point H).

Our aim is to build a model and analyse this pattern. Unfortunately, the pattern

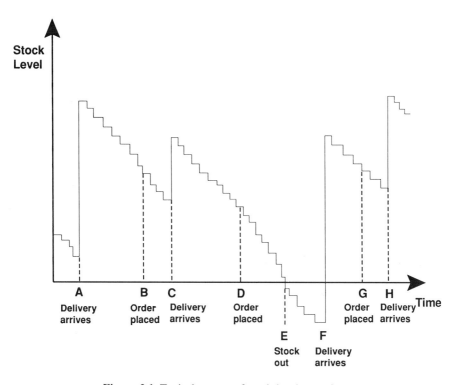

Figure 2.1 Typical pattern of stock level over time

is fairly complicated, so we start with a basic analysis which makes a number of simplifying assumptions. Most importantly, we assume that demand is known exactly, is continuous and constant over time, as shown in Figure 2.2.

The basic model makes a number of other assumptions, the main ones being:

- a single item is considered
- all costs are known exactly and do not vary
- no shortages are allowed
- lead time is zero (so a delivery is made as soon as the order is placed)

Some other assumptions are implicit in the model, including:

- purchase price and reorder costs do not vary with the quantity ordered
- a single delivery is made for each order
- replenishment is instantaneous, so that all of an order arrives in stock at the same time and can be used immediately
- each stock item is independent and money cannot be saved by substituting other items or grouping several items into a single order.

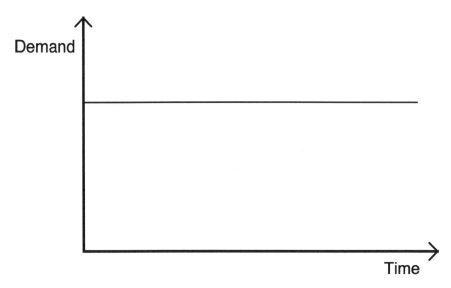

Figure 2.2 Demand is continuous and constant over time

These assumptions seem unrealistic and could make us doubt the validity of the model. In practice, however, we should remember two points.

- Firstly, all models are simplifications of reality. Their main purpose is to give useful results rather than be exact representations of actual circumstances. The results obtained from the classic analysis are very widely used, and we can infer that the model is accurate enough for many purposes. The results may not be optimal in the strict mathematical sense, but they are good approximations and do, at worst, give useful guidelines.
- Secondly, this is a basic model which can be extended in many ways. In the following two chapters we will remove some of the assumptions and develop more complex models. These show how a range of realistic features can be added.

The assumptions made in the classic analysis give an idealised pattern of stock level which is easier to analyse. If lead time is zero, an order need never be placed before stock actually runs out: placing an order when there is stock remaining would leave a residue of stock which is never used and incurs unnecessary holding costs. Conversely, the assumption that no shortages are allowed means there are no lost sales and the stock level will never go below zero. The resulting stock level follows the pattern shown in Figure 2.3. This assumes that the quantity ordered will vary, but later we show there is an optimal order size, and the best policy is always to order the same amount.

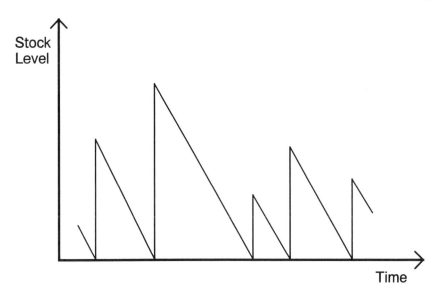

Figure 2.3 Simplified stock level pattern with varying order size

In Summary

The classic analysis defines a relationship between order size, demand for an item, and costs. By making a number of assumptions an optimal order size (EOQ) can be calculated.

2.1.2 Variables Used in the Analysis

We have now laid the groundwork for the model and can introduce some details, starting with a definition of variables used. The costs have already been described in Chapter 1, and if you have forgotten any of these it would be worth reviewing them.

Order Quantity (Q)

When an order is placed and stock is replenished the quantity ordered is Q. The main purpose of this analysis is to find an optimal value for the order quantity.

Cycle Time (T)

The cycle time is the time between two consecutive replenishments. This depends on the order quantity, with larger orders leading to longer cycle times.

Demand (D)

This is the number of units to be supplied from stock in a given time period (for example, ten units a week). The demand is assumed to be known, continuous and constant.

Unit Cost (UC)

This is the price charged by the suppliers for one unit of the item, or the total cost to the organisation of acquiring one unit.

Reorder Cost (RC)

The reorder cost is the cost of placing a routine order for the item and might include allowances for drawing up an order, computer time, correspondence, telephone costs, receiving, use of equipment, expediting, delivery, quality checks, and so on. If the item is made internally, this becomes a batch set-up cost.

Holding Cost (HC)

This is the cost of holding one unit of an item in stock for one period of time. The usual period for calculating stock costs is a year, so a holding cost might be expressed as, say, £10 a unit a year.

Shortage Cost (SC)

If demand for an item cannot be met because stocks have been exhausted, there is usually some associated shortage cost. In this analysis we have said that no shortages are allowed, so SC does not appear (it is effectively so large that any shortage would be prohibitively expensive).

Variables used:

Q = order quantity
T = cycle length
D = demand per unit time
UC = unit cost
RC = reorder cost
HC = holding cost

The only variable which is directly under our control is the reorder quantity. We can give this any value we like. Then the value given to the reorder quantity determines the cycle time. All the other variables are outside our direct control. We might be able to influence some of them (changing the price, for example might influence the demand) but we cannot control them directly. In this analysis, we assume that all other variables are fixed. Then our aim is to find an equation for the optimal value for Q (and hence T) in terms of the other variables. In this sense an optimal value is defined as one which minimises the total costs.

2.1.3   Derivation of the Economic Order Quantity

This derivation uses a standard approach which can be used for many inventory control problems. It has three steps which:

- find the total cost of one stock cycle
- divide this total cost by the cycle length to give a cost per unit time
- minimise this cost per unit time.

Consider one stock cycle, as shown in Figure 2.4. At some point an order is placed for a quantity, Q, which arrives instantly and is used at a constant rate, D, until no stock remains. At this point another order is placed and arrives immediately. The cycle has a length T. We know that during the cycle the amount entering stock is Q, while the amount leaving is $D * T$. These must be equal as the stock level at both the start and finish of the cycle is zero.

$$\text{amount entering stock} = \text{amount leaving stock}$$
$$\text{in cycle} \qquad \text{in cycle}$$

so

$$Q = D * T$$

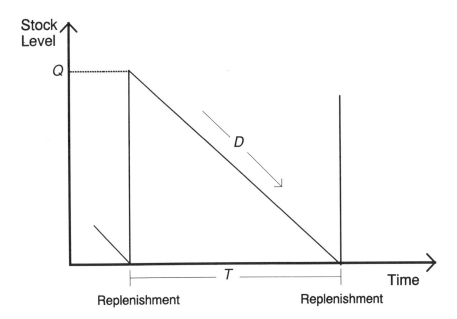

Figure 2.4 One cycle of the saw-tooth stock level pattern

The first step of the analysis calculates a total cost for the cycle. This is found by adding the three separate components of cost for units, reorders and holdings (remembering there are no shortage costs). Hence:

$$\begin{array}{ccccc} \text{total cost per} = & \text{unit cost} & + \text{reorder cost} & + \text{holding cost} \\ \text{cycle} & \text{component} & \text{component} & \text{component} \end{array}$$

These separate components are calculated as follows:

- unit cost component   = unit cost (UC)   * number of units ordered (Q)

$$= UC * Q$$

- reorder cost component = reorder cost (RC)   * number of orders (1)

$$= RC$$

- holding cost component = holding cost (HC) * average stock level ($Q/2$) * time held (T)

$$= \frac{HC * Q * T}{2}$$

Adding these three components gives the total cost per cycle as:

$$\text{total cost per cycle} = UC * Q + RC + \frac{HC * Q * T}{2}$$

This completes the first step of the analysis. The second step divides this cost by the cycle length, T, to give a total cost per unit time, TC.

$$\text{total cost per unit time} = TC = \frac{UC * Q}{T} + \frac{RC}{T} + \frac{HC * Q}{2}$$

We know that $Q = D * T$ or $D = Q/T$ so substituting this gives:

$$TC = UC * D + \frac{RC * D}{Q} + \frac{HC * Q}{2}$$

The demand and all costs are fixed, so the only variable on the right-hand side of this equation is Q. We can plot a graph to show how TC, the total cost per unit time, varies with Q, the reorder quantity. The most convenient way of doing this is to plot each of the cost components separately against Q and then add them together as shown in Figure 2.5. The unit cost component ($UC * D$) is independent of order quantity and can be considered "fixed". The other two components vary with order quantity and form the "variable" cost, VC.

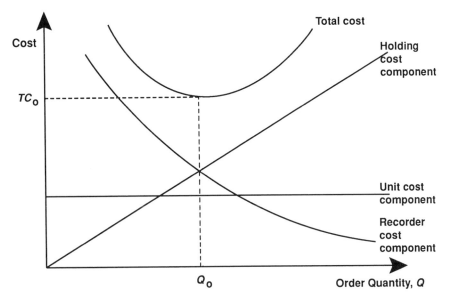

Figure 2.5 Variation of costs with order quantity, Q

$$\begin{array}{ccc} \text{total cost per} & = \text{fixed cost per} & + \text{ variable cost} \\ \text{unit time} & \text{unit time} & \text{per unit time} \end{array}$$

$$TC = UC * D + VC$$

with

$$VC = \frac{RC * D}{Q} + \frac{HC * Q}{2}$$

The holding cost component rises linearly with Q while the reorder cost component falls as Q increases. This confirms the observation that large, infrequent orders give low reorder costs but high holding costs; small, frequent orders give low holding costs but high reorder costs.

Adding the three components together gives a total cost curve which is an asymmetric "U" shape with a distinct minimum. This minimum corresponds to the optimal order size, which is called the "economic order quantity", EOQ. In other words, the best policy is always to place orders of the same size. With smaller orders than this, costs are high because of the reorder cost component, and with larger orders they are high because of the holding cost component.

The minimum value for TC is found by differentiating with respect to Q and setting the result equal to zero.

$$\frac{d(TC)}{dQ} = -\frac{RC * D}{Q^2} + \frac{HC}{2} = 0$$

$$Q_o = \sqrt{\frac{2 * RC * D}{HC}}$$

This gives the optimal order size, or economic order quantity (EOQ), which we will call Q_o.

$$Q_o = \sqrt{\frac{2 * RC * D}{HC}} = \text{economic order quantity}$$

This is the most important result of the analysis and answers the question, "How much should be ordered?". We know that if orders are placed with size Q_o the total cost per unit time is minimised, but if orders are placed which are either larger or smaller than this the total cost will be higher. The best policy is clearly to place orders which are always of size Q_o. Figure 2.3 assumed order quantities would vary, so we can now revise this to the result shown in Figure 2.6.

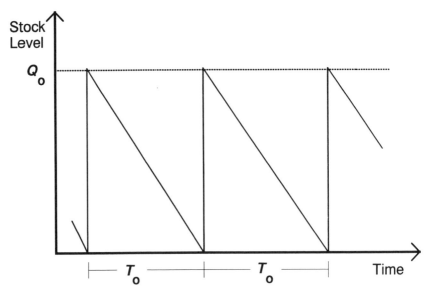

Figure 2.6 Regular pattern of stock level when orders of size Q_o are always placed

The optimal length of the stock cycle can be found from the equation $Q = D * T$. If we substitute Q_o for Q we can find the optimal cycle length, T_o.

$$T_0 = Q_0/D$$

$$T_0 = \frac{1}{D} * \sqrt{\frac{2 * RC * D}{HC}}$$

$$T_o = \sqrt{\frac{2 * RC}{D * HC}} = \text{optimal cycle length}$$

By similar substitution we can find the optimal cost per unit time, TC_0. If we consider only the variable cost (by definition the fixed cost does not change so we need not worry about it) we have:

$$VC_0 = \frac{RC * D}{Q_0} + \frac{HC * Q_0}{2}$$

Then substitution for Q_0 gives:

$$VC_0 = RC * D * \sqrt{\frac{HC}{2 * RC * D}} + \frac{HC}{2} * \sqrt{\frac{2 * RC * D}{HC}}$$

$$= \sqrt{\frac{RC * HC * D}{2}} + \sqrt{\frac{RC * HC * D}{2}} \qquad (a)$$

$$VC_o = \sqrt{2 * RC * HC * D} = \text{optimal variable cost}$$

Total cost is the sum of variable cost and fixed cost, so:

$$TC_o = UC * D + VC_o = \text{optimal total cost}$$

An interesting point in this derivation is found in line (a). This clearly shows that for the economic order quantity the reorder cost component equals the holding cost component, with both having the value $\sqrt{(RC * HC * D/2)}$.

In Summary

We have now:

- described an idealised view of an inventory system
- built a model of this, relating order size to demand and costs
- found an optimal order size which minimises the total cost per unit time: this is the economic order quantity
- shown that for large infrequent orders the holding cost component is high, so the total cost is also high
- shown that for small frequent orders the reorder cost component is high, so the total cost is also high
- found optimal values for the cycle length and costs per unit time.

Worked Example 2.1

A Company buys 6000 units of an item every year with a unit cost of £30. It costs £125 to process an order and arrange delivery, while interest and storage costs amount to £6 a year for each unit held. What is the best ordering policy for the item?

Solution

Listing the values we know:

D = 6000 units a year
UC = £30 a unit
RC = £125 an order
HC = £6 a unit a year

Substituting these into the economic order quantity equation gives:

$$Q_o = \sqrt{\frac{2 * RC * D}{HC}} = \sqrt{\frac{2 * 125 * 6000}{6}} = 500 \text{ units}$$

The optimal time between orders is found from:

$$T_o = \sqrt{\frac{2 * RC}{D * HC}} = \sqrt{\frac{2 * 125}{6000 * 6}} = 0.083 \text{ years } = 1 \text{ month}$$

The associated variable cost is:

$$VC_o = \sqrt{2 * RC * HC * D} = \sqrt{2 * 125 * 6 * 6000} = £3000 \text{ a year}$$

This gives a total cost of (see Figure 2.7):

$$TC_o = UC * D + VC_o = 30 * 6000 + 3000 = £183\,000 \text{ a year}$$

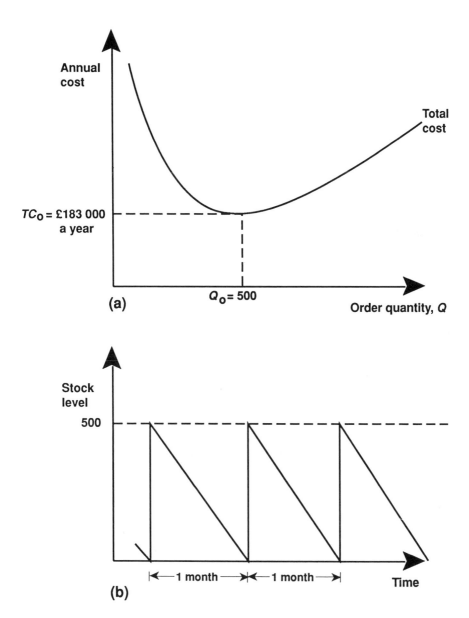

Figure 2.7 Illustrating the solution to Worked Example 2.1. (a) Variation of total cost with order quantity. (b) Variation of stock level over time

These calculations could have been done in a number of ways. Having found Q_o, for example, we could have found T_o by substitution in $Q_o = D * T_o$. Then:

$$T_o = Q_o/D = 500/6000 = 0.083 \text{ years}$$

The variable cost could also be found from the equation:

$$VC_o = \frac{RC * D}{Q_o} + \frac{HC * Q_o}{2}$$

$$= \frac{125 * 6000}{500} + \frac{6 * 500}{2}$$

$$= £3000 \text{ a year}$$

Other ways of calculating the variable cost come from the observation that at Q_o the reorder cost component equals the holding cost component, so:

$$\text{variable cost} = 2 * \text{reorder cost component}$$

and

$$= 2 * \text{holding cost component.}$$

Then $VC_o = \dfrac{2 * RC * D}{Q_o}$ $= \dfrac{2 * 125 * 6000}{500}$ $= £3000 \text{ a year}$

or $VC_o = HC * Q_o$ $= 6 * 500$ $= £3000 \text{ a year}$

It does not matter which versions of the equations are used as they always lead to the same results. The best advice is simply to use the most convenient calculation.

Worked Example 2.2

(a) A company operating a 50-week year is concerned about its stocks of copper cable. This costs £8 a metre and there is a demand for 8000 metres a week. Each replenishment costs £35 for administration and £55 for delivery, while holding costs are estimated at 25% of value held a year. Assuming no shortages are allowed, what is the optimal inventory policy for the cable?

(b) How would this analysis differ if the company wanted to maximise profit rather than minimise costs? What is the gross profit if the company sells cable for £12 a metre?

Solution

(a) Listing the variables we know, and making sure the units are consistent, gives:

$D = 8000 * 50 = 400\,000$ metres a year

$UC \qquad\quad = £8$ a unit

$RC = 35 + 55 = £90$ an order

$HC = 0.25 * 8 = £2$ a metre a year

Substituting these values gives the economic order quantity:

$$Q_o = \sqrt{\frac{2 * RC * D}{HC}} = \sqrt{\frac{2 * 90 * 400\,000}{2}} = 6000 \text{ metres}$$

The optimal time between orders:

$$
\begin{aligned}
T_o = Q_o/D \quad &= 6000/400\,000 \\
&= 0.015 \text{ years} \\
&= 0.75 \text{ weeks}
\end{aligned}
$$

Associated variable cost:

$$
\begin{aligned}
VC_o = HC * Q \quad &= 2 * 6000 \\
&= £12\,000 \text{ a year}
\end{aligned}
$$

Total cost:

$$
\begin{aligned}
TC_o = UC * D + VC_o \quad &= 8 * 400\,000 + 12\,000 \\
&= £3\,212\,000 \text{ a year}
\end{aligned}
$$

This last figure shows one reason why inventory control is sometimes overlooked. With a turnover in excess of three million pounds a year inventory costs are only £12 000, or 0.4%. This figure is unusually low, but any well-run organisation should try to make all the savings it can, however small.

(b) If the company wanted to maximise profit rather than minimise costs the analysis used would remain exactly the same. We can demonstrate this by defining SP as the selling price per unit so that gross profit per unit time becomes:

profit = revenue − costs

$$= SP * D - (UC * D + RC * D/Q + HC * Q/2)$$

When this is maximised by differentiating with respect to Q and setting the result equal to zero, we get the same results as before.

If the company sells the cable for £12 a metre its revenue is $12 * 400\,000 =$ £4 800 000 a year. Direct costs of £3 212 000 must be subtracted from this to give a gross profit of £1 588 000 a year.

Worked Example 2.3

A manufacturing company makes a number of parts for marine engines. It has 20 assembly lines on which it makes 60 different products in a total of 1500 batches a year. Every time a new batch is started a team of three fitters takes two hours to set up equipment. The lines work two shifts of eight hours a day for five days a week, but 10% of this time is needed for maintenance and training, and is unavailable for productive work. Once a batch is completed, it is tested and transferred to a finished goods store. The accounting department has estimated the following annual figures.

Total value of output	= £54 000 000
Total cost of materials	= £18 000 000
Total cost of overheads	= £12 000 000
Wages of fitters	= £30 000
Wages of testers, transfer and clerical staff =	£60 000

The company looks for a return of 20% a year on capital.

One product has an annual demand of 1250 units. The selling price is £300, 60% of which is direct material and production costs. What is the optimal batch size for this product?

Solution

We must start by finding values for the variables in the EOQ equation.

- The annual demand is given directly as 1250 units.
- As 60% of the selling price is made up of direct costs, the unit cost becomes $0.6 * 300 =$ £180.
- The only information about holding costs is that the company looks for a return of 20% a year on capital. Then the annual holding cost is 20% of unit cost, or $0.2 * 180 =$ £36.
- Reorder, or in these circumstances batch set-up, cost is a little more complicated. There are two components due to lost production and direct wages. The value of an hour of production time can be found from:

$$\text{value of 1 h} = \frac{\text{value of output} - \text{overheads} - \text{material cost}}{\text{no. of lines} * \text{productive hours worked}}$$

$$= \frac{54\,000\,000 - 12\,000\,000 - 18\,000\,000}{20 * 2 * 8 * 5 * 52 * 0.9}$$

$$= £320.51$$

Hence two hours of set-up costs £641. There are additional costs of wages for fitters and other staff which amount to $(30\,000 + 60\,000)/1500 = £60$ a batch. Then the batch set-up cost is $641 + 60 = £701$.

Now we have all the variables needed:

D = 1250 units a year
UC = £180 a unit
RC = £701 a batch
HC = £36 a unit a year

Substituting these gives the optimal order size:

$$Q_o = \sqrt{\frac{2 * RC * D}{HC}} = \sqrt{\frac{2 * 701 * 1250}{36}} = 220 \text{ units (about)}$$

The optimal time between orders is:

$$T_o = Q_o/D = 220/1250 = 0.176 \text{ years}$$

$$= 9 \text{ weeks (about)}$$

The best policy is to make a batch of 220 units of the item every 9 weeks.

SELF-ASSESSMENT QUESTIONS

2.1 What is the purpose of the analysis described above?
2.2 What assumptions are made in the calculation of an economic order quantity?
2.3 What costs may be taken into account in quantitative models of stock holdings?
2.4 What is meant by the EOQ?
2.5 In the model developed above, is the variable cost:
   (a) greater than the fixed cost?
   (b) equal to the fixed cost?
   (c) less than the fixed cost?
   (d) either greater than or less than the fixed cost?
2.6 If small orders are placed frequently (rather than placing large orders infrequently), is the total cost:
   (a) increased?

(b) reduced?
(c) either increased or reduced?
(d) minimised?
2.7 If orders are placed with size determined by the economic order quantity, is the reorder cost component:
(a) equal to the holding cost component?
(b) greater than the holding cost component?
(c) less than the holding cost component?
(d) either greater than or less than the holding cost component?

2.2   ADJUSTING THE ECONOMIC ORDER QUANTITY

2.2.1   Limitations of the Classic Analysis

Although it is widely used, the analysis for finding an economic order quantity has several weaknesses. The obvious one is the number of unrealistic assumptions. This can easily be avoided by designing more complex models, a number of which are described in following chapters. Unfortunately, these models almost inevitably need more computation and a balance must be struck between the improved quality of results and the effort needed to get them.

A more difficult problem is that the calculations are based on estimated costs and forecast demand which may contain significant errors. The unreliability of some data means that more complex models do not necessarily give better results.

Another common criticism of the EOQ analysis is met in manufacturing companies, where batch set-up costs are high. This can lead to very large batches, which complicate production scheduling, need too much capacity, give long lead times to customers, need excessive storage capacity, and leave too much capital tied up in stocks. These problems can be avoided to some extent by putting an artificially high value on the holding cost and allowing smaller "uneconomic" batches to be made. The cost of these is higher than optimal, but they allow a balance between conflicting objectives.

These criticisms reinforce the point that the EOQ should be treated as a good guideline whose use can give considerable benefits. Often the data collection and analysis needed for the EOQ calculation give the secondary benefit of allowing a much better understanding of the stock holdings.

2.2.2   Moving Away from the Economic Order Quantity

Even when available data allows a reliable EOQ to be calculated, there are several reasons why this may not be used.

• The EOQ might suggest fractional value for things which come in discrete units: an order for 2.7 computer systems, for example, makes no sense and we would either buy two or three systems.

- Suppliers may be unwilling to split standard package sizes: 227 kg of cement, for example, would be rounded to the nearest 50 kg.
- Deliveries are made by vehicles with fixed capacities, so that 12 tonnes, say, might fit onto one lorry but the EOQ of 13 tonnes would need two lorries and hence double delivery costs.
- It is simply more convenient to round order sizes to a convenient number.

In Worked Example 2.1 we found an economic order quantity of 500 units. Suppose the company in this example updated some of its accounting conventions and raised holding costs from £6 to £7 a unit a year. The variables become:

D = 6000 units a year
UC = £30 a unit
RC = £125 an order
HC = £7 a unit a year

Substituting these values into the standard equations gives:

$$Q_o = \sqrt{\frac{2 * RC * D}{HC}} = \sqrt{\frac{2 * 125 * 6000}{7}} = 462.91 \text{ units}$$

$$VC_o = HC * Q = 7 * 462.91 = £3240.37 \text{ a year}$$

It is unlikely that anyone would place orders for 463 units (and certainly not 462.91), so it would be useful to know how sensitive costs are to small changes around Q_o. If we move a small distance away from the optimal value do the costs rise very quickly or are they stable, allowing wide movements with only small penalties? In this example we can look at the variable costs of buying batches of, say, 450 or 500 units.

Orders of 450 units

$$VC = \frac{RC * D}{Q} + \frac{HC * Q}{2} = \frac{125 * 6000}{450} + \frac{7 * 450}{2} = £3241.67$$

Orders of 500 units

$$VC = \frac{RC * D}{Q} + \frac{HC * Q}{2} = \frac{125 * 6000}{500} + \frac{7 * 500}{2} = £3250.00$$

Batches of 450 units (which is 2.8% below the EOQ) raise variable costs by £1.30 or 0.04%: batches of 500 units (which is 8% above the EOQ) raise variable costs by £9.63 or 0.3%. In this example the variable cost is clearly stable for order sizes around the optimal value. We can generalise this result by comparing the minimum variable cost, VC_0, from ordering batches of size Q_0, with the variable cost, VC, of ordering any other quantity, Q.

We know that:

$$VC_0 = \sqrt{2 * RC * HC * D} \qquad \text{and} \qquad VC = \frac{RC * D}{Q} + \frac{HC * Q}{2}$$

If we take the ratio of these we get:

$$\frac{VC}{VC_0} = \frac{RC * D}{Q * VC_0} + \frac{HC * Q}{2 * VC_0}$$

We found earlier that VC_0 can be found from either:

$$\text{(a) } VC_0 = \frac{2 * RC * D}{Q_0} \qquad \text{or} \qquad \text{(b) } VC_0 = HC * Q_0$$

Substituting VC_0 from (a) in the first term on the right-hand side of this ratio and VC_0 from (b) in the second term gives:

$$\frac{VC}{VC_0} = \frac{RC * D * Q_0}{Q * 2 * RC * D} + \frac{HC * Q}{2 * HC * Q_0}$$

or:

$$\frac{VC}{VC_0} = \frac{1}{2} * \left(\frac{Q_0}{Q} + \frac{Q}{Q_0} \right)$$

As VC_0 is the lowest possible value for the variable cost this equation can only take values greater than one.

Suppose we could tolerate variable costs within 5% of optimal, by how much could the order quantity vary? Substituting $VC = 1.05 * VC_0$ in the equation and expressing Q as a fraction of Q_0 (so $Q = k * Q_0$) we have:

$$\frac{1.05 * VC_0}{VC_0} = \frac{1}{2} * \left(\frac{Q_0}{k * Q_0} + \frac{k * Q_0}{Q_0} \right)$$

$$1.05 = \frac{1}{2} * \left(\frac{1}{k} + \frac{k}{1} \right)$$

$$2.1 * k = 1 + k^2$$

which can be solved to give two values of:

$$k = 1.37 \quad \text{or} \quad k = 0.73$$

In other words, orders can be placed up to 37% more than Q_o or down to 27% less than Q_o and still keep variable costs within 5% of optimal. This shows that the variable cost is always stable around the optimal. We might try moving even further away from Q_o by accepting variable costs within 10% of optimal. Then repeating the calculation for $VC = 1.1 * VC_o$ gives:

$$\frac{1.10 * VC_o}{VC_o} = \frac{1}{2} * \left(\frac{Q_o}{k * Q_o} + \frac{k * Q_o}{Q_o} \right)$$

$$1.10 = \frac{1}{2} * \left(\frac{1}{k} + \frac{k}{1} \right)$$

$$2.2 * k = 1 + k^2$$

and

$$k = 1.56 \quad \text{or} \quad k = 0.64$$

Orders can be placed up to 56% more than Q_o or down to 36% less than Q_o and still keep variable costs within 10% of optimal (see Figure 2.8). This result shows why the economic order quantity calculation is so popular. The analysis may be based on a number of assumptions and approximations, but provided the quantity ordered is somewhere close to the EOQ, costs will be close to optimal. If, for example, the calculated EOQ for an item is 123 units and orders are placed for 120 or 130 the costs will be very close to optimal; if orders are placed for 100 or 150 the costs will still be acceptable, but if orders are being placed for 30 or 300 it is probably time to review the ordering policy.

In Summary

One of the main strengths of the EOQ analysis is that costs rise slowly for order sizes near to optimal. If there is uncertainty in data, or some other factor which prevents the calculated EOQ from being used, a close approximation will give good results.

Worked Example 2.4

Each unit of an item costs a company £40. Annual holding costs are 18% of unit cost for interest charges, 1% for insurance, 2% allowance for obsolescence, £2 for building overheads, £1.50 for damage and loss, and £4 miscellaneous costs. Annual demand for the item is constant at 1000 units and each order costs £100 to place.

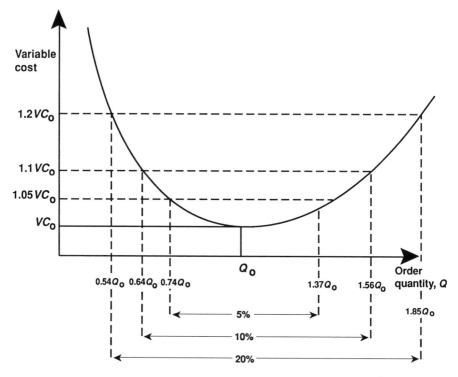

Figure 2.8 Illustrating the shallow variable cost curve around Q_0

(a) Calculate the economic order quantity and the total costs associated with stocking the item.
(b) If the supplier of the item will only deliver batches of 250 units, how are the stock holding costs affected?
(c) If the supplier relaxes his order size requirement, but the company has limited warehouse space and can stock a maximum of 100 units at any time, what would be the optimal ordering policy and associated costs?

Solution

The annual holding cost equals $(18 + 1 + 2)\%$ of unit cost plus £$(2 + 1.50 + 4)$ a year. Then:

D = 1000 units a year
UC = £40 a unit
RC = £100 an order
HC = $(0.21 * 40) + 7.50 = £15.90$ a unit a year

(a) Substituting these values gives:

$$Q_o = \sqrt{\frac{2 * RC * D}{HC}} = \sqrt{\frac{2 * 100 * 1000}{15.9}} = 112.15 \text{ units}$$

$$VC_o = HC * Q_o = 112.15 * 15.9 = £1783.26 \text{ a year}$$

(b) If Q must equal 250 units, the variable cost can be found from:

$$\frac{VC}{VC_o} = \frac{1}{2} * \left(\frac{Q_o}{Q} + \frac{Q}{Q_o} \right)$$

$$VC = \frac{1783.26}{2} * \left(\frac{112.15}{250} + \frac{250}{112.15} \right)$$

$$= £2387.57 \text{ a year}$$

(c) The highest stock level occurs when an order has just arrived. If the maximum permissible stock level is 100 units, this sets an upper limit on the amount which can be ordered. The order size should be as near Q_o as possible and this is now equal to 100, so:

$$\frac{VC}{VC_o} = \frac{1}{2} * \left(\frac{Q_o}{Q} + \frac{Q}{Q_o} \right)$$

$$VC = \frac{1783.26}{2} * \left(\frac{112.15}{100} + \frac{100}{112.15} \right)$$

$$= £1795.00 \text{ a year}$$

Worked Example 2.5

A baker works 6 days a week for 49 weeks a year. Flour is delivered directly to the bakery with a charge of £7.50 for each delivery. The baker uses an average of 10 sacks of flour a day, for which he pays £12 a sack. He has an overdraft at the bank which costs 16% a year, with spillage, storage, loss and insurance costing 2.75% a year.

(a) What size of delivery should the baker use and what are the consequent costs?
(b) How much should be ordered if the flour has a shelf life of two weeks?
(c) How much should be ordered if the bank imposes a maximum order value of £1500?
(d) If the mill only delivers on Mondays how much should be ordered and how often?
(e) If the mill offers a 10% discount on all orders of 200 sacks or over should the baker take advantage of this offer?

Solution

Working in consistent units gives:

$$D = 10 * 6 * 49 = 2940 \text{ sacks a year}$$
$$UC = £12 \text{ a sack}$$

$RC = £7.50$ an order

$HC = (0.16 + 0.0275) * 12 = £2.25$ a sack a year

(a) Substituting these values:

$$Q_o = \sqrt{\frac{2 * RC * D}{HC}} = \sqrt{\frac{2 * 7.50 * 2940}{2.25}} = 140 \text{ units}$$

$VC_o = HC * Q_o = 2.25 * 140 = £315$ a year

(b) If flour has a shelf life of two weeks, buying more than $2 * 6 * 10 = 120$ sacks at a time will mean the excess is wasted. The further the actual order size is away from EOQ the higher the cost will be, so the baker should aim to have batches as near to 140 sacks as possible. In this case the baker should buy batches of 120 sacks. Then:

$$VC = \frac{VC_o}{2} * \left(\frac{Q_o}{Q} + \frac{Q}{Q_o} \right) = \frac{315}{2} * \left(\frac{140}{120} + \frac{120}{140} \right)$$

$$= £318.75 \text{ a year}$$

(c) A maximum order value of £1500 implies 125 sacks. Again the baker should aim to buy as near to 140 as possible, in this case 125 sacks (see Figure 2.9). Then:

$$VC = \frac{VC_o}{2} * \left(\frac{Q_o}{Q} + \frac{Q}{Q_o} \right) = \frac{315}{2} * \left(\frac{140}{125} + \frac{125}{140} \right)$$

$$= £317.03 \text{ a year}$$

(d) The baker should aim for deliveries of 140 sacks which is between 2 and 3 weeks' supply. If deliveries are only weekly, he has a choice of ordering every 2 weeks or ordering every 3 weeks. The cost for each of these is:

• order every 2 weeks

$Q = 120$

$VC = £318.75$ as calculated in part (b).

• order every 3 weeks

$Q = 180$

$$VC = \frac{VC_o}{2} * \left(\frac{Q_o}{Q} + \frac{Q}{Q_o} \right) = \frac{315}{2} * \left(\frac{140}{180} + \frac{180}{140} \right)$$

$= £325$ a year

Ordering every 2 weeks is cheaper and this should be the baker's policy.

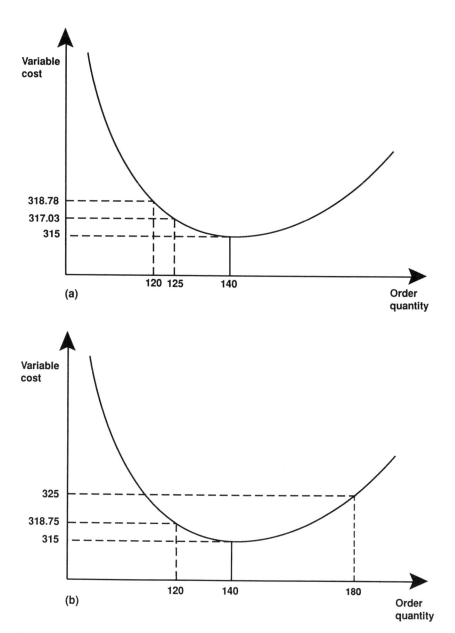

Figure 2.9 Results for the baker. (a) Variation of cost with order size. (b) Costs of ordering for either two or three weeks

(e) In the original scheme the baker could order in batches of 140 and incur a variable cost of £315 a year and a fixed cost of 2940 * 12 = £35 280 a year. Then:

$$\text{total cost} = \text{fixed cost} + \text{variable cost}$$
$$= 35\,280 + 315$$
$$= £35\,595 \text{ a year.}$$

If the baker orders 200 sacks at a time, his unit cost is reduced to 0.9 * 12 = £10.80 a sack while his holding cost is reduced to 0.1875 * 10.80 = £2.025 a sack a year. Substituting these figures to find a new EOQ gives:

$$Q_0 = \sqrt{\frac{2 * RC * D}{HC}} = \sqrt{\frac{2 * 7.50 * 2940}{2.025}} = 147.57 \text{ units}$$

The baker must order at least 200 units to get the discount. He cannot order the EOQ but should try to get as near this as possible, so he should send orders for 200 sacks. Then:

$$VC = \frac{RC * D}{Q} + \frac{HC * Q}{2} = \frac{7.50 * 2940}{200} + \frac{2.025 * 200}{2}$$

$$= £312.75$$

$$\text{total cost} = UC * D + VC$$
$$= 10.80 * 2940 + 312.75$$
$$= £32\,064.75 \text{ a year}$$

This is considerably cheaper than the original option and the baker should accept the offered discount.

2.2.3   Uncertainty in Demand and Costs

The stability of costs around EOQ is particularly useful when the demand or costs are not known exactly, but are approximations or contain errors. Suppose, for example, the demand is forecast and contains a proportional error, E, so that an actual demand of D is forecast to be $D * (1 + E)$. Then the EOQ we should be using is:

$$Q_0 = \sqrt{\frac{2 * RC * D}{HC}}$$

but we are actually using:

$$Q_0 = \sqrt{\frac{2 * RC * D * (1 + E)}{HC}}$$

The resulting error in the variable cost can be found from:

$$\frac{VC}{VC_o} = \frac{1}{2} * \left(\frac{Q_o}{Q} + \frac{Q}{Q_o} \right)$$

Substituting the values for Q_o and Q and cancelling the common terms gives:

$$\frac{VC}{VC_o} = \frac{1}{2} * \left(\frac{1}{\sqrt{1 + E}} + \frac{\sqrt{1 + E}}{1} \right)$$

Table 2.1 shows the increase in variable cost for various errors in forecast. Again it is clear that large errors in forecast demand lead to relatively small movements away from the minimum value of VC_o. We can see from this table that the variable cost is asymmetric and rises more quickly to the left of the EOQ than the right. This means that if demand is uncertain it is better to *over*-estimate the EOQ than to *under*-estimate it. Moving 40% above EOQ, for example, raises variable cost by 1.42% but moving 40% below EOQ raises variable cost by 3.28% (see Figure 2.10).

Similar analyses can be done for variations in costs. If, for example, an actual reorder cost of RC is approximated by $RC * (1 + E_1)$ while an actual holding cost of HC is approximated $HC * (1 + E_2)$ then an order quantity of:

$$Q_o = \sqrt{\frac{2 * RC * D}{HC}}$$

is approximated by:

$$Q_o = \sqrt{\frac{2 * RC * (1 + E_1) * D}{HC * (1 + E_2)}}$$

Then substitution into:

$$\frac{VC}{VC_o} = \frac{1}{2} * \left(\frac{Q_o}{Q} + \frac{Q}{Q_o} \right)$$

gives:

$$\frac{VC}{VC_o} = \frac{1}{2} * \left(\frac{\sqrt{1 + E_2}}{\sqrt{1 + E_1}} + \frac{\sqrt{1 + E_1}}{\sqrt{1 + E_2}} \right)$$

Some values for these variations are given in Table 2.2.

Table 2.1

Percentage error in D	Percentage increase in VC	Percentage error in D	Percentage increase in VC
−95	134.79	95	5.63
−90	73.93	90	5.19
−85	48.46	85	4.77
−80	34.16	80	4.35
−75	25.00	75	3.94
−70	18.67	70	3.54
−65	14.10	65	3.15
−60	10.68	60	2.77
−55	8.08	55	2.41
−50	6.07	50	2.06
−45	4.50	45	1.73
−40	3.28	40	1.42
−35	2.33	35	1.13
−30	1.59	30	0.86
−25	1.04	25	0.62
−20	0.62	20	0.42
−15	0.33	15	0.24
−10	0.14	10	0.11
−5	0.03	5	0.03

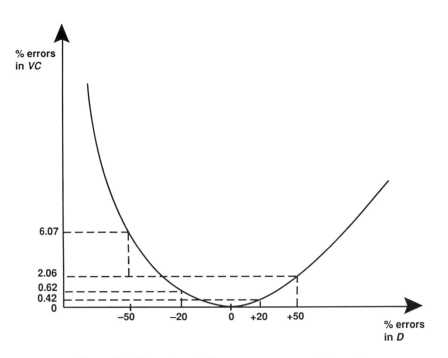

Figure 2.10 Errors in variable cost versus errors in demand

Table 2.2 Errors in EOQ with values of errors E_1 and E_2

		E_1							
		−0.8	−0.6	−0.4	−0.2	0.0	0.2	0.4	0.6	0.8
E_2	−0.8	0.00	6.07	15.47	25.00	34.16	42.89	51.19	59.10	66.67
	−0.6	0.07	0.00	2.06	6.07	10.68	15.47	20.27	25.00	29.64
	−0.4	15.47	2.06	0.00	1.04	3.28	6.07	9.11	12.27	15.47
	−0.2	25.00	6.07	1.04	0.00	0.62	2.06	3.94	6.07	8.33
	0	34.16	10.68	3.28	0.62	0.00	0.42	1.42	2.77	4.35
	0.2	42.89	15.47	6.07	2.06	0.42	0.00	0.30	1.04	2.06
	0.4	51.19	20.27	9.11	3.94	1.42	0.30	0.00	0.22	0.79
	0.6	59.10	25.00	12.27	6.07	2.77	1.04	0.22	0.00	0.17
	0.8	66.67	29.64	15.47	8.33	4.35	2.06	0.79	0.17	0.00

Sometimes when costs are difficult to find they may be inferred from current operations. Suppose, for example, an organisation is uncertain of its reorder cost. It might be possible to examine the ordering policy for an item and then work backwards to find an implicit reorder cost from:

$$Q_o = \sqrt{\frac{2 * RC * D}{HC}} \qquad \text{or} \qquad RC = \frac{Q_o^2 * HC}{2 * D}$$

If the organisation does not know its reorder cost it cannot be using economic order quantities. The calculated reorder cost is, therefore, only an approximation. If the calculation is repeated for a range of products it may be possible to get a more reliable value.

When more accurate values are used in stock control models, the results will be closer to optimal. There is a school of thought, however, which suggests that quantitative analyses can give guidelines for inventory control, but final decisions must be made by managers. Because of the large amount of data manipulation, it would be unreasonable to give managers the "optimal" results from an automated stock control system and ask them to make adjustments by hand. A better solution would be for the system automatically to produce the results desired. In other words, the purpose of stock control models should not be to calculate "optimal" values, but to give systems with the characteristics wanted by managers. This often leads to models with additional factors, K, of the kind:

$$Q = K * \sqrt{\frac{2 * RC * D}{HC}} \qquad \text{or} \qquad Q = \sqrt{\frac{2 * RC * D}{HC + K}}$$

A more straightforward adjustment is for managers to substitute values for costs which are not actual costs, but which give the characteristics they want. If, for example, they prefer orders which are larger than the economic order quantity, they can substitute artificially high reorder costs or low holding costs.

Such adjustments should only be made if there are genuine reasons, and after careful analysis. For the rest of this book we will present calculations of optimal values, but recognise that organisations may adjust these to suit individual circumstances.

Worked Example 2.6

Demand for an item is 10 units a week. Orders are always placed for 40 units of the item. What can you infer about the costs? If the reorder cost is £160 what is the implied holding cost?

Solution

We are only told that $D = 10$ units a week and $Q = 40$ units. If the organisation used economic order quantities, it would find:

$$Q_0 = \sqrt{\frac{2 * RC * D}{HC}} \quad \text{or} \quad 40 = \sqrt{\frac{2 * RC * 10}{HC}}$$

In other words:

$$RC/HC = 80$$

We can conclude that a system where the reorder cost is 80 times the holding cost gives the characteristics desired by managers.

If the reorder cost is £160 the implied holding cost is £2 a unit a week.

In Summary

The increased variable cost resulting from errors in costs and forecast demand can be calculated. This increase is usually quite small. It may be argued that any reasonable values for costs can be used, provided they give a system with the characteristics wanted by managers.

2.2.4 Orders for Discrete Units

In Worked Example 2.5, a baker ordered sacks of flour, and at one point the optimal order size was calculated at 147.57 sacks. It is normally impossible to order batches of this size and the baker must, at best, round to the nearest integer. We already know that costs rise slowly around EOQ, so the additional cost is likely to be small.

Sometimes the rounding of order quantities can make a significant difference, particularly when dealing with small numbers of expensive items, such as machines, planes, engines, vehicles, jewels, drums of chemicals, and so on. An organisation might, for example, have to decide whether it is better to order two computer systems or three, when the unit cost is £250 000.

The obvious approach to this problem is to calculate the economic order quantity, and then calculate the costs of rounding-up to the next integer and rounding-down. Suppose the economic order quantity is calculated as Q_0 which is between the integers $Q' - 1$ and Q' (as shown in Figure 2.11). Orders should be rounded *up* when the variable cost of ordering Q' units is less than the variable cost of ordering $Q' - 1$ units. That is:

$$\frac{RC * D}{Q'} + \frac{HC * Q'}{2} \leq \frac{RC * D}{Q' - 1} + \frac{HC * (Q' - 1)}{2}$$

This can be simplified by multiplying both sides by $2 * Q' * (Q' - 1)$ and cancelling to give:

$$HC * Q'^2 - HC * Q' \leq 2 * RC * D$$

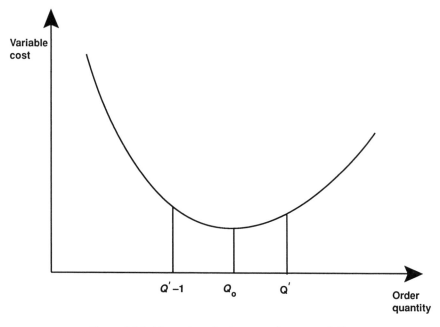

Figure 2.11 Alternatives for integer values around Q_o

$$HC * Q' * (Q' - 1) \leq 2 * RC * D$$

$$Q' * (Q' - 1) \leq 2 * RC * D/HC$$

or $\qquad Q' * (Q' - 1) \leq Q_o^2$

This defines a procedure for determining whether it is better to round-up or round-down discrete order quantities. This has:

- calculate the EOQ, Q_o
- find the integers Q' and $Q' - 1$ which surround Q_o
- if $Q' * (Q' - 1)$ is less than or equal to Q_o^2, order Q'
- if $Q' * (Q' - 1)$ is greater than Q_o^2, order $Q' - 1$

Worked Example 2.7

A company works for 50 weeks a year and stocks electric motors with the following characteristics:

D = 20 a week
UC = £2500 a unit

RC = £50 an order
HC = £660 a unit a year

What is the optimal order quantity? Would it make much difference if this number were rounded up or down to the nearest integer?

Solution

Substituting the given values allows an EOQ of:

$$Q_o = \sqrt{\frac{2 * RC * D}{HC}} = \sqrt{\frac{2 * 50 * 20 * 50}{660}} = 12.31 \text{ units}$$

The company cannot order 12.31 motors so its alternatives are to order 12 or 13. Here Q' equals 13 and the rule developed above would suggest ordering 13 when:

$$Q' * (Q' - 1) \le Q_o^2$$

$$13 * 12 \le 12.31^2$$

$$156 \le 151.54$$

This is not true so the best policy would be to order motors in batches of 12. This decision can be checked by calculating the cost of ordering in batches of 12 or 13 as follows:

- *order size 12 motors*

$$VC = \frac{RC * D}{Q} + \frac{HC * Q}{2} = \frac{50 * 1000}{12} + \frac{660 * 12}{2} = £8126.67$$

- *order size 13 motors*

$$VC = \frac{RC * D}{Q} + \frac{HC * Q}{2} = \frac{50 * 1000}{13} + \frac{660 * 13}{2} = £8136.15$$

As expected, the difference is quite small (about 0.1%).

SELF-ASSESSMENT QUESTIONS

2.8 Do the assumptions and other limitations of the economic order quantity calculation mean it has no practical value?

2.9   If an economic order quantity is calculated, but an order is then placed which is smaller than this, will the variable cost:
(a) increase?
(b) decrease?
(c) either increase or decrease?
(d) not change?

2.10   If an optimal order size, Q_0, is calculated but is found to be of an inappropriate size, would the total cost per unit time:
(a) rise quickly around Q_0?
(b) rise slowly around Q_0?
(c) fall quickly around Q_0?
(d) fall slowly around Q_0?
(e) either rise or fall?

2.11   If estimated values are used to find Q_0 and the result is uncertain, would it generally be better to *under*-estimate or *over*-estimate the order quantity?

2.12   Must accurate values for costs always be used in inventory control models?

2.13   What procedure should be followed to determine whether it is better to round-up the EOQ to the nearest integer or to round-down?

2.3   ADDING A FINITE LEAD TIME

2.3.1   Reorder Level

We have, so far, assumed that lead time is zero. Then, as soon as an order is placed the delivery arrives and is immediately available. In practice, this almost never happens and there are delays between placing an order and receiving the goods in stock. The lead time for an item may be anywhere from a few minutes to several years, and is typically between a few days and several weeks. If we assume the lead time is constant, a modification can be made to the previous analysis.

Consider the effect of a finite lead time, *LT*, on the standard saw-tooth stock level pattern shown in Figure 2.6. With a constant demand there is no benefit in carrying stock from one cycle to the next, so each order should be timed to arrive just as existing stock is exhausted. To achieve this, orders must be placed a time *LT* before they are needed, as shown in Figure 2.12. The optimal order quantity, Q_0, remains unchanged, but the time at which orders are placed is brought forward by *LT*. Although, it is easy to say, "place an order at time *LT* before it is needed", the method of achieving this might be less clear. The easiest way is to define a "reorder level". Then, when stock declines to this reorder level it is time to place an order.

When an order is placed the stock on hand must just cover demand until the order arrives. Here both demand and lead time are assumed constant, so the amount of stock needed to cover the lead time will also be constant, and is calculated from:

$$\text{lead time} * \text{demand per unit time}$$

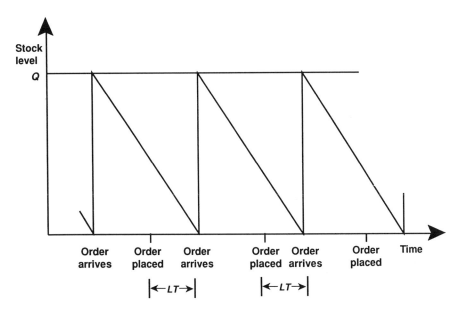

Figure 2.12 Relationship of lead time, *LT*, to order placing and arrival

This defines the reorder level, where an order should be placed.

$$\text{reorder level} = \text{lead time demand}$$

$$= \text{lead time} * \text{demand per unit time}$$

$$ROL = LT * D = \text{reorder level}$$

The simple rule, then, is to order in batches of size Q_o whenever the stock level falls to $LT * D$ (see Figure 2.13).

In Summary

An optimal inventory policy is to order an amount equal to the economic order quantity, whenever the stock level falls to the reorder level.

Worked Example 2.8

Demand for an item is constant at 100 units a week and the EOQ has been calculated as 250 units. What is the best ordering policy if lead time is:

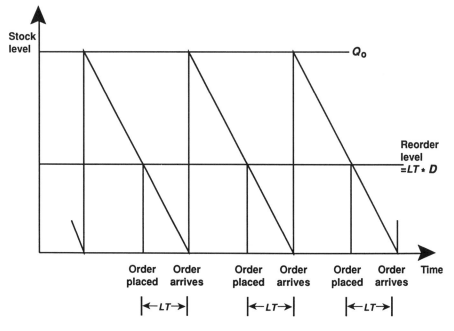

Figure 2.13 Illustrating the reorder level

(a) one week
(b) two weeks

Solution

(a) Substituting values $LT = 1$ and $D = 100$ gives:

$$ROL = LT * D = 1 * 100 = 100 \text{ units}$$

As soon as the stock level declines to 100 units an order for 250 units should be placed (see Figure 2.14).

(b) Substituting $LT = 2$ and $D = 100$ gives:

$$ROL = LT * D = 2 * 100 = 200 \text{ units}$$

As soon as the stock level declines to 200 units an order for 250 units should be placed.

This rule of ordering when stock level declines to lead time demand works well provided the lead time is shorter than the stock cycle. If the lead time is longer than the cycle time, some other adjustment is needed. This can be demonstrated for Worked Example 2.8 where the cycle time was:

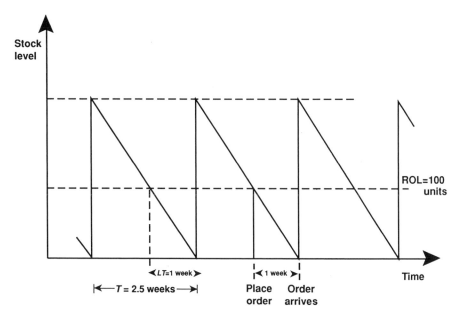

Figure 2.14 Reorder level for Worked Example 2.7 with lead time equal to one week

$$T = Q/D = 250/100 = 2.5 \text{ weeks}$$

The simple rule works well when the lead time was less than this, but if lead time is increased to 3 weeks the reorder level calculation becomes:

$$ROL = LT * D = 3 * 100 = 300$$

The problem is that the stock level never actually rises to 300 units, but varies between zero and 250 units. Because the lead time is longer than the cycle time, as shown in Figure 2.15, there will always be one order outstanding. This observation suggests a revised rule for setting the reorder level. Order B should be placed when there is enough stock, either on hand or on order and arriving before B is due, exactly to meet the lead time demand. Thus an order is placed when:

$$\text{stock on hand} + \text{stock on order} = 300 \text{ units}$$

When B is ordered there is one order, A, of 250 units outstanding so order B should be placed when:

$$\text{stock on hand} + 250 = 300$$

or

$$\text{stock on hand} = 50 \text{ units}$$

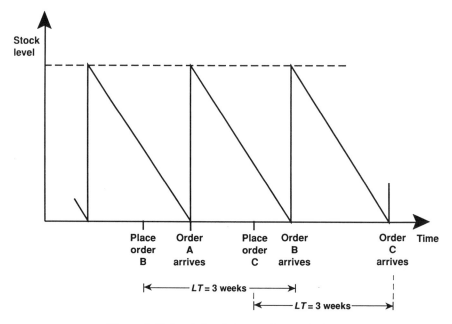

Figure 2.15 Lead time is longer than cycle time

From this observation we can generalise the simple rule to say:

- place an order when stock on hand plus stock on order equals lead time demand, or
- place an order when stock on hand falls to lead time demand minus stock on order.

Thus:

> recorder level = lead time demand − stock on order

When lead time is particularly long the number of orders outstanding at any time can be quite high, as illustrated in Figure 2.16. When the lead time is several times the stock cycle it is easy to lose track of the amount of goods on order. Based on the observations above, we can suggest a general rule:

> When lead time is between $n*T$ and $(n+1)*T$ order an amount Q_o whenever stock on hand falls to $LT*D − n*Q_o$

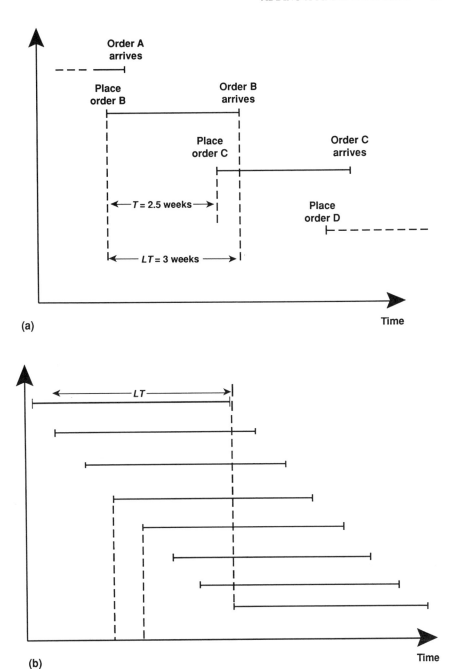

Figure 2.16 Timing of orders when lead time is longer than cycle length. (a) Timing of orders when $T = 2.5$ weeks and $LT = 3$ weeks. (b) Increasing number of orders outstanding as LT increases (here $LT = 7T$)

This recognises the fact that there will always be n orders outstanding when a new order has to be placed. When n equals zero, this reduces to the first simple rule we described.

In Summary

A reorder level can be used to find when an order should be placed. For constant lead time and demand, the reorder level equals lead time demand minus stock on order.

Worked Example 2.9

Demand for an item is steady at 1200 units a year with ordering cost of £16 and holding cost estimated at £0.24 a unit a year. Determine an appropriate inventory policy if lead time is constant at:

(a) 3 months
(b) 9 months
(c) 18 months

Solution

The values given are:

D = 1200 units a year
RC = £16 an order
HC = £0.24 a unit a year

Substituting these values gives the economic order quantity:

$$Q_o = \sqrt{\frac{2 * RC * D}{HC}} = \sqrt{\frac{2 * 16 * 1200}{0.24}} = 400 \text{ units}$$

$$T_o = Q_o/D = 400/1200 = 0.33 \text{ years or 4 months}$$

With lead time between $n * T_o$ and $(n+1) * T_o$ there will be n orders outstanding when it is time to place the next order. Then the reorder level is found from:

$$ROL = LT * D - n * Q_o$$

(a) A lead time of 3 months is less than the cycle time, so n = 0 and the reorder level is:

$$ROL = LT * D = 3 * 100 = 300 \text{ units}$$

Every time the stock on hand declines to 300 units an order for 400 units is placed.

(b) A lead time of 9 months is between 2 and 3 stock cycles, so $n = 2$ and the reorder level is:

$$ROL = LT * D - n * Q_o = 9 * 100 - 2 * 400 = 100 \text{ units}$$

Every time the stock on hand declines to 100 units an order for 400 units is placed.

(c) A lead time of 18 months is between 4 and 5 stock cycles, so $n = 4$ and the reorder level is:

$$ROL = LT * D - n * Q_o = 18 * 100 - 4 + 400 = 200 \text{ units}$$

Every time the stock on hand declines to 200 units an order for 400 units is placed.

2.3.2 Limitations of the Reorder Level

Despite the ease of calculation, there may be practical difficulties with using the reorder level. These include the following.

- We have assumed the lead time is known exactly and is constant. In practice there may be some variation, or the lead time may be difficult to determine exactly (it may, for example, differ considerably from a supplier's quoted lead time). Problems with variable lead time are described in Chapter 4.
- The reorder level may be difficult to identify accurately; in other words, it may be impossible to notice the point at which stock on hand declines to the reorder level. This happens with, say, oil tanks or coal tips where stock on hand is only known approximately.
- Stock levels may not be recorded continuously. Then the exact time an item reaches its reorder level may be missed, and the order delayed. Many inventories are checked periodically. Then, if a stock level is checked every week, say, stock on hand could decline well below the reorder level before anyone notices.
- Orders may not be possible when stock falls exactly to the reorder level. This is true when, for example, customers demand several units of an item. Then a single order for several units may suddenly reduce stocks to below the reorder level.
- We have assumed that reorder levels and reorder quantities are independent of each other.

2.3.3 Two-Bin System

The reorder level calculation answers the fundamental question, "When should orders be placed?". Now we know how much to order (the economic order quantity) and when to place orders (from the reorder level), so we have the basis for a useful inventory control system.

Most large stocks are controlled automatically by computer, but simple procedures can be used for any store, even very small ones. A practical way of implementing the reorder level is a "two-bin system". This is a simple procedure for controlling stock without either computer assistance or continuous monitoring of stock levels.

Stock of an item is kept in two distinct bins, A and B. Bin B contains an amount equal to the reorder level with all remaining stock in bin A. Stock is used from bin A until it is empty. At this point only the reorder level remains and an order should be placed immediately. Stock is used from bin B until the order arrives, at which point B is again filled with the reorder level and all extra units are put into A. This system can work well for cheap goods with long cycle times and can be modified so that the "bins" are locations on shelves, liquids in containers and so on (see Figure 2.17).

In Summary

Although widely used, there may be some practical difficulties with reorder level calculations. Some of these can be removed by simple two-bin systems.

SELF-ASSESSMENT QUESTIONS

2.14 What is meant by a "reorder level"?

2.15 If demand for an item is 10 units a week, the optimal order size is 30 units and the lead time is 7 weeks how many orders will be outstanding when it is time to place another order?

2.16 Orders should be placed when stock on hand declines to the reorder level; does this mean that continuous monitoring of stock levels is needed?

SUMMARY OF CHAPTER

In this chapter we have introduced the basic ideas and methods of "scientific inventory control". In particular we have:

- discussed the purpose and approach of the "classic analysis" of inventory control
- listed the assumptions made in this analysis
- built a model of an idealised inventory system

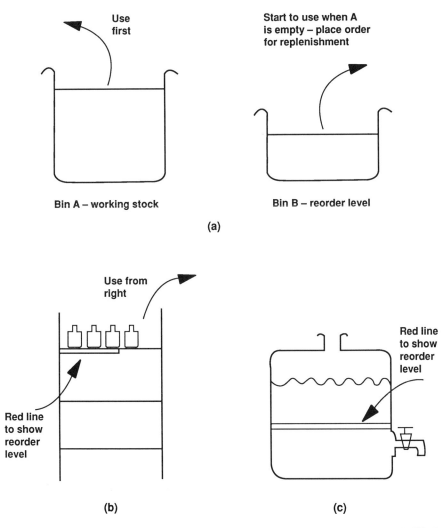

Figure 2.17 Versions of the two-bin system. (a) Standard system with "bins". (b) Modified for rack storage. (c) Modified for liquids in tank

- calculated an economic order quantity and related values
- found how sensitive this model is to changes in order quantities and errors in variables
- considered orders for integer numbers of units
- calculated reorder levels
- described a two-bin system

The result is a means of controlling stock which is based on the following relationships.

$$Q_o = \sqrt{\frac{2 * RC * D}{HC}}$$

$$T_o = \sqrt{\frac{2 * RC}{D * HC}}$$

$$VC_o = \sqrt{2 * RC * HC * D}$$

$$TC_o = UC * D + VC_o$$

$$ROL = LT * D - n * Q_o$$

ADDITIONAL PROBLEMS

2.1 Demand for an item is known to be constant at 1000 units a year. Unit cost is £50, reorder cost is £100, holding cost is 25% of value a year and no shortages are allowed. Describe an optimal inventory policy for the item.

2.2 For the item described in problem 2.1, find the order size which will give variable costs within 10% of optimal. What would be the cost if suppliers only made deliveries of 200 units?

2.3 Demand for an item is forecast to be around 110 units next year, but because forecasts are never entirely accurate we can only say that demand is likely to be between 100 and 120 units. Similarly, costs are uncertain and the best we can say is that reorder cost is somewhere between £12.50 and £17.50, with holding cost between 20% and 25% of unit value a year. If unit cost is £100 and all other conditions for the classic analysis hold, what can be said about the order quantity?

2.4 A wholesaler sells 16 computer systems a week over a 52-week year. Each system costs £5000 to buy, while order administration costs and delivery from the Far East cost £1000. Holding costs are estimated at 16% a year. What is the optimal order size for the systems?

2.5 Demand for an item is constant at 40 units a week, and the economic order quantity is calculated to be 100 units. What is the reorder level if lead time is constant at (a) 2 weeks (b) 4 weeks (c) 6 weeks?

REFERENCES FOR FURTHER READING

• Early work:
Harris, F. (1915) *Operations and Cost*, A.W. Shaw Co. Factory Management Series, Chicago.
Wilson, R.H. (1934) A Scientific Routine for Stock Control, *Harvard Business Review*, XIII.

- The EOQ analysis can be found in all specialist books on stock control or general books which include a chapter on the subject.

- Specialist books

Aft, L.S. (1987) *Production and Inventory Control*, Harcourt, Orlando, FL.

Buffa, E.S. and Miller, J.G. (1979) *Production-Inventory Systems: Planning and Control* (3rd edn), Irwin, Homewood, IL.

Fogarty, D.W. and Hoffman, T.R. (1983) *Production and Inventory Management*, South-Western Publishing, Dallas, TX.

Greene, J.H. (1970) *Production and Inventory Control Handbook*, McGraw-Hill, New York.

Hadley, G. and Whitin, T.M. (1963) *Analysis of Inventory Systems*, Prentice Hall, Englewood Cliffs, NJ.

Hax, A.C. and Candea, D. (1984) *Production and Inventory Management*, Prentice Hall, Englewood Cliffs, NJ.

Lewis, C.D. (1970) *Scientific Inventory Control*, Butterworth, London.

Love, S.F. (1979) *Inventory Control*, McGraw-Hill, New York.

McLeavy, D.W. and Seetharama, L.N. (1985) *Production Planning and Inventory Control*, Allyn and Bacon, Boston, MA.

Silver, E.A. and Peterson, R. (1985) *Decision Systems for Inventory Management and Production Planning* (2nd edn), John Wiley, New York.

Tersine, R.J. (1987) *Principles of Inventory and Materials Management* (3rd edn), North Holland, New York.

Thomas, A.B. (1980) *Stock Control in Manufacturing Industries* (2nd edn), Gower Press, London.

- General books include:

Buffa, E.S. and Sarin, R.K. (1987) *Modern Production/Operations Management*, John Wiley, New York.

Chase, R.B. and Aquilano, N.J. (1989) *Production and Operations Management* (5th edn), Irwin, Homewood, IL.

Davis, K.R., McKeown, P.G. and Rakes, T.R. (1986) *Management Science: an Introduction*, Kent Publishing, Boston, MA.

Eppen, G.D., Gould, F.J. and Schmidt, C.P. (1987) *Introductory Management Science* (2nd edn), Prentice Hall, Englewood Cliffs, NJ.

Gaither, N. (1990) *Production and Operations Management* (4th edn), The Dryden Press, Chicago, IL.

Schroeder, R.G. (1989) *Operations Management* (3rd edn), McGraw-Hill, New York.

Stevenson, W.J. (1986) *Production/Operations Management* (2nd edn), Irwin, Homewood, IL.

Waters, C.D.J. (1989) *A Practical Introduction to Management Science*, Addison-Wesley, Wokingham.

Waters, C.D.J. (1991) *Introduction to Operations Management*, Addison-Wesley, Wokingham.

3
DETERMINISTIC MODELS FOR INVENTORY CONTROL

SYNOPSIS

Chapter 2 described the classic analysis, leading to an economic order quantity. Although this analysis gives useful results it is based on a number of assumptions. In Chapters 3 and 4 we will describe models where some of these assumptions are removed. In particular:

- Chapter 3 keeps the condition that all variables take values which are known exactly (i.e. deterministic models)
- Chapter 4 removes the condition of certainty and allows probabilities to be assigned to variables (i.e. probabilistic models).

There are literally hundreds of models for different inventory systems. It would be impossible to describe all of them, so the chapters illustrate general principles by concentrating on a number of widely used models.

This chapter starts with a model for discounted unit cost. Many suppliers quote lower prices for larger orders, so a procedure is described for finding the overall lowest cost. Similar models can be developed when other costs change with order size.

The next model describes a system with a finite replenishment rate. This is typical of a finished goods store at the end of a production line. Here units arrive at a finite rate and stock accumulates during a production run. For this analysis we remove the assumption of instantaneous replenishment used for the economic order quantity and calculate new optimal batch sizes.

Sometimes, particularly with expensive items, it is too expensive to hold stocks which are large enough to meet all demand. Then some demand cannot be met from stock, and planned shortages are introduced. These are particularly useful when customers are willing to wait for back-orders to arrive. An analysis is described which balances holding and shortage costs to find an optimal number of back-orders. If customers are not willing to wait for back-orders, shortages lead to lost sales.

The next analysis examines the question of how much to buy if there is a single opportunity to purchase before an impending price rise. Finally, the chapter outlines some problems with constrained systems.

OBJECTIVES

After reading this chapter and completing the numerical exercises you should be able to:

- appreciate the ways that costs can vary with order quantity
- draw a valid total cost curve for discounted unit cost
- find the best ordering policy with discounted unit cost
- extend this analysis to other discounted costs
- describe the characteristics of production systems with finite replenishment rates
- calculate optimal batch sizes for systems with finite replenishment rates
- appreciate the use of planned shortages
- calculate optimal numbers of back-orders with time-dependent shortage costs
- determine a policy for maximising revenue with lost sales
- calculate the amount to buy before an impending price rise
- appreciate problems with constrained systems.

3.1 QUANTITY DISCOUNTS IN UNIT COST

3.1.1 Discounted Costs

One assumption of the economic order quantity analysis is that all costs are fixed; they have constant values which never change. In this section we will remove this assumption and look at problems where costs vary with the quantity ordered. In practice, this occurs most commonly with discounted unit costs, where a supplier quotes lower prices for larger order size. A particular microcomputer, for example, might cost £2500, but this is reduced to £2250 for orders of 10 or more, and to £2000 for orders of 50 or more.

The reorder cost might also vary with order quantity. Many of the costs of arranging an order and making a delivery are independent of order size, so smaller orders generally have higher reorder costs per unit than larger ones. Conversely, there are some reorder costs which increase with order quantity, such as quality control inspections of incoming products. Other costs have completely different patterns. Transport, for example, may cost a fixed amount for orders up to a certain limit which corresponds to the capacity of a delivery vehicle, but any larger orders need a second vehicle which doubles delivery cost.

Finally, the holding cost may also vary with order size. If the economic order quantity is large, there may be insufficient warehouse space to receive a full order. Then extra space must be rented or some other action taken. This problem is particularly relevant in manufacturing industry where high set-up costs often lead to very large batches.

We have now suggested that unit, reorder and holding costs can all vary with order size. We could build models for any situation with varying costs, but the analyses are all similar. We will, therefore, illustrate the approach with problems where the unit cost declines in discrete steps with increasing order quantity.

In Summary

All costs can vary with the quantity ordered. Models for calculating optimal order sizes with variable costs are similar, so we are concentrating on discounted unit cost.

3.1.2   Valid Total Cost Curve

Occasionally a sliding scale of unit costs is used, so that every unit bought has a different price. If a batch of ten units is bought the first unit might cost £10, the second £9.80, the third £9.70, and so on. In these circumstances the analysis is only slightly different from the classic analysis described in Chapter 2. Much more frequently the unit cost decreases in steps, with a supplier offering a reduced price on *all* units if more than a certain number are bought. More than one discount can be given, so the unit cost varies as shown in Figure 3.1. The basic unit cost is UC_1, but if more than Q_a are bought this falls to UC_2 for all units: if more than Q_b are bought the unit cost falls to UC_3, and so on (Table 3.1).

If we look at the most expensive unit cost, UC_1, we can draw a total cost curve, as done for economic order quantity analysis. In this case, however, the curve will only be valid for order quantities in the range zero to Q_a. In Figure 3.2 the continuous line shows the section of the total cost curve which applies to this unit cost, while the broken line shows the part of the curve which does not apply. If an order is placed for some quantity which is not between zero and Q_a the unit cost will be different, and we should be working on a different total cost curve.

If we now consider the next highest unit cost, UC_2, we can draw a second total cost curve. Figure 3.3 shows the relationship between the two total cost curves corresponding to UC_1 and UC_2. As UC_2 is lower than UC_1, this second curve will always be lower than the original one. It will only be valid in the range Q_a to Q_b and if orders are placed with a size outside this range we should be working on a different curve.

Now, continuing this process, we can draw a series of similar total cost curves for every unit cost. Each of these is only valid in a prescribed range, and outside this range one of the other curves must be used. The position of the curves is determined largely by the unit cost, so higher unit costs give curves which are further up the cost axis. This means that the total cost curves never cross each

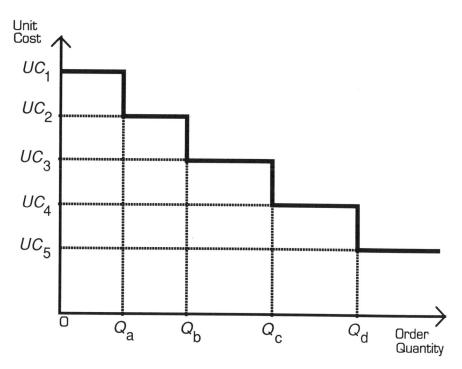

Figure 3.1 Stepped decrease in unit cost with reorder quantity

Table 3.1

Unit cost	Order quantity	
	Lower limit	Upper limit
UC_1	0	Q_a
UC_2	Q_a	Q_b
UC_3	Q_b	Q_c
UC_4	Q_c	Q_d
etc.		

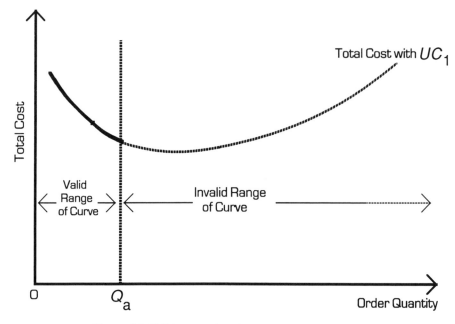

Figure 3.2 Valid range of total cost curve using UC_1

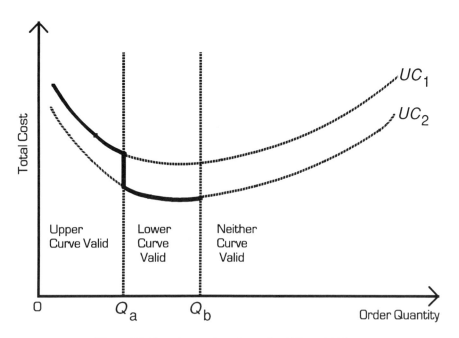

Figure 3.3 Superimposed total cost for UC_1 and UC_2

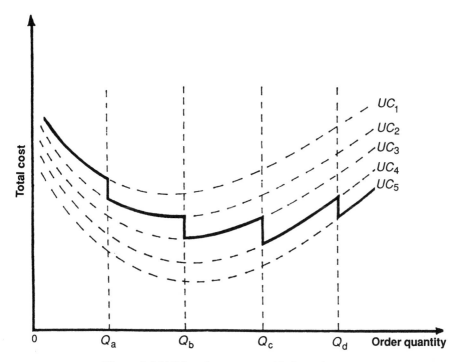

Figure 3.4 Valid total cost curve with five unit costs

other but remain separate as shown in Figure 3.4. The continuous line on this graph shows the overall valid total cost curve. As usual, in this analysis we are looking for the order quantity which minimises total cost. In other words, we are looking for the optimal value of Q which corresponds to the lowest point on the valid total cost curve.

We know from Chapter 2 that in general:

$$Q_o = \sqrt{\frac{2 * RC * D}{HC}}$$

The holding cost, HC is often expressed as an equivalent interest rate, I, multiplied by the unit cost, UC, so the lowest point on each curve is given by:

$$Q_{oi} = \sqrt{\frac{2 * RC * D}{I * UC_i}}$$

Then Q_{o1} is the lowest point on the total cost curve for UC_1, Q_{o2} is the lowest point on the total cost curve for UC_2, and so on. For any particular curve with unit cost UC_i this minimum can either be 'valid' or 'invalid'.

- *Valid minimum.* The minimum point on the cost curve is within the range of valid order quantities for this particular unit cost.
- *Invalid minimum.* The minimum point on the cost curve falls outside the valid order range for this particular unit cost.

Every set of cost curves will have at least one valid minimum, and a variable number of invalid minima, as shown in Figure 3.5.

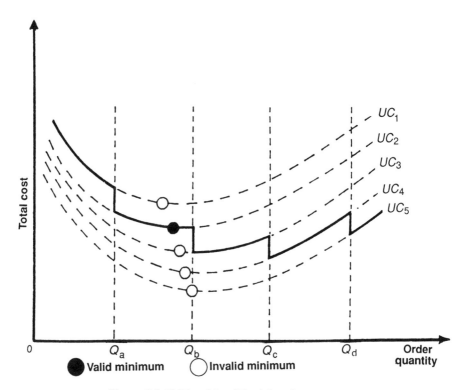

Figure 3.5 Valid and invalid minima for cost curves

Two other interesting features can be seen in the valid cost curve.

- Firstly, the valid total cost curve always rises to the left of a valid minimum; this means that when we search for an overall minimum cost it is either *at* the valid minimum or somewhere to the right of it.
- Secondly, there are only two possible positions for the overall minimum cost: either it is at a valid minimum, or else it is at a cost break point (see Figure 3.6).

These observations suggest a method of solution. All we have to do is find the total cost at the valid minimum and compare this with the total cost at each break

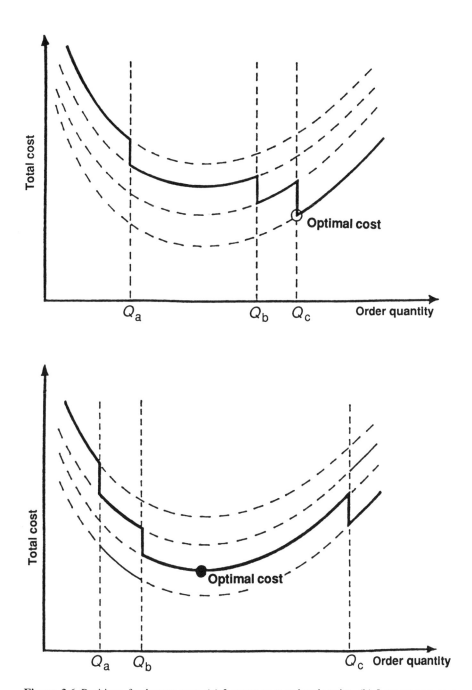

Figure 3.6 Positions for lowest cost. (a) Lowest cost at break point. (b) Lowest cost at a valid minimum

point to the right of the valid minimum. The optimal order quantity is found from the lowest of these costs.

In Summary

A valid total cost curve can be drawn for quantity discounts in unit cost. The lowest point on this curve occurs either at a valid minimum, or a cost break point to the right of the valid minimum.

3.1.3 Solution Procedure

We have now described the general principles for finding an optimal ordering policy. A more formalised version of this is shown in the flow diagram in Figure 3.7. Starting with the lowest unit cost we find the minimum point on the corresponding total cost curve. If this is valid, it must be the optimal solution. If it is invalid the total cost is calculated at the break point at the smaller end of the valid range. This process is repeated for each cost curve in turn until a valid minimum is found. Then a set of costs has been calculated (one from each unit cost curve examined) and these are compared. The optimal solution is the one with the lowest total cost.

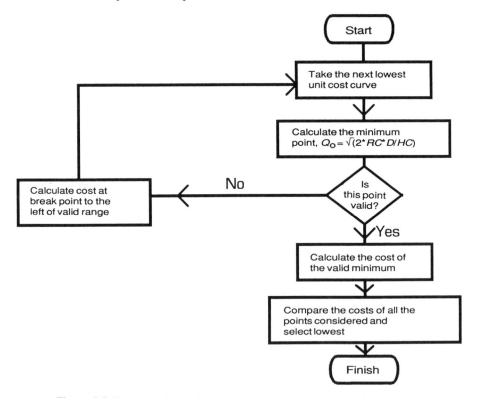

Figure 3.7 Procedure for finding the lowest total cost with varying unit cost

The best way to illustrate this process is with an example.

Worked Example 3.1

Annual demand for an item is 2000 units, each order costs £10 to place and annual holding cost is 40% of unit cost. The unit cost depends on the quantity ordered as follows:

- unit cost is £1 for order quantities less than 500
- £0.80 for quantities between 500 and 999 each
- £0.60 for quantities of 1000 or more

What is the optimal ordering policy?

Solution

Listing the variables we know:

D = 2000 units a year
RC = £10 an order
I = 40% of unit cost a year
$HC = I * UC = 0.4 * UC$ a unit a year
UC varies as shown in Figure 3.8

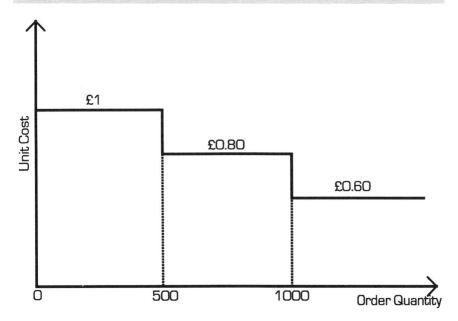

Figure 3.8 Variation of unit cost with order quantity for Worked Example 3.1

We should also remember that:

- total cost, TC_o, for an optimal order quantity, Q_o, is:

$$TC = UC * D + \sqrt{2 * RC * HC * D}$$

- total cost, TC, for any other order quantity, Q, is:

$$TC = UC * D + \frac{RC * D}{Q} + \frac{HC * Q}{2}$$

Now we can follow the procedure shown in Figure 3.7.

Taking the lowest cost curve:

UC = £0.60, valid for Q of 1000 or more
$Q_o = \sqrt{(2 * RC * D / HC)} = \sqrt{(2 * 10 * 2000 / 0.4 * 0.60)} = 408.2$
This is an *invalid* minimum as Q_o is not greater than 1000.
Calculating the cost of the break point at the smaller end of the valid range
(i.e. $Q = 1000$):
$TC = UC * D + (RC * D)/Q + (HC * Q)/2$
$\quad = 0.60 * 2000 + (10 * 2000)/1000 + (0.4 * 0.60 * 1000)/2$
$\quad = $ £1340 a year (point A in Figure 3.9)

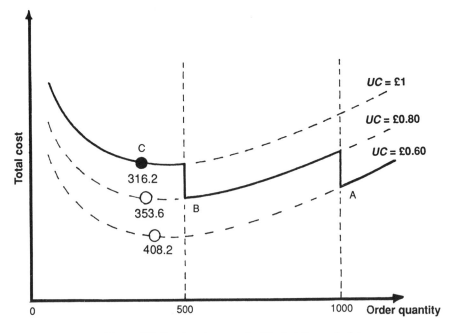

Figure 3.9 Total cost curves for Worked Example 3.1

Taking the next lowest cost curve:

$UC = £0.80$, valid for Q between 500 and 1000
$Q_o = \sqrt{(2 * RC * D / HC)} = \sqrt{(2 * 10 * 2000/0.4 * 0.80)} = 353.6$
This is an *invalid* minimum as Q_o is not between 500 and 1000.
Calculating the cost of the break point at the lower end (i.e. $Q = 500$):
$TC = UC * D + (RC * D)/Q + (HC * Q)/2$
$= 0.80 * 2000 + (10 * 2000)/500 + (0.4 * 0.80 * 500)/2$
$= £1720$ a year (point B in Figure 3.9)

Taking the next lowest cost curve:

$UC = £1.00$ valid for Q less than 500
$Q_o = \sqrt{(2 * RC * D / HC)} = \sqrt{(2 * 10 * 2000/0.4 * 1.00)} = 316.2$
This is a *valid* minimum as Q_o is less than 500.
Calculating the cost at this valid minimum:
$TC_o = UC * D + \sqrt{2 * RC * HC * D}$
$= 1.00 * 2000 + \sqrt{2 * 10 * 0.4 * 1.00 * 2000}$
$= £2126.49$ a year (point C)

Even if there were more cost curves we would not need to examine them: once a valid minimum is found there is no need to examine curves with higher unit costs. This leads to the final part of the analysis, which is to look at the solutions obtained and find the best.

The choice is between:

- point A $Q = 1000$ cost = £1340 a year
- point B $Q = 500$ cost = £1720 a year
- point C $Q = 316.2$ cost = £2126.49 a year

The best policy is to order batches of 1000 units, placing one order every six months, with total annual costs of £1340. The discounts offered on the unit cost more than offset the increased cost of carrying extra stock.

Worked Example 3.2

A company works for 50 weeks a year during which demand for a product is constant at 10 units a week. The cost of placing an order, including delivery charges, is estimated to be £150. The company aims for 20% annual return on assets employed. The supplier of the item quotes a basic price of £250 a unit, with discounts of 10% on orders of 50 units or more, 15% on orders of 150 units or more and 20% on orders of 500 units or more. What is the optimal order quantity for the item?

Solution

Listing the variables given in consistent units:

D = 10 * 50 = 500 units a year
RC = £150 an order
I = 20% of unit cost a year
$HC = I * UC = 0.2 * UC$ a unit a year

The variation of unit cost is shown in Figure 3.10.

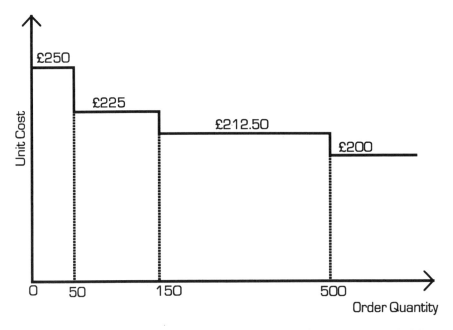

Figure 3.10 Variation of unit cost with reorder quantity for Worked Example 3.2

Now we can follow the standard solution procedure.

Taking the lowest cost curve:

UC = £200, valid for Q of 500 or more
$Q_o = \sqrt{(2 * RC * D / HC)} = \sqrt{(2 * 150 * 500 / 0.2 * 200)} = 61.2$
This is an *invalid* minimum as Q_o is not greater than 500.
Calculating the cost at the break point to the left (Q = 500):
$TC = UC * D + (RC * D)/Q + (HC * Q)/2$
  = 200 * 500 + (150 * 500)/500 + (0.2 * 200 * 500)/2
  = £110 150 a year (point A in Figure 3.11)

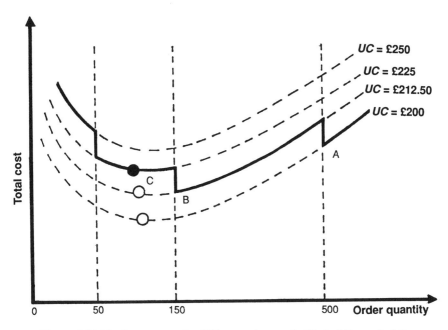

Figure 3.11 Total cost curve for different unit costs in Worked Example 3.2

Taking the next lowest cost curve:

$UC = £212.50$ valid for Q between 150 and 500
$Q_o = \sqrt{(2 * 150 * 500/0.2 * 212.50)} = 59.4$
This is an *invalid* minimum as Q_o is not between 150 and 500.
Calculating the cost at the break point to the left ($Q = 150$):
$TC = 212.50 * 500 + (150 * 500)/150 + (0.2 * 212.50 * 150)/2$
$= £109\ 938$ a year (point B in Figure 3.11)

Taking the next lowest cost curve:

$UC = £225$ valid for Q between 50 and 150
$Q_o = \sqrt{(2 * 150 * 500/0.2 * 225)} = 57.7$
This is a *valid* minimum as Q_o is between 50 and 150.
Calculating the cost at this valid minimum:
$TC = UC * D + \sqrt{2 * RC * HC * D}$
$= 225 * 500 + \sqrt{2 * 150 * 0.2 * 225 * 500}$
$= £115\ 098$ a year (point C)

As a valid minimum has been reached the procedure stops and we can compare
the solutions found so far.

- point A $Q = 500$ cost = £110 150 a year
- point B $Q = 150$ cost = £109 938 a year
- point C $Q = 57.7$ cost = £115 098 a year

The best choice is to order in batches of 150 units with annual costs of almost £110 000 a year. The difference is small in this case and some other factor, such as limitations in available storage space, capital tied-up, or delivery problems might be considered.

3.1.4   Rising Delivery Cost

The last section described an approach to problems where unit cost falls in discrete steps as the quantity ordered increases. We said earlier that other costs could vary in the same way. Bulky items, for example, often include an element for delivery in the reorder cost, and this might rise in steps as more delivery vehicles are needed. It would be useful to extend the discounted price analysis to cover variations in other costs. In practice this extension is very easy as all analyses with discretely changing costs are similar. We can illustrate this by an example with increasing reorder cost.

Worked Example 3.3

A company uses 4 tonnes of fine industrial sand every day. This sand costs £20 a tonne to buy, and £1.90 a tonne to store for a day. Deliveries are made by modified lorries which carry up to 15 tonnes, and each delivery of a load or part load costs £200. Find the cheapest way to ensure continuous supplies of sand.

Solution

Here the unit cost is constant, but the reorder (i.e. delivery) cost is £200 for each lorry load. Thus, orders up to 15 tonnes need one lorry with a reorder cost of £200, orders between 15 and 30 tonnes need two lorries with a reorder cost of £400, orders between 30 and 45 tonnes need three lorries with reorder costs of £600, and so on (see Figure 3.12).
Other variables are:

D = 4 tonnes a day
UC = £20 a tonne
HC = £1.90 a tonne a day

We can plot a family of total cost curves with the general form shown in Figure 3.13. The continuous line again shows the valid total cost curve while broken lines show invalid sections. This curve is the reverse of the valid total cost curve with unit cost discounts; it is lower when the quantity ordered is small and rises with increasing order size.

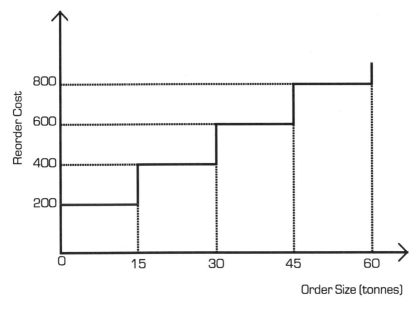

Figure 3.12 Rising reorder cost with order size in Worked Example 3.3

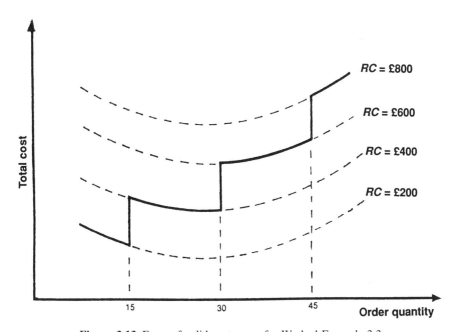

Figure 3.13 Form of valid cost curve for Worked Example 3.3

To find the lowest point on the valid cost curve we again use the observation that this lowest point must either be at a valid minimum or at a cost break point. We can, therefore, follow the same procedure as before. The only difference is that the valid cost curve is reversed, so we look for optimal order quantities to the *left* of a valid minimum and calculate the cost of break points at the upper limit of valid ranges.

Taking the lowest cost curve:

RC = £200, valid for Q less than 15 tonnes
$Q_o = \sqrt{(2 * RC * D/HC)} = \sqrt{(2 * 200 * 4/1.90)} = 29.0$ tonnes
This is an *invalid* minimum as Q_o is not less than 15 tonnes.
Calculating the cost at the break point (in this case you can see from Figure 3.13 that the lowest cost is to the right of the range at 15 tonnes):
$TC = UC * D + (RC * D)/Q + (HC * Q)/2$
$\quad = 20 * 4 + (200 * 4)/15 + (1.9 * 15)/2$
$\quad = $ £147.58 a day (point A in Figure 3.14)

Taking the next lowest cost curve:

RC = £400, valid for Q between 15 and 30 tonnes

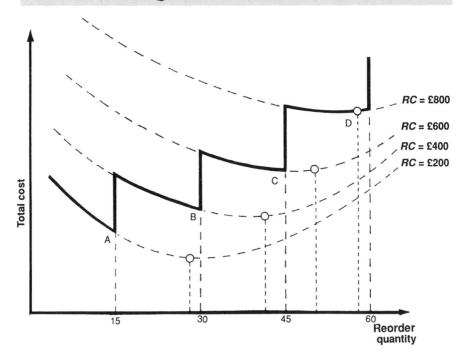

Figure 3.14 Variation in costs with reorder quantity for Worked Example 3.3

$Q_o = \sqrt{(2 * RC * D/HC)} = \sqrt{(2 * 400 * 4/1.9)} = 41.0$ tonnes

This is an *invalid* minimum as Q_o is not between 15 and 30 tonnes.

Calculating the cost at the cost break point (again to the right of the range):

$TC = UC * D + (RC * D)/Q + (HC * Q)/2$

$\qquad = 20 * 4 + (400 * 4)/30 + (1.9 * 30)/2$

$\qquad = £161.83$ a day (point B in Figure 3.14)

Taking the next lowest cost curve:

$RC = 600$ valid for Q between 30 and 45 tonnes

$Q_o = \sqrt{(2 * RC * D/HC)} = \sqrt{(2 * 600 * 4/1.9)} = 50.3$ tonnes

This is an *invalid* minimum as Q_o is not between 30 and 45 tonnes.

Calculating the cost at the break point (again to the right of the range):

$TC = UC * D + (RC * D)/Q + (HC * Q)/2$

$\qquad = 20 * 4 + (600 * 4)/45 + (1.9 * 45)/2$

$\qquad = £176.08$ a day (point C)

Taking the next lowest cost curve:

$RC = £800$, valid for Q between 45 and 60 tonnes

$Q_o = \sqrt{(2 * RC * D/HC)} = \sqrt{(2 * 800 * 4/1.9)} = 58.0$ tonnes

This is a *valid* minimum as Q_o is between 45 and 60 tonnes.

Calculating the cost at this valid minimum:

$TC = UC * D + \sqrt{2 * RC * HC * D}$

$\qquad = 20 * 4 + \sqrt{2 * 800 * 1.9 * 4}$

$\qquad = £190.27$ a day (point D)

As a valid minimum has been reached we stop the process, compare the calculated costs and select the lowest.

- point A $Q = 15$ tonnes   cost = £147.58 a day
- point B $Q = 30$ tonnes   cost = £161.83 a day
- point C $Q = 45$ tonnes   cost = £176.08 a day
- point D $Q = 58$ tonnes   cost = £190.27 a day

The best choice is to order 15 tonnes at a time, with deliveries needed every $15/4 = 3.75$ days.

In Summary

The procedure developed for finding optimal order quantities with discounted unit cost can be used for other discretely varying costs.

SELF-ASSESSMENT QUESTIONS

3.1 Which costs can vary with order quantity:
   (a) unit cost only?
   (b) reorder cost only?
   (c) holding cost only?
   (d) none of these?
   (e) all of these?

3.2 If a 10% discount in unit cost is available for all orders larger than 500 units, what is the "valid" range of order quantities for:
   (a) the original unit cost
   (b) the discounted unit cost

3.3 What is a "valid minimum"?

3.4 How many valid minima would you expect to find on the total cost curve (assuming unit cost decreases in discrete steps with increasing order quantity)?

3.5 Where must the point of minimum cost be on a valid total cost curve:
   (a) anywhere?
   (b) at a valid minimum?
   (c) at an invalid minimum?
   (d) at a cost break?
   (e) at a valid minimum or at a cost break?

3.6 If we find a valid minimum on a total cost curve with discounted unit cost, is the optimal order size:
   (a) at this valid minimum?
   (b) at or to the left of this minimum?
   (c) at or to the right of this minimum?
   (d) anywhere?

3.7 If we find a valid minimum on a total cost curve with increasing reorder cost is the optimal order size:
   (a) at this valid minimum?
   (b) at or to the left of this minimum ?
   (c) at or to the right of this minimum?
   (d) anywhere?

3.2 PRODUCTION SYSTEMS WITH FINITE REPLENISHMENT RATES

3.2.1 Finite Replenishment Rates

The economic order quantity analysis describes a typical situation met by wholesalers: a large delivery of an item instantaneously raises the stock level and then a series of smaller demands slowly reduces it. Consider, though, the stock of finished goods at the end of a production line. If the rate of production is greater than demand, goods will accumulate at a finite rate while the line is operating. This gives a situation where the instantaneous replenishment of the classic analysis is replaced by a finite replenishment rate. A similar pattern is met with stocks of work in progress between two machines: the first machine builds up stock at a finite rate while the second machine creates demand to reduce it.

If the rate of production is less than demand, each unit arriving is immediately transferred to a customer and no stocks are held. Stock only accumulates if the production rate is greater than demand. Then the stock level rises at a rate which is the difference between production and demand. If we call the rate of production P, stocks will build up at a rate $P - D$, as shown in Figure 3.15. Stock will continue to accumulate as long as production continues. This means that a decision must be made at some point to stop production of this item and transfer facilities to making other items. The purpose of this analysis is to find the best time for this transfer, which is equivalent to finding an optimal batch size.

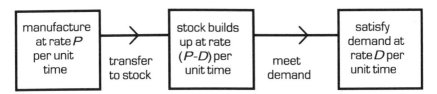

Figure 3.15 A manufacturer producing for stock with finite replenishment rate

The main assumptions we retain here are:

- a single item is considered
- demand is known, constant and continuous
- all costs are known exactly and do not vary
- no shortages are allowed

With production at a rate P and demand at a rate D, stocks will build up at a rate $P - D$. After some time, PT, a decision is made to stop production. Then, stock is used to meet demand and declines at a rate D. After some further time, DT, all stock has been used and production must start again. The resulting variation in stock level is shown in Figure 3.16. This diagram assumes there is an optimal value for PT (corresponding to an optimal batch size) which is always used.

In Summary

Replenishment of stock often occurs at a finite rate rather than instantaneously. This gives a cycle with stock levels rising at a rate $P-D$ in the first part and falling at a rate D in the second part.

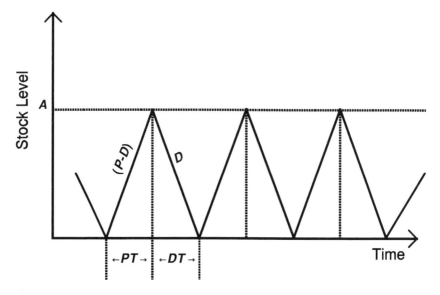

Figure 3.16 Variation in stock level with finite production rate

3.2.2   Derivation of Optimal Batch Size

The overall approach of this analysis is the same as the classic analysis, and involves:

- finding the total cost for one stock cycle
- dividing this total cost by the cycle length to get a cost per unit time
- minimising this cost per unit time.

Consider one cycle of the modified saw-tooth pattern shown in Figure 3.17. If a batch of size Q is made, the maximum stock level with instantaneous replenishment would also be Q. With a finite replenishment rate, however, this level is never reached, as units are continuously being removed to meet demand. The maximum stock level will be lower than Q and will occur at the point where production is stopped. The highest actual stock level, A, can be found in terms of other variables as follows.

Looking at the productive part of the cycle we have:

$$A = (P - D) * PT$$

We also know that total production during the period is:

$$Q = P * PT \qquad \text{or} \qquad PT = Q/P$$

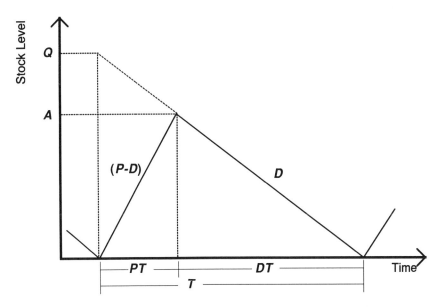

Figure 3.17 One stock cycle with finite production rate

Substituting for PT into the equation for A gives:

$$A = Q * \frac{(P - D)}{P}$$

Now we can continue the analysis, remembering that RC, the reorder cost, may really be a production set-up cost. Individual cost components (unit, set-up and holding) are as follows.

- unit cost component: = number of units made (Q)∗ unit cost (UC)
  $= UC * Q$
- set-up cost component: = number of production set-ups (1)∗ set-up cost (RC)
  $= RC$
- holding cost component: = average stock level ($A/2$)∗ time held (T)∗ holding cost (HC)

$$= \frac{HC * A * T}{2} = \frac{HC * Q * T}{2} * \frac{(P - D)}{P}$$

Adding these three components gives the total cost for the cycle as:

$$UC * Q + RC + \frac{HC * Q * T}{2} * \frac{(P - D)}{P}$$

Dividing this by the cycle length, T, gives a total cost per unit time, TC:

$$TC = \frac{UC * Q}{T} + \frac{RC}{T} + \frac{HC * Q}{2} * \frac{(P - D)}{P}$$

Then substitution of $Q = D * T$, or $T = Q/D$, gives:

$$TC = UC * D + \frac{RC * D}{Q} + \frac{HC * Q}{2} * \frac{(P - D)}{P}$$

If we compare this with the classic analysis, the only difference is the factor $(P - D)/P$. We could again draw a graph of this total cost against batch size and get an asymmetric "U"-shaped curve with a distinct minimum. We need not actually draw the graph, but can find the optimal batch quantity, Q_o, by differentiating TC with respect to Q and equating the derivative to zero.

$$\frac{\mathrm{d}(TC)}{\mathrm{d}Q} = -\frac{RC * D}{Q_o^2} + \frac{HC}{2} * \left(\frac{P - D}{P}\right) = 0$$

or

$$Q_o^2 = \left(\frac{2 * RC * D}{HC}\right) * \left(\frac{P}{P - D)}\right)$$

Then:

$$Q_o = \sqrt{\frac{2 * RC * D}{HC}} * \sqrt{\frac{P}{P - D}}$$

This result again differs from the economic order quantity by the factor $\sqrt{P/(P - D)}$. An optimal cycle time, T_o, can be found by substituting the value for Q_o in $Q_o = D * T_o$. Then PT is found from $Q_o = P * PT$. These results are summarised in Table 3.2. They again show the compromise between large, infrequent batches (with high holding cost component) and small frequent batches (with high set-up cost component). With a finite production rate the stock level is somewhat lower than it would be with instantaneous replenishment, so we would expect, all other things being equal, to make larger batches.

In Summary

An optimal batch size can be calculated for finite replenishment rates. This, and related results vary from the classic analysis by the factor $\sqrt{P/(P - D)}$.

Table 3.2

Finite production rate	Classic analysis
$Q_o = \sqrt{\dfrac{2 * RC * D}{HC}} * \sqrt{\dfrac{P}{P - D}}$	$Q_o = \sqrt{\dfrac{2 * RC * D}{HC}}$
$T_o = \sqrt{\dfrac{2 * RC}{HC * D}} * \sqrt{\dfrac{P}{P - D}}$	$T_o = \sqrt{\dfrac{2 * RC}{HC * D}}$
$VC_o = \sqrt{2 * RC * HC * D} * \sqrt{\dfrac{P - D}{P}}$	$VC_o = \sqrt{2 * RC * HC * D}$
$TC_o = UC * D + VC_o$	$TC_o = UC * D + VC_o$
$PT = Q_o / P$	

Worked Example 3.4

Demand for an item is constant at 1800 units a year. The item can be made at a constant rate of 3500 units a year. Unit cost is £50, batch set-up cost is £650, and holding cost is 30% of value a year. What is the optimal batch size for the item? If production set-up time is 2 weeks, when should this be started?

Solution

Listing the variables we know:

D = 1800 units a year
P = 3500 units a year
UC = £50 a unit
RC = £650 a batch
HC = 0.3 * 50 = £15 a unit a year

Substituting these values gives the order quantity:

$$Q_o = \sqrt{\frac{2 * RC * D}{HC}} * \sqrt{\frac{P}{P - D}} = \sqrt{\frac{2 * 650 * 1800}{15}} * \sqrt{\frac{3500}{3500 - 1800}} = 566.7$$

Production time, *PT*, is:

$$PT = Q_o / P = 566.7 / 3500 = 0.16 \text{ years} = 8.4 \text{ weeks}$$

Cycle time, T_o, is:

$$T_o = \sqrt{\frac{2 * RC}{HC * D}} * \sqrt{\frac{P}{P - D}} = \sqrt{\frac{2 * 650}{15 * 1800}} * \sqrt{\frac{3500}{3500 - 1800}}$$

$$= 0.31 \text{ years}$$

$$= 16.4 \text{ weeks}$$

Variable cost, VC_o, is:

$$VC_o = \sqrt{2 * RC * HC * D} * \sqrt{\frac{P - D}{P}}$$

$$= \sqrt{2 * 650 * 15 * 1800} * \sqrt{\frac{3500 - 1800}{3500}}$$

$$= \pounds 4129 \text{ a year}$$

Total cost is:

$$TC_o = UC * D + VC_o = 50 * 1800 + 4129$$

$$= \pounds 94\,129 \text{ a year.}$$

If it takes two weeks to set up production, the time to start this can be found from the reorder level calculation. The cycle time is longer than lead time, so:

$$\text{ROL} = LT * D = 2 * (1800/52) = 70 \text{ (rounding up to the nearest integer)}$$

Then the best policy is to start making a batch of 567 units whenever stocks fall to 70 units.

Worked Example 3.5

The demand for a product is constant at 20 units a month. Each unit costs £100. Last year the cost of running the company's purchasing department (which sent out 2000 orders) was £50 000. Annual holding costs are 20% of unit cost for capital, 5% for storage space, 3% for deterioration and obsolescence and 2% for insurance. All other costs associated with stocking the item are combined into a fixed annual cost of £2400. Calculate the economic order quantity for the item, the time between orders and the corresponding total cost.

By making the item itself the company could avoid the fixed cost of £2400 a year. With a production rate of 40 units a month, each unit costs £75 and batch set-up costs are £1000. Would it be better for the company to make the item rather than buy it?

Solution

Listing the variables we know in consistent units:

D = 20 * 12 = 240 units a year
UC = £100 a unit
RC = 50 000/2000 = £25 an order
HC = (0.2 + 0.05 + 0.03 + 0.02) * 100 = 0.3 * 100 = £30 a unit a year

Substituting these values gives:

$$Q_o = \sqrt{\frac{2 * RC * D}{HC}} = \sqrt{\frac{2 * 25 * 240}{30}} = 20 \text{ units}$$

$$T_o = Q_o/D = 20/240 = 0.083 \text{ years} \qquad = 1 \text{ month}$$

$$VC_o = \sqrt{2 * RC * HC * D} = \sqrt{2 * 25 * 30 * 240} \qquad = £600 \text{ a year}$$

$$TC_o = UC * D + VC_o = 100 * 240 + 600 \qquad = £24\,600 \text{ a year}$$

Adding the fixed cost of £2400 a year to give a total cost of £27 000 a year. The company could make the item itself with:

P = 40 * 12 = 480 units a year
UC = £75 a unit
RC = £1000 a batch
HC = 0.3 * 75 = £22.5 a unit a year

This has costs of:

$$VC_o = \sqrt{2 * RC * HC * D} * \sqrt{\frac{P - D}{P}}$$

$$= \sqrt{2 * 1000 * 22.5 * 240} * \sqrt{\frac{480 - 240}{480}}$$

$$= £2324 \text{ a year}$$

$$TC_o = UC * D + VC_o = 75 * 240 + 2324 = £20\,324 \text{ a year}$$

This is lower than the cost of purchases and it would be better for the company to make the item itself. Then:

$$Q_o = \sqrt{\frac{2 * RC * D}{HC}} * \sqrt{\frac{P}{P - D}}$$

$$= \sqrt{\frac{2 * 1000 * 240}{22.5}} * \sqrt{\frac{480}{480 - 240}} = 206.6 \text{ units}$$

$T_o = Q_o/D = 206.6/240$ $= 0.86$ years $= 45$ weeks

$PT = Q_o/P = 206.6/480$ $= 0.43$ years $= 22.4$ weeks

SELF-ASSESSMENT QUESTIONS

3.8   We have just described a situation with a finite replenishment rate and demand reducing the stock level over time. Why did we not describe a situation where stocks are removed instantaneously (when, for example, they are transferred in a batch to another store)?

3.9   What is the maximum stock level when demand is greater than production rate?

3.10 Is DT (the part of a cycle when there is no production):
      (a) greater than PT?
      (b) less than PT?
      (c) either greater than or less than PT?

3.11 When compared with instantaneous replenishment, does a finite replenishment rate lead to:
      (a) the same size batches?
      (b) larger batches?
      (c) smaller batches?
      (d) either larger or smaller batches?

3.3   PLANNED SHORTAGES WITH BACK-ORDERS

3.3.1   Back-orders

The models described so far have assumed that all demand must be met. The implication is that shortages are very expensive and must be avoided. There are, however, situations where planned shortages are beneficial, and an obvious example of this occurs when the cost of keeping an item in stock is higher than the gross profit made from selling it.

When there is customer demand for an item which cannot be met immediately there are shortages, and each customer has a choice:

- he can wait for the item to come into stock, in which case it is met by a back-order, or
- he can withdraw his order and go to another supplier, in which case there are lost sales.

Once a sale has been lost a customer is likely to divert at least some future business to more reliable suppliers. These alternatives with shortages are shown in Figure 3.18. Surveys of customer attitudes suggest that one poor experience is likely to make a customer change suppliers, and it takes 14 good experiences fully to restore confidence.

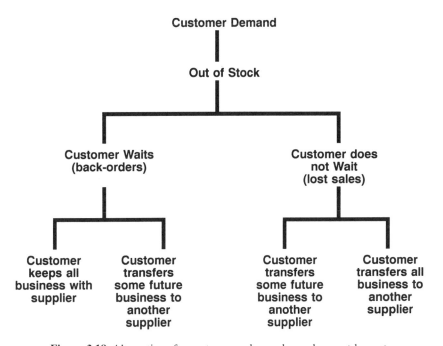

Figure 3.18 Alternatives for customers when a demand cannot be met

In this section we will look at situations where customers are prepared to wait and shortages are back-ordered. Section 3.4 looks at situations where sales are lost as customers transfer their business to another supplier.

An example of back-orders is found in furniture showrooms. Each showroom carries a selection of furniture which customers can examine to choose what they want, but usually there is not enough in stock to cover all demand. Customers are asked to wait for deliveries from suppliers or regional distribution centres, and they are given a likely date to cover the lead time. A slightly different illustration exists in car showrooms where each showroom carries only a selection of cars, but not a complete range. Customers cannot examine the car they want, including all the options, but must make some selections and hope the result meets their expectations. The showroom places an order with its supplier, and the customer is promised delivery as soon as possible, preferably from the next batch of cars arriving.

These examples suggest that back-ordering is common when:

- the unit cost of inventory items is high
- there are many different items which could be stocked
- it would be too expensive to hold complete stocks
- lead times from suppliers are short
- there is limited competition
- customers are willing to wait for delivery.

In extreme cases an organisation keeps no stock at all and meets *all* demand by back orders. We will look at the more common case where some stock is kept, but not enough to cover all demand. The key question is how much of the demand should be met from stock and how much from back-orders.

In Summary

Sometimes it is beneficial to have planned shortages. This is particularly true when customer demand is not lost but can be met from back-orders.

3.3.2   Time-Dependent Shortage Cost

Suppose customers demand an item which is out of stock, but they are all willing to accept back-orders. There will be an associated cost to allow for administration, loss of goodwill, some loss of future orders, expediting, and so on. This cost is likely to rise with increasing delay. We can, then, define a shortage cost, SC, which is time-dependent and is a cost per unit per unit time delayed.

Figure 3.19 shows the variation of stock level when shortages are back-ordered. In this diagram back-orders are shown as negative stock levels, and we again assume that optimal values can be found to make all cycles the same.

The analysis starts by taking the costs of a single cycle (as shown in Figure 3.20). There are four cost components for each cycle:

- unit cost component: $UC * Q$

- reorder cost component: RC

- holding cost component: $\dfrac{HC * (Q - S) * T_1}{2}$

  (an average stock of $(Q - S)/2$ held for a time T_1)

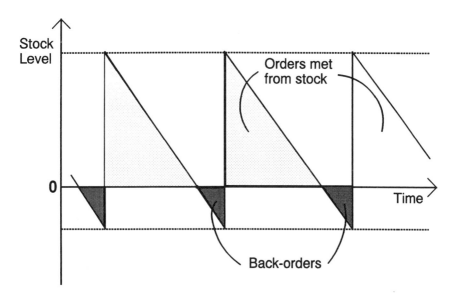

Figure 3.19 Stock level with back-orders

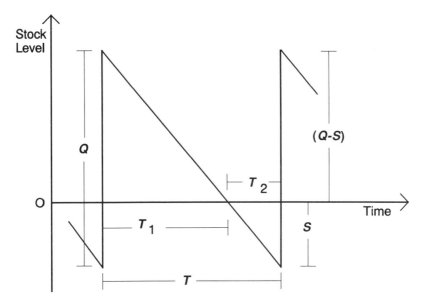

Figure 3.20 A single stock cycle with back-orders

- shortage cost component: $\dfrac{SC * S * T_2}{2}$

(an average shortage of S held for a time T_2)

Adding these together gives the total cost per cycle:

$$UC * Q + RC + \frac{HC * (Q - S) * T_1}{2} + \frac{SC * S * T_2}{2}$$

During the first part of the cycle all demand is met from stock, so the amount supplied is $Q - S$, which equals the demand of $D * T_1$. During the second part of the cycle all demand is back-ordered, so the shortage, S, equals the demand of $D * T_2$. Substituting:

$$T_1 = (Q - S)/D \qquad \text{and} \qquad T_2 = S/D$$

gives the total cost per cycle as:

$$UC * Q + RC + \frac{HC * (Q - S)^2}{2 * D} + \frac{SC * S^2}{2 * D}$$

Then dividing by T gives the total cost per unit time, TC:

$$TC = UC * D + \frac{RC * D}{Q} + \frac{HC * (Q - S)^2}{2 * Q} + \frac{SC * S^2}{2 * Q}$$

This equation has two variables, Q and S, so we can differentiate with respect to both of these and set the results to zero:

$$\frac{\delta(TC)}{\delta Q} = 0 = -\frac{RC * D}{Q^2} + \frac{HC}{2} - \frac{HC * S^2}{2 * Q^2} - \frac{SC * S^2}{2 * Q^2}$$

and

$$\frac{\delta(TC)}{\delta S} = 0 = -HC + \frac{HC * S}{Q} - \frac{SC * S}{Q}$$

After some manipulation, which we need not describe in detail, these simultaneous equations can be solved to give optimal values:

$$\text{Optimal order size} = Q_o = \sqrt{\frac{2 * RC * D * (HC + SC)}{HC * SC}}$$

$$\text{Optimal amount to be back-ordered} = S_o = \sqrt{\frac{2 * RC * HC * D}{SC * (HC + SC)}}$$

In addition we know:

$$
\begin{aligned}
T_1 &= (Q_o - S_o)/D & &= \text{time during which demand is met}\\
T_2 &= S_o/D & &= \text{during which demand is back-ordered}\\
T &= T_1 + T_2 & &= \text{cycle time}
\end{aligned}
$$

In Summary

When products can be supplied through back-orders there is a time-dependent shortage cost. This can be used to find optimal values for the order size and amount to be back-ordered.

Worked Example 3.6

Demand for an item is constant at 100 units a month. Unit cost is £50, reorder cost is £50, holding cost is 25% of value a year, shortage cost for back-orders is 40% of value a year. Find an optimal inventory policy for the item.

Solution

Listing the variables given in consistent units:

$$
\begin{aligned}
D &= 100 * 12 = 1200 \text{ units a year}\\
UC &= £50 \text{ a unit}\\
RC &= £50 \text{ an order}\\
HC &= 0.25 * 50 = £12.5 \text{ a unit a year}\\
SC &= 0.4 * 50 = £20 \text{ a unit a year}
\end{aligned}
$$

Then substitution gives:

$$
Q_o = \sqrt{\frac{2 * RC * D * (HC + SC)}{HC * SC}} = \sqrt{\frac{2 * 50 * 1200 * (12.5 + 20)}{12.5 * 20}}
$$

$$
= 125 \text{ units}
$$

$$
S_o = \sqrt{\frac{2 * RC * HC * D}{SC * (HC + SC)}} = \sqrt{\frac{2 * 50 * 12.5 * 1200}{20 * (12.5 + 20)}}
$$

$$
= 48 \text{ units}
$$

$$T_1 = (Q_o - S_o)/D = (125 - 48)/1200 = 0.064 \text{ years} = 3.3 \text{ weeks}$$
$$T_2 = S_o/D = 48/1200 = 0.04 \text{ years} = 2.1 \text{ weeks}$$
$$T = T_1 + T_2 = 5.4 \text{ weeks}$$

In this example the shortage cost is relatively low, so the item is out of stock almost 40% of the time.

SELF-ASSESSMENT QUESTIONS

3.12 When are inventory items back-ordered?

3.13 What do you think would be the major problem in using the back-order analysis described?

3.14 Are inventory systems with back-orders:
   (a) always more expensive than those without back-orders?
   (b) always less expensive than those without back-orders?
   (c) either more or less expensive than those with back-orders?

3.4 LOST SALES

The previous analysis assumed that if customers' demands could not be met from stock they would wait for a back-order to arrive. The alternative would have the customer going to another supplier, in which case sales would be lost. The pattern of stock level for this situation is shown in Figure 3.21.

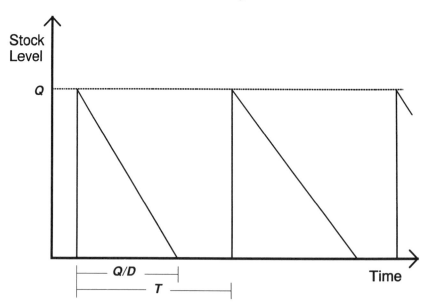

Figure 3.21 Stock level with lost sales

An initial stock of Q runs out after a time Q/D, and all subsequent demand is lost until the next replenishment arrives. In these circumstances the equality $Q = D * T$ no longer applies as some demand is unsatisfied and Q (the amount supplied in a cycle) is less than $D * T$ (the amount of demand in a cycle). In particular, the unsatisfied demand in a cycle is $D * T - Q$.

We should also notice that when shortages are allowed the aims of minimising costs and maximising revenue are no longer the same. If shortages are allowed we might, for example, minimise costs by holding no stock at all. A more appropriate objective would be to maximise net revenue.

If we define SP as the selling price per unit of an item, each unit of lost sales has a cost which can be considered in two parts:

- loss of profit. This is a notional cost which can be defined as $SP - UC$ per unit of sales lost.
- direct costs. This is an actual cost which includes loss of goodwill, loss of future custom, remedial action, and so on. We will define this as DC per unit of sales lost.

If we are aiming to minimise costs, only the direct costs should be included as the loss of profit will appear later in the analysis. Then the four cost components per stock cycle are:

- unit cost component: $UC * Q$

- reorder cost component: RC

- holding cost component: $\dfrac{HC * Q}{2} * \dfrac{Q}{D}$

  (an average stock of $Q/2$ held for time Q/D)

- lost sales cost component: $DC * (D * T - Q)$

  ($D * T - Q$ lost sales each costing DC)

Then the net revenue per cycle is the gross revenue ($SP * Q$) minus the sum of these costs:

$$SP * Q - UC * Q - RC - \frac{HC * Q^2}{2 * D} - DC * (D * T - Q)$$

Dividing this by T gives the net revenue per unit time:

$$R = \frac{1}{T} * \left[Q * (DC + SP - UC) - RC - \frac{HC * Q^2}{2 * D} - DC * D * T \right]$$

Now we can define:

LC = cost of each unit of lost sales *including* loss of profit
$\quad = DC + SP - UC$
and Z = proportion of demand satisfied
$\quad = Q/(D*T)$

Then we can concentrate on the variable cost (ignoring the fixed cost $DC*D$) to get:

$$R = Z * \left[D*LC - \frac{RC*D}{Q} - \frac{HC*Q}{2} \right]$$

Differentiating this with respect to Q and setting the result to zero gives a maximum value for net revenue:

$$\frac{dR}{dQ} = 0 = -\frac{Z*RC*D}{Q^2} - \frac{Z*HC}{2}$$

or

$$Q_0 = \sqrt{\frac{2*RC*D}{HC}}$$

which is the standard economic order quantity. When this is substituted into the revenue equation we get the optimal value for R, which we will call R_0:

$$R_0 = Z * \left[D*LC - \sqrt{2*RC*HC*D} \right]$$

Now Z is the proportion of demand met, so we can set this to any value in the range $0 \le Z \le 1$. We want to adjust Z so that R_0 is maximised. This means:

- if the term in brackets is positive, we want to make Z as large as possible (i.e. set Z to 1 and meet all demand)
- if the term in brackets is negative, we want to make Z as small as possible (i.e. set Z to zero and meet none of the demand)
- if the term in brackets is zero the revenue is zero whatever value is given to Z (i.e. Z can be set to any value, and any convenient proportion of demand can be met).

These conditions can be formalised into a general rule, as follows.

- If $D*LC > \sqrt{2*RC*HC*D}$ (i.e. revenue is positive) set $Z = 1$
- If $D*LC < \sqrt{2*RC*HC*D}$ (i.e. revenue is negative) set $Z = 0$
- If $D*LC = \sqrt{2*RC*HC*D}$ (i.e. revenue is zero) set Z to any convenient value

Worked Example 3.7

Find the best ordering policy for the following three items.

Item	D	RC	HC	DC	SP	UC
1	50	150	80	20	110	90
2	100	400	200	10	200	170
3	50	500	400	30	350	320

Solution

For each item we have to calculate $D * LC$ and compare this with $\sqrt{2 * RC * HC * D}$. We should also remember that, by definition,

$$LC = DC + SP - UC$$

Item 1:
$LC = DC + SP - UC = 20 + 110 - 90 = 40$
$D * LC = 50 * 40 = 2000$
$\sqrt{2 * RC * HC * D} = \sqrt{2 * 150 * 80 * 50} = 1095$
$D * LC > \sqrt{2 * RC * HC * D}$ so net revenue is positive and we set $Z = 1$.
All demand is met and no sales are lost. Then:
$R_o = Z * \left[D * LC - \sqrt{2 * RC * HC * D} \right] = 1 * [2000 - 1095] = 905$
$Q_o = \sqrt{(2 * RC * D / HC)} = \sqrt{(2 * 150 * 50/80)} = 13.7$

Item 2:
$LC = DC + SP - UC = 10 + 200 - 170 = 40$
$D * LC = 100 * 40 = 4000$
$\sqrt{2 * RC * HC * D} = \sqrt{2 * 400 * 200 * 100} = 4000$
$D * LC = \sqrt{2 * RC * HC * D}$ so we set Z to any convenient value.
The net revenue is zero whatever value we choose for Z, provided all orders are of size:
$Q_o = \sqrt{(2 * RC * D / HC)} = \sqrt{(2 * 400 * 100/200)} = 20$

Item 3:
$LC = DC + SP - UC = 30 + 350 - 320 = 60$
$D * LC = 50 * 60 = 3000$
$\sqrt{2 * RC * HC * D} = \sqrt{2 * 500 * 400 * 50} = 4472$
$D * LC < \sqrt{2 * RC * HC * D}$ so net revenue is negative and we set $Z = 0$.
The item is not stocked at all.

In Summary

When shortages lead to lost sales rather than back-orders we can build a model for maximising net revenues, rather than minimising total costs. This gives a simple rule which determines whether or not an item should be stocked.

SELF-ASSESSMENT QUESTIONS

3.15 When will sales be lost?

3.16 When sales are lost is:
   (a) $Q = D * T$?
   (b) $Q < D * T$?
   (c) $Q > D * T$?
   (d) any of the above?

3.17 What would be the optimal value of Z if $D * LC = \sqrt{2 * RC * HC * D}$?

3.18 Why does the analysis for lost sales maximise revenue rather than minimise costs?

3.19 How would the classic analysis be changed if its objective were to maximise revenue?

3.5   ONE OPPORTUNITY TO BUY BEFORE A PRICE RISE

Suppose an organisation is about to place an order to replenish an item, when the suppliers say their quoted price is about to rise. There is one opportunity to buy at the current price, and all subsequent orders will have a higher price. It may be sensible to place a single large order and take advantage of the current lower price. The next question is, "How big should this single order be?"

Suppose the unit cost is about to rise from UC to a new level NUC and the new economic order quantity becomes Q_0. If we place a single large order of Q (assuming there is no stock remaining) the stock pattern is shown in Figure 3.22.

A reasonable objective would be to order an amount which minimises costs over some long period. We could, for example, look at the total costs over some time horizon TH. During this time there will be:

- a single special cycle of length T, corresponding to the single order for Q units
- a number of ordinary cycles with total length $TH - T$, corresponding to the regular orders of size Q_0. The total demand during this period is $D * (TH - T)$, so the number of orders is $D * (TH - T)/Q_0$.

Now we can find the three cost components for the period TH as shown in Table 3.3 (assuming no shortages are allowed and the holding cost is a proportion, I, of the unit cost). Substituting $Q = D * T$ and adding these components gives the total cost over time TH of:

$$Q * UC + D * TH * NUC - Q * NUC + RC + \frac{D * TH * RC}{Q_0} - \frac{Q * RC}{Q_0}$$

$$+ \frac{I * UC * Q^2}{2 * D} + \frac{I * NUC * Q_0 * TH}{2} - \frac{I * NUC * Q_0 * Q}{2 * D}$$

This can be differentiated with respect to Q and set equal to zero for a minimum:

$$0 = (UC - NUC) - \frac{RC}{Q_0} + \frac{I * UC * Q}{D} - \frac{I * NUC * Q_0}{2 * D}$$

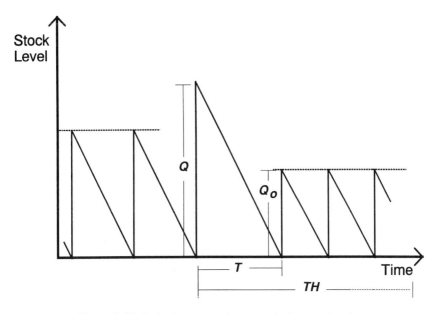

Figure 3.22 A single opportunity to buy before a price rise

Table 3.3

	First cycle	Remaining cycles
• unit cost component:	$D * T * UC$	$D * (TH - T) * NUC$
• reorder cost component:	RC	$\dfrac{D * (TH - T)}{Q_0} * RC$
• holding cost component:	$\dfrac{I * UC * Q * T}{2}$	$\dfrac{I * NUC * Q_0 * (TH - T)}{2}$

After some manipulation, which we need not describe in detail, this simplifies to give the size of the single order as:

$$Q = \frac{(NUC - UC) * D}{I * NUC} + Q_0 * \sqrt{\frac{NUC}{UC}}$$

This analysis assumes we make the decision to buy Q when there is no stock left. If there is some stock remaining the amount is simply subtracted from the calculated quantity for Q.

Worked Example 3.8

The demand for an item is 400 units a year. Reorder cost is £50, holding cost is 20% of value a year. Lead time is effectively zero, so an order is about to be placed when there is no remaining stock. The quoted unit cost is about to rise from £9 to £10. How much should be bought in this single order? How much should be bought if there are still 50 units of stock remaining when the single order is placed?

Solution

Listing the variables given:

D = 400 units a year
UC = £9 a unit
NUC = £10 a unit
RC = £50 an order
I = 0.2

The new economic order quantity is:

$$Q_0 = \sqrt{\frac{2 * RC * D}{I * NUC}} = \sqrt{\frac{2 * 50 * 400}{0.2 * 10}} = 141.4$$

Then substitution gives the optimal amount for a single order as:

$$Q = \frac{(NUC - UC) * D}{I * NUC} + Q_0 * \sqrt{\frac{NUC}{UC}}$$

$$= \frac{(10 - 9) * 400}{0.2 * 10} + 141.4 * \sqrt{\frac{10}{9}}$$

$$= 349 \text{ units}$$

If there are already 50 units in stock we subtract this from the 349 and order 299 units (or more probably 300).

In Summary

If there is a single opportunity to buy before an impending price rise we can calculate the order quantity that minimises total costs over an arbitrarily long time horizon.

SELF-ASSESSMENT QUESTIONS

3.20 If the unit cost rises, will optimal order quantity:
(a) increase?
(b) decrease?
(c) either increase or decrease?
3.21 If unit cost is about to rise, why do we not buy as many units as possible at the lower price?

3.6 INVENTORY SYSTEMS WITH CONSTRAINTS

3.6.1 Interactions between Items

The models developed so far have assumed that each inventory item is completely independent. Then the size of order for each item is the economic order quantity and there is no need to consider interactions with other items. In practice there are several situations where, although demand for each item is independent, it may be necessary to consider interactions between different items. Examples of this are:

- when several items are ordered from the same supplier; delivery costs may be reduced by combining orders for these items in a single delivery;
- when there are constraints on the system, such as limited warehouse space or a maximum acceptable investment in stock.

Analyses of this type can become complex, and the amount of arithmetic can be excessive. For this reason we will limit our discussion to examples where constraints are put on stock levels. There are several types of constraints which are common in stock control. They include:

- limited storage space
- maximum acceptable investment in stock
- maximum number of deliveries which can be accepted
- maximum number of orders which can be placed
- maximum size of delivery which can be handled
- and so on

Most analyses of constraints are similar, and we will illustrate two of these. The first shows an intuitive approach to problems where there is a limited amount of storage space. The second is a more formal analysis for constrained investment.

In Summary

There are several situations in which inventory items cannot be treated in isolation. Typical examples of this have constraints on stock levels.

3.6.2 Constraints on Storage Space

If the economic order quantity is used for all items in an inventory, it is possible that the resulting total stock will exceed the available storage capacity. Then we need some means of reducing the stock until it is within acceptable limits. One approach would put an additional cost on space used. Then the holding cost would be in two parts:

- the original holding cost, HC, which we have used before
- an additional cost, AC, related to the storage area used by each unit of the item

Then the total holding cost per unit per unit time becomes:

$$HC + AC * S_i$$

where S_i is the amount of space occupied by one unit of item i. When this revised cost is used in the economic order quantity calculation it gives the result:

$$Q_i = \sqrt{\frac{2 * RC_i * D_i}{HC_i + AC * S_i}}$$

In this equation we have used subscripts for all variables to ensure generality and allow all values to vary for different items.

If there are no constraints on space, a value of zero can be given to AC, and the result is the standard economic order quantity. If, however, space is constrained AC can be given a positive value and order quantities of all items are reduced from Q_{oi} to Q_i. As the average stock level is $Q_i/2$, this automatically reduces the amount of stock held. The reduction necessary in stock and the consequent value of AC depend on the severity of space constraints. One way of finding appropriate solutions is iteratively to adjust AC until the space required exactly matches available capacity. This approach is illustrated in the following worked example.

Worked Example 3.9

An organisation is concerned with the space occupied by three items which have the characteristics shown in Table 3.4. Reorder cost for the items is constant at £1000, while holding cost is 20% of value a year. If the company wants to allocate an average space of 300 cubic metres to the items, what would be the best ordering policy? How much would this constraint on space increase variable inventory costs?

Table 3.4

Item	Unit cost	Demand	Space per unit (m^3)
1	100	500	1
2	200	400	2
3	300	200	3

Solution

We should start by calculating the reorder quantities to see if the space constraint is limiting.

- Item 1
  $Q_{o1} = \sqrt{(2 * RC * D_1/HC_1)} = \sqrt{(2 * 1000 * 500/20)} = 223.6$ units
  Average space $= S_1 * Q_{o1}/2 = 1 * 223.6/2 = 111.8$ cubic metres

- Item 2
  $Q_{o2} = \sqrt{(2 * RC * D_2/HC_2)} = \sqrt{(2 * 1000 * 400/40)} = 141.4$ units
  Average space $= S_2 * Q_{o2}/2 = 2 * 141.2/2 = 141.4$ cubic metres

- Item 3
  $Q_{o3} = \sqrt{(2 * RC * D_3/HC_3)} = \sqrt{(2 * 1000 * 200/60)} = 81.6$ units
  Average space $= S_3 * Q_{o3}/2 = 3 * 81.6/2 = 122.4$ cubic metres

Using economic order quantities, the average space occupied is 375.6 cubic metres. This is above the limit of 300 cubic metres set by the company, so stocks must be reduced. Thus we set the additional cost for space, AC, to an arbitrary value, say 1, and calculate modified order quantities.

- Item 1
  $Q_1 = \sqrt{(2*RC*D_1/(HC_1+AC*S_1))} = \sqrt{(2*1000*500/(20+1*1))} = 218.2$ units
  Average space $= S_1 * Q_{o1}/2 = 1 * 218.2/2 = 109.1$ cubic metres

- Item 2
  $$Q_2 = \sqrt{(2 * RC * D_2/(HC_2 + AC * S_2))} = \sqrt{(2 * 1000 * 400/(40 + 1 * 2))}$$
  $$= 138.0 \text{ units}$$
  Average space $= S_2 * Q_{o2}/2 = 2 * 138.0/2 = 138.0$ cubic metres

- Item 3
  $$Q_3 = \sqrt{(2 * RC * D_3/(HC_3 + AC * S_3))} = \sqrt{(2 * 1000 * 200/(60 + 1 * 3))}$$
  $$= 79.7 \text{ units}$$
  Average space $= S_3 * Q_{o3}/2 = 3 * 79.7/2 = 119.6$ cubic metres

This gives an average stock of 366.7 cubic metres. Although this is less than before, it is still above the limits set by the company. We should repeat the calculations, iteratively increasing AC until we get results which satisfy the constraint. Illustrative results are shown in Table 3.5. This table shows that the space constraint is met when AC is around 11 (actually 11.37). To ensure the stock is kept within the specified limit, we might set AC to 12. The variable costs of this policy can be calculated as follows.

Table 3.5

AC	Q_1	Q_2	Q_3	Space needed
0	223.6	141.4	81.6	375.6
1	218.2	138.0	79.7	366.7
5	200.6	126.5	73.0	336.0
10	182.6	115.5	66.7	306.8
11	179.6	113.6	65.6	301.8
12	176.8	111.8	64.5	297.0
13	174.0	110.1	63.6	292.5

- Item 1
  Using economic order quantity:
  $$VC_{o1} = \sqrt{(2 * RC * HC_1 * D_1)} = \sqrt{(2 * 1000 * 20 * 500)} = £4472$$
  Using the revised order quantity:
  $$VC_1 = RC * D_1/Q_1 + HC_1 * Q_1/2 = 1000 * 500/176.8 + 20 * 176.8/2$$
  $$= £4596$$

- Item 2
  Using economic order quantity:
  $$VC_{o2} = \sqrt{(2 * RC * HC_2 * D_2)} = \sqrt{(2 * 1000 * 40 * 400)} = £5657$$
  Using the revised order quantity:
  $$VC_2 = RC * D_2/Q_2 + HC_2 * Q_2/2 = 1000 * 400/111.8 + 40 * 111.8/2$$
  $$= £5814$$

- Item 3
  Using economic order quantity:
  $VC_{o3} = \sqrt{(2 * RC * HC_3 * D_3)} = \sqrt{(2 * 1000 * 60 * 200)} = £4899$
  Using the revised order quantity:
  $VC_3 = RC * D_3/Q_3 + HC_3 * Q_3/2 = 1000 * 200/64.5 + 60 * 64.5/2$
  $\quad = £5036$

Thus, to meet the space constraint the total variable cost has risen from $(4472 + 5657 + 4899) = £15\ 028$ to $(4596 + 5814 + 5036) = £15\ 446$, which is a rise of less than 3%.

In Summary

For inventory systems with constraints on space, revised order quantities can be found by adding additional costs for the space used. This reduces order quantities, and hence average stock levels.

3.6.3   Constraints on Average Investment in Stock

In the analysis for constrained space we calculated revised order quantities by including an additional cost for space occupied. This procedure gives optimal solutions, and its derivation is usually found from more formal analysis. We can demonstrate this by considering a similar problem with constraints on the average investment allowed in stocks.

Suppose an organisation stocks N items and enforces an upper limit, UL, on the total average investment. The calculated economic order quantity for each item i is Q_{oi}, but again we need some means of calculating the best, lower amount Q_i which allows for the constraint.

The average stock of item i is $Q_i/2$ and the average investment in this item is $UC * Q_i/2$. The problem then becomes one of constrained optimisation:

Minimise: total variable cost
Subject to: upper limit on average investment

That is:

$$\text{Minimise: } VC = \sum_{i=1}^{N} \left[\frac{RC_i * D_i}{Q_i} + \frac{HC_i * Q_i}{2} \right]$$

$$\text{Subject to: } \sum_{i=1}^{N} \frac{UC_i * Q_i}{2} \leq UL$$

The usual way of solving problems of this type is to eliminate the constraint by introducing a Lagrange multiplier and incorporating the constraint into a revised objective function. In particular, the constraint is adjusted to make it less than or equal to zero, and the result is multiplied by the Lagrange multiplier, $\mathcal{L}$. This is incorporated in the revised objective function:

$$\text{Minimise} \sum_{i=1}^{N} \left[\frac{RC_i * D_i}{Q_i} + \frac{HC_i * Q_i}{2} \right] + \mathcal{L} * \left[\sum_{i=1}^{N} \frac{UC_i * Q_i}{2} - UL \right]$$

Although it is quite straightforward, solving this equation is rather messy. The objective function is differentiated with respect to both Q_i and $\mathcal{L}$. Then setting both of these derivatives to zero gives two simultaneous equations. The Lagrange multiplier can be eliminated from these to give the overall result:

$$Q_i = Q_{oi} * \frac{2 * UL * HC}{UC * \sum_{i=1}^{N} VC_{oi}}$$

When the holding cost is a fixed proportion of the unit cost this solution has the best order quantity for each item as a fixed proportion of the economic order quantity. This approach is demonstrated in the following worked example.

Worked Example 3.10

A company is concerned with the stock of three items with the characteristics shown in Table 3.6. The items have a reorder cost of £100 and a holding cost of 20% of value a year. What would be the best ordering policy if the company wants to limit average investment in these items to £4000?

Table 3.6

Item	Demand	Unit cost
1	100	100
2	300	60
3	200	40

Solution

To start this analysis we need to calculate the total variable cost if economic order quantities are used.

- Item 1
  $Q_{o1} = \sqrt{(2 * RC * D_1/HC_1)} = \sqrt{(2 * 100 * 100/20)} = 31.62$ units
  $VC_{o1} = \sqrt{(2 * RC * HC_1 * D_1)} = \sqrt{(2 * 100 * 20 * 100)} = £632.46$ a year
  Average stock $= Q_{o1}/2 = 31.62/2 = 15.81$ units
  Average investment $= UC_1 *$ average stock $= 100 * 15.81$
  $\qquad = £1581.00$

- Item 2
  $Q_{o2} = \sqrt{(2 * RC * D_2/HC_2)} = \sqrt{(2 * 100 * 300/12)} = 70.71$ units
  $VC_{o2} = \sqrt{(2 * RC * HC_2 * D_2)} = \sqrt{(2 * 100 * 12 * 300)} = £848.53$ a year
  Average stock $= Q_{o2}/2 = 70.71/2 = 35.36$ units
  Average investment $= UC_2 *$ average stock $= 60 * 35.36$
  $\qquad = £2121.60$

- Item 3
  $Q_{o3} = \sqrt{(2 * RC * D_3/HC_3)} = \sqrt{(2 * 100 * 200/8)} = 70.71$ units
  $VC_{o3} = \sqrt{(2 * RC * HC_3 * D_3)} = \sqrt{(2 * 100 * 8 * 200)} = £565.69$ a year
  Average stock $= Q_{o2}/2 = 70.71/2 = 35.36$ units
  Average investment $= UC_2 *$ average stock $= 40 * 35.36$
  $\qquad = £1414.40$

Using economic order quantities, average investment in the three items is $(1581.00+2121.60+1414.40) = £5117$. This is above the limit of £4000 imposed by the company, so the order quantities must be reduced.

The sum of variable costs is:

$$632.46 + 848.53 + 565.69 = 2046.68$$

Then substitution of the values given gives revised order quantities as follows.

- Item 1

$$Q_1 = Q_{o1} * \frac{2 * UL * HC}{UC * \sum_{i=1}^{N} VC_{oi}}$$

$$= 31.62 * \frac{2 * 4000 * 20}{100 * 2046.68} = 24.72$$

  Average investment $= UC * Q_1/2 = 100 * 12.36 = £1236$

- Item 2

$$Q_2 = Q_{o2} * \frac{2 * UL * HC}{UC * \sum_{i=1}^{N} VC_{oi}}$$

$$= 70.71 * \frac{2 * 4000 * 12}{60 * 2046.68} = 55.28$$

Average investment $= UC * Q_2/2 = 60 * 27.64 = £1658.40$

- Item 3

$$Q_3 = Q_{o3} * \frac{2 * UL * HC}{UC * \sum_{i=1}^{N} VC_{oi}}$$

$$= 70.71 * \frac{2 * 4000 * 8}{40 * 2046.68} = 55.28$$

Average investment $= UC * Q_3/2 = 40 * 27.64 = £1105.60$

Thus the total average investment is $(1236.00 + 1658.40 + 1105.60) = £4000$.

In this example the holding cost was defined as 20% of unit cost, so we could have saved some effort by simply multiplying the economic order quantities by:

$$2 * 4000 * 0.2/2046.68 = 0.78$$

In Summary

When limits are placed on average investment in stock, reduced order quantities can be calculated. When the holding cost is a fraction of unit cost, the revised order quantities are fixed proportions of the economic order quantities.

SELF-ASSESSMENT QUESTIONS

3.22 If demand for inventory items is independent, does this mean there are never any interactions which need to be considered?

3.23 How might the average stock level be reduced when storage space is limited?

3.24 If the total investment in stock is limited will the best order quantity for each item:
(a) equal the economic order quantity?
(b) be greater than the EOQ?
(c) be less than the EOQ?
(d) be either greater or less than the EOQ?

SUMMARY OF CHAPTER

This chapter has described a number of inventory models, where demand and other variables are known with certainty. In particular it has:

- discussed how costs might vary with changing order size
- described how to find the optimal policy when discounted unit costs are available
- extended this analysis to changing reorder costs
- calculated optimal batch sizes with finite replenishment rates
- examined back-orders and calculated optimal values with time-dependent shortage costs
- defined an optimal policy when shortages lead to lost sales
- calculated an optimal order size when there is one chance to buy before a price rise
- discussed problems with constraint
- calculated order quantities with constraints on space and investment

ADDITIONAL PROBLEMS

3.1 Demand for an item is constant at 400 units a month. The reorder cost (including delivery charges) is £1240 and the cost of holding stock is 30% of value a year. A supplier quotes costs as follows:

Order quantity:	0–1499	1500–1999	2000–2499	2500 or more
Unit cost:	£12.60	£12.20	£11.80	£11.20

A second supplier quotes a basic price of £12, but with a discount to £11.40 for orders of 1500 or more. What would be the best ordering policy?

3.2 The unit cost of an item is as follows:

Order quantity:	0–99	100–399	400–999	1000 or more
Unit cost:	£20	£19.40	£18.80	£18

Demand for the item is constant at 2000 a year, reorder cost is £50 and holding cost is 40% of value a year. What is the best ordering policy? If it were possible to reduce reorder costs so that they were effectively zero, how would this effect the ordering policy?

3.3 Demand for an item is 500 units a month, while the production rate is 1000 units a month. Unit cost is £10, batch set-up cost is £2000 and holding cost is £1 a unit a month. What is the optimal batch size and corresponding cost?

3.4 An item of inventory has a constant demand of 2500 units a year. It costs £500 to set up each production run and the variable cost is £30 a unit. Holding costs are 20% of value a year and the production rate is 10 000 units a year. There is a lead time of two months from receiving a production requisition until finished units begin to come from the production line. Find the optimal batch size and the reorder level (assuming shortages are not allowed). What are the costs of this policy?

3.5 A company examines one inventory item and decides that the holding cost is about 25% of value a year, while the shortage cost for back-orders is 150% of value a year. Unit cost is £400 and reorder cost is £100. Demand is constant at 300 units a year and all shortages are met by back-orders. What is the optimal policy for this item? What proportion of time is demand met by back-orders, and what is the cost of this policy?

3.6 Demand for an item is constant at 100 units a year. Unit cost is £50, reorder cost is £40 and holding cost is 40% of value a year. Any demand which occurs when no stock remains is lost. What is the minimum selling price which makes it profitable to stock the item?

3.7 Demand for an item is 250 units a year. The current unit cost is £100 but this is about to rise to £110. Reorder cost is £100 and holding cost is 25% of value a year. If there is one opportunity to place an order at the current price, how big should this order be?

3.8 A company stocks four items with the characteristics shown in Table 3.7. Describe the effects of constrained space and investment on this system.

Table 3.7

Item	Demand	Unit cost	Holding cost	Reorder cost	Space used (m³)
1	500	200	35	80	4
2	300	100	20	100	3
3	200	300	45	120	6
4	400	200	40	80	5

REFERENCES FOR FURTHER READING

- Many operations management and management science books describe a range of inventory models. Some of these, together with specialised inventory control books, are listed below.

Aft, L.S. (1987) *Production and Inventory Control*, Harcourt, Orlando, FL.

Buffa, E.S. and Miller, J.G. (1979) *Production-Inventory Systems: Planning and Control* (3rd edn), Irwin, Homewood, IL.

Buffa, E.S. and Sarin, R.K. (1987) *Modern Production/Operations Management*, John Wiley, New York.

Chase, R.B. and Aquilano, N.J. (1989) *Production and Operations Management* (5th edn), Irwin, Homewood, IL.

Davis, K.R., McKeown, P.G. and Rakes, T.R. (1986), *Management Science: An Introduction*, Kent Publishing, Boston, MA.

Fogarty, D.W. and Hoffman, T.R. (1983) *Production and Inventory Management*, South-Western Publishing, Dallas, TX.

Gaither, N. (1990) *Production and Operations Management* (4th edn), The Dryden Press, Chicago.

Greene, J.H. (1970) *Production and Inventory Control Handbook*, McGraw-Hill, New York.

Hadley, G. and Whitin, T.M. (1963) *Analysis of Inventory Systems*, Prentice Hall, Englewood Cliffs, NJ.

Hax, A.C. and Candea, D. (1984) *Production and Inventory Management*, Prentice Hall, Englewood Cliffs, NJ.

Hoyt, J. (1973) Order Points Tailored to Suit Your Business, *Production and Inventory Management*, Fourth Quarter, 42.

Lewis, C.D. (1970) *Scientific Inventory Control*, Butterworth, London.

Love, S.F. (1979) *Inventory Control*, McGraw-Hill, New York.

Mayer, R.R. (1972) Selection of Rules-of-Thumb in Inventory Control, *Journal of Purchasing*, May, 19.

McLeavy, D.W. and Seetharama, L.N. (1985) *Production Planning and Inventory Control*, Allyn and Bacon, Boston, MA.

Porteus, E.L. (1985) Investing in Reduced Setups in the EOQ Model, *Management Science*, **31**, 998.

Schroeder, R.G. (1989) *Operations Management* (3rd edn), McGraw-Hill, New York.

Silver, E.A. and Peterson, R. (1985) *Decision Systems for Inventory Management and Production Planning* (2nd edn), John Wiley, New York.

Tersine, R.J. (1987) *Principles of Inventory and Materials Management* (2nd edn), North-Holland, New York.

Thomas, A.B. (1980) *Stock Control in Manufacturing Industries* (2nd edn), Gower Press, London.

Trueman, R.E. (1971) Incremental (Marginal) Analysis of Basic Inventory Models, *Decision Sciences*, **2**, 341.

Waters, C.D.J. (1989) *A Practical Introduction to Management Science*, Addison-Wesley, Wokingham.

Waters, C.D.J. (1991) *Introduction to Operations Management*, Addison-Wesley, Wokingham.

4
PROBABILISTIC MODELS FOR INVENTORY CONTROL

SYNOPSIS

The last two chapter have developed a number of models for inventory control. Chapter 2 showed how a quantitative model could relate demand and costs to calculate an optimal order quantity. Chapter 3 removed some of the assumptions of this economic order quantity analysis and developed more general models. These were based on certainty, in that all variables took fixed values which were known in advance. This chapter will introduce uncertainty and develop models where variables are not known exactly but follow some probability distribution.

The chapter starts by discussing the reasons why uncertainty exists in inventory systems. The most common form of uncertainty is in demand. Some analyses for this are described, starting with discrete demand models. The first of these finds an optimal order quantity based on marginal costs. A more formal version of this is presented as the Newsboy Problem. The next analysis finds an optimal stock level for spare parts with known shortage costs. This is followed by a method for jointly calculating the optimal order quantity and reorder level.

It is almost invariably difficult to find reliable shortage costs and most organisations prefer systems where these are not used explicitly. The most common alternative specifies an acceptable service level which describes the percentage of demand which is met directly from stock. Service level models are developed for uncertainty in both demand and lead time.

All the models described so far have been based on fixed order quantities. The chapter ends with a description of the alternative periodic review system.

OBJECTIVES

After reading this chapter and completing the exercises you should be able to:

- discuss areas of uncertainty in inventory systems
- appreciate the need for probabilistic models to describe uncertain demand
- use a marginal analysis to find the best order quantity for a single period
- extend this analysis in a more formal definition of the Newsboy Problem
- calculate an optimal stock level for spare parts when shortage costs are known
- calculate joint reorder quantities and reorder levels with shortages
- understand the principles of service level and safety stock
- determine the best policy for a system with Normally distributed demand
- determine an optimal policy when lead time is uncertain
- determine optimal policies when both demand and lead time are Normally distributed
- describe periodic review systems and calculate target stock levels
- discuss the advantages of alternate ordering policies

4.1 UNCERTAINTY IN INVENTORY SYSTEMS

The economic order quantity analysis described in Chapter 2 assumes costs, demand and lead time are all known exactly and are constant. In Chapter 3 we extended this analysis and developed some models for variable costs, but still assumed the costs and demand were known exactly. In other words, there was no uncertainty in the system.

In practice, almost every inventory system contains uncertainty. Prices rise with inflation, and this alone is enough to give uncertainty about future costs. At the same time, there can be considerable uncertainty in demand (introduced by apparently random fluctuations in customer requirements). In this chapter we will develop some models which allow for uncertainty.

We should start by defining the term "uncertainty". In inventory systems this means that a value is not known exactly, but follows a known probability distribution. Long-term demand for a product might, for example, be Normally distributed with a mean of 10 units a week and standard deviation 2 units a week. We cannot say what demand in a particular week will be, but know it is a random figure drawn from this distribution.

Now we can classify problems according to variables which are:

- unknown—in which case we have complete ignorance of the system and any analysis is difficult
- known (and either constant or variable)—in which case deterministic models are used
- uncertain—in which case probabilistic models are used.

We have already mentioned uncertainty in price and demand, but there are several possible areas for uncertainty. These include:

- *demand.* Aggregate demand for an item often comes from a large number of individual customers. Random fluctuations in the number and size of their orders is translated into a variable and uncertain overall demand.
- *costs.* In recent years there has been a trend for costs to rise continually. The size and timing of increases cannot be predicted, so future inventory costs are uncertain. In addition, conventional accounting practices do not directly identify the costs used by inventory models so some approximations must be used.
- *lead time.* The lead time consists of several parts, including order preparation, location or production of the item by suppliers, packaging, documentation, shipment, transport, checking on arrival, and so on. There are so many steps in this chain of activities that some variability is inevitable. If the item has to be made and shipped internationally the uncertainty in timing may be high, but if it is supplied from a local store the uncertainty should be low.
- *supplied quantity.* Although orders are placed for a certain number of units, there are times when the number actually delivered is different. Obvious reasons for this are checks on quality which reject some delivered units, damage or losses during shipping, and mistakes. Conversely, the supplier might allow some overage and send more units than requested.

Some of the uncertainty in a system (such as lead time, quantity and quality) is directly dependent on suppliers. If they introduce too much uncertainty, corrective action should be taken. One of the dominant themes in recent management thinking is that efficient operations can only be achieved if uncertainty is reduced to a minimum. Problems of supplier reliability are not really part of inventory management, but form part of the wider procurement or quality assurance functions. Although they have direct implications for stock holdings, we must take the view that they cannot be dealt with in the limited field of inventory management.

Some uncertainty in an inventory system is not introduced by suppliers and is attributable to customers, economic conditions, and so on. Often this uncertainty is small and can be ignored. In Chapter 2 we saw how quite large errors in demand, for example, gave relatively small increases in costs. Sometimes, however, the amount of uncertainty is large enough to make results from deterministic models of questionable quality. When this happens we must use alternative probabilistic models.

A key element in probabilistic models is the lead time demand. It does not matter how demand varies outside the lead time, as this is allowed for by the timing of the next order. Once an order is placed, however, and we are working within the lead time it is too late to make allowances for any variation. If demand outside the lead time is higher than expected all that happens is the reorder level is reached sooner than expected: if demand inside the lead time is higher than expected it is too late to make adjustments and there will be shortages. This means that uncertainty in demand and lead time are particularly important for inventory systems.

In Summary

Uncertainty exists in almost all inventory systems. This might appear in costs, demand, lead time or amount supplied. Provided the uncertainty is small, deterministic models give good results. If there is significant uncertainty, probabilistic analyses should be used.

SELF-ASSESSMENT QUESTIONS

4.1 Where might you find uncertainty in an inventory system?

4.2 Because inventory systems usually contain uncertainty, deterministic models are of little use. Is this statement true?

4.3 What is the difference between variability, uncertainty and ignorance in an inventory system?

4.2 UNCERTAIN DEMAND

Independent demand inventory systems rely on forecasts of demand. Unfortunately, these forecasts are likely to contain some uncertainty, and when this is sufficiently large, we must use models based on probabilistic demand. Many such models have been developed and this section will describe some of the more useful ones.

Aggregate demand for an item is often made up of small demands from a large number of customers. In these circumstances it is reasonable to assume that overall demand is Normally distributed. Then we can easily show why deterministic models can give unsatisfactory results. Deterministic models would use mean values, so that reorder level is calculated as:

reorder level = mean demand * mean lead time

Then three things can happen:

- Actual demand during the lead time exactly matches expected demand. This gives the ideal pattern of stock shown in Figure 4.1(a).
- Actual demand during the lead time is less than expected demand. The resulting stock level is higher than expected and this incurs unnecessary holding costs, as shown in Figure 4.1(b).
- Actual demand during the lead time is greater than expected demand. This gives shortages which may have very high costs, as shown in Figure 4.1(c).

Unfortunately, a Normally distributed demand will be above the mean value in 50% of cycles. Then high costs from shortages and many unsatisfied customers are inevitable. This level of performance must be considered unacceptable, and we need to look for a model which will take the uncertainty into account. The following sections develop models based on uncertain demand.

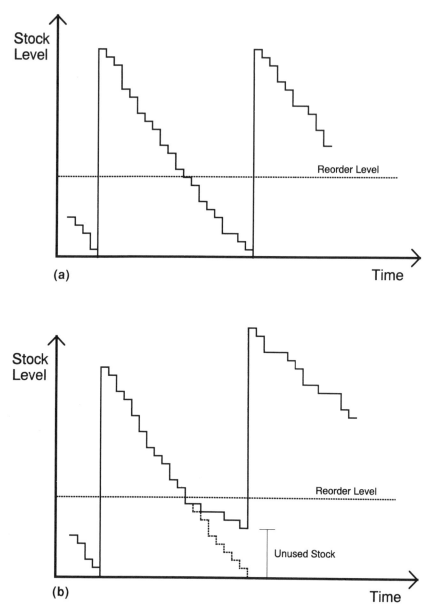

Figure 4.1 Effects of varying demand. (a) Demand during lead time gives the ideal outcome. (b) Demand during lead time is less than expected giving unused stock

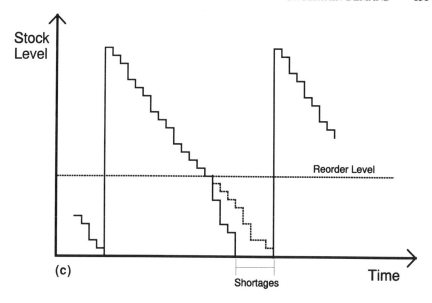

Figure 4.1 (continued) (c) Demand during lead time is greater than expected giving shortages

Worked Example 4.1

Demand for an item over the past six months has been 20, 80, 240, 120, 100 and 40 units respectively. The reorder cost is £50 an order and holding cost is £1 a unit a month. No shortages are allowed and lead time is constant at 1 month. Describe an ordering policy for this item based on average values. How satisfactory is this policy?

Solution

Listing the values given:

D = 100 units a month (taking the average value)
RC = £50 an order
HC = £1 a unit a month
LT = 1 month

Then substitution gives:

Q_o = $\sqrt{(2 * RC * D/HC)} = \sqrt{(2 * 50 * 100/1)} = 100$ units
T_o = $Q_o/D = 100/100 = 1$ month
ROL = $LT * D = 1 * 100 = 100$ units

The optimal policy is to order 100 units whenever gross stock (stock on hand + stock on order) declines to 100 units. On average, this happens once a month.

Table 4.1

Month	1	2	3	4	5	6	7
Opening stock	0	80	100	0	0	0	60
Replenishment	100	100	0	100	100	100	
Demand	20	80	240	120	100	40	
Closing stock	80	100	−140	−20	0	60	

If this policy had been used for the past 6 months the inventory pattern would be as shown in Table 4.1. These figures assume:

- an opening stock of zero, but an order of 100 units arrives at the start of month 1
- replenishments arrive at the beginning of the month and are available during the month they arrive
- no order is placed in month 2 as the reorder level is only reached at the end of the month
- all unmet demand (i.e. negative closing stock) is lost

The stock pattern is shown in Figure 4.2.

This policy is unlikely to be satisfactory. Provided demand is below 100 units a month the system avoids shortages, but gives unnecessary stock. Whenever demand rises above 100 units there are shortages. During the six months, 160 units of demand were not met, despite the statement that no shortages are allowed.

In Summary

Uncertain demand is very common in inventory systems. Probabilistic models for dealing with significant uncertainty assume demand follows a known probability distribution.

4.3   MODELS FOR DISCRETE DEMAND

This section describes some models for demand which is both uncertain and discrete. In the following section we will extend these analyses to cover continuous demand.

4.3.1   Marginal Analysis

The models developed in Chapters 2 and 3 look at stable, unchanging situations where the objective is to minimise costs over the long term. Sometimes, however,

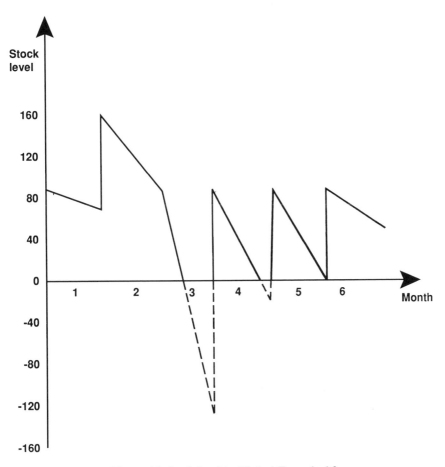

Figure 4.2 Stock level in Worked Example 4.2

models are needed for the shorter term, and in extreme cases for a single period. The first probabilistic model we consider finds an optimal order quantity to satisfy demand for a single period. This kind of analysis is particularly useful for items which have a strong seasonal demand. A baker, for example, may want to know how many Christmas cakes to make, knowing that any cakes left unsold will have a much lower value immediately after Christmas.

We will tackle this problem using a marginal analysis which is based on the expected profit and cost of each unit. Here:

$$\begin{array}{l} \text{expected profit} \\ \text{on a unit} \end{array} = \begin{array}{l} \text{probability of} \\ \text{selling the unit} \end{array} * \begin{array}{l} \text{profit made by} \\ \text{selling a unit} \end{array}$$

$$\begin{array}{l} \text{expected loss} \\ \text{on a unit} \end{array} = \begin{array}{l} \text{probability of not} \\ \text{selling the unit} \end{array} * \begin{array}{l} \text{cost incurred when} \\ \text{a unit is not sold} \end{array}$$

If a small order of size Q is placed, the probability of selling the Qth unit is high and the expected profit is greater than the expected cost. If a large order is placed, the probability of selling the Qth unit is low and the expected profit is less than the expected cost. We might suggest, based on intuition, that the optimal order size is the largest quantity which gives a net expected profit on the Qth unit (and a net expected loss on the $(Q + 1)$th and all following units). Ordering less than this value of Q will lose some potential profit, while ordering more will incur net costs.

We will assume:

- a number of units, Q, are bought
- some of these are sold in the period to meet demand, D
- any units left unsold, $Q - D$, at the end of the period are scrapped at a lower value
- Prob $(D > Q)$ = probability demand in the period is greater than Q
- UC = unit cost
- SP = selling price of a unit during the period
- SV = scrap value of an unsold unit at the end of the period
- profit on each unit sold is $(SP - UC)$
- loss on each unit scrapped is $(UC - SV)$

Then an order of size Q has:

- expected profit on the Qth unit = $\text{Prob}(D \geq Q) * (SP - UC)$
- expected loss on the Qth unit = $\text{Prob}(D < Q) * (UC - SV)$

We will only buy Q units if the expected profit is greater than the expected loss. In other words:

$$\text{Prob}(D \geq Q) * (SP - UC) \geq \text{Prob}(D < Q) * (UC - SV)$$

$$\geq (1 - \text{Prob}(D \geq Q)) * (UC - SV)$$

This gives us the general rule, that an order of size Q is placed so that Q is the largest value which ensures:

$$\text{Prob}(D \geq Q) \geq \frac{UC - SV}{SP - SV}$$

As Q increases the expected profit continues to rise provided the inequality remains valid. At some point the inequality becomes invalid, showing the last units would have an expected loss, and net profit begins to fall. This confirms the optimal solution as the largest value of Q which ensures the inequality is still valid.

Worked Example 4.2

A shop is about to order some industrial heaters for a forecast spell of cold weather. The shop pays £1000 for each heater, and during the cold spell they sell for £2000 each. Demand for the heaters declines markedly after a cold spell, and any unsold units are sold at £500. Previous experience suggests the likely demand for heaters is as follows.

Demand:	1	2	3	4	5
Probability:	0.2	0.3	0.3	0.1	0.1

How many heaters should the shop buy?

Solution

Listing the variables given:

UC = £1000 a unit
SP = £2000 a unit
SV = £500 a unit

Then:

$$\frac{UC - SV}{SP - SV} = \frac{1000 - 500}{2000 - 500} = 0.33$$

Prob($D \geq Q$) is the cumulative probability, and we are looking for the largest value of Q which makes this less than 0.33.

- If $Q = 1$, Prob($D \geq 1$) = 1.0. This is greater than 0.33, so the inequality is valid and we increase Q.
- If $Q = 2$, Prob($D \geq 2$) = 0.8. This is greater than 0.33, so the inequality is valid and we increase Q.
- If $Q = 3$, Prob($D \geq 3$) = 0.5. This is greater than 0.33, so the inequality is valid and we increase Q.
- If $Q = 4$, Prob($D \geq 4$) = 0.2. This is less than 0.33, so the inequality is no longer valid.

This identifies $Q = 3$ as the highest value where the inequality is valid and this is the optimal solution.

In Summary

A marginal analysis can be used to find the optimal order quantity for a single period. An order is placed for the largest value of Q which makes:

$$\text{Prob}(D \geq Q) \geq \frac{UC - SV}{SP - SV}$$

4.3.2 Newsboy Problem

The marginal analysis described above is particularly useful for seasonal goods, and a standard illustration is phrased in terms of a newsboy selling papers on a street corner. The newsboy has to decide how many papers to buy from his supplier when customer demand is uncertain. If he buys too many papers he is left with unsold stock which has no value at the end of the day: if he buys too few papers he has unsatisfied demand which could have given a higher profit. Because of this illustration, single period problems are usually referred to as Newsboy Problems. Although, it is a widely occurring problem, we will stick to the original description of a newsboy selling papers.

The marginal analysis described above is based on intuitive reasoning, and its derivation was not particularly rigorous. In this section, therefore, we will use a slightly more formal approach to confirm the results. We start this by assuming the newsboy buys Q papers, and then:

- if demand is greater than Q the newsboy will sell all his papers and make a profit of $Q * (SP - UC)$ (assuming there is no penalty for lost sales)
- if demand, D, is less than Q, the newsboy will only sell D of his papers at full price, and will get the scrap value, SV, for each of the remaining $Q - D$. Then his profit is $D * SP + (Q - D) * SV - Q * UC$

The optimal value for Q would maximise expected profit. To simplify the arithmetic we will assume there is no scrap value, so $SV = 0$, and we get the demands, profits and probabilities shown in Table 4.2. The overall expected profit is the sum of the profits multiplied by their probabilities. If the newsboy buys Q papers, the expected profit, $EP(Q)$, is:

Table 4.2

Demand	Profit	Probability
0	$0 * SP - Q * UC$	Prob(0)
1	$1 * SP - Q * UC$	Prob(1)
2	$2 * SP - Q * UC$	Prob(2)
$\vdots$	$\vdots$	$\vdots$
$Q - 1$	$(Q - 1) * SP - Q * UC$	Prob($Q - 1$)
Q	$Q * (SP - UC)$	Prob(Q)
$Q + 1$	$Q * (SP - UC)$	Prob($Q + 1$)
$\vdots$	$\vdots$	$\vdots$
∞	$Q * (SP - UC)$	Prob(∞)

$EP(Q)$ = sum of (profit * probability)

$$= \sum \begin{array}{c} \text{(expected profits} \\ \text{when } D < Q) \end{array} + \sum \begin{array}{c} \text{(expected profits} \\ \text{when } D \geq Q) \end{array}$$

$$= \sum_{D=0}^{Q} [D * SP - Q * UC] * \text{Prob}(D) + \sum_{D=Q+1}^{\infty} Q * [SP - UC] * \text{Prob}(D)$$

$$= SP * \left\{ \sum_{D=0}^{Q} D * \text{Prob}(D) + Q * \sum_{D=Q+1}^{\infty} \text{Prob}(D) \right\} - Q * UC$$

Substituting $Q - 1$ for Q gives the expected profit if the newsboy buys $Q - 1$ papers:

$$EP(Q-1) = SP * \left\{ \sum_{D=0}^{Q-1} D * \text{Prob}(D) + (Q-1) * \sum_{D=Q}^{\infty} \text{Prob}(D) \right\} - (Q-1) * UC$$

Subtracting the second of these from the first and doing some rearranging gives:

$$EP(Q) - EP(Q-1) = SP * \left\{ \sum_{D=Q}^{\infty} \text{Prob}(D) - UC/SP \right\}$$

This gives a guideline for an optimal number of newspapers (see Figure 4.3):

- if $EP(Q) - EP(Q-1)$ is positive the profit is still increasing with additional papers
- if $EP(Q) - EP(Q-1)$ is negative the profit is decreasing with additional papers.

The optimal order quantity, Q_o, is the point where the profit would begins to decline if another unit were bought. Then:

$$EP(Q_o - EP(Q_o - 1) > 0 \quad \text{and} \quad EP(Q_o + 1) - EP(Q_o) < 0$$

or

$$EP(Q_o + 1) - EP(Q_o) < 0 < EP(Q_o) - EP(Q_o - 1)$$

Substituting the derived value for $EP(Q) - EP(Q-1)$ gives:

$$EP(Q_o) - EP(Q_o - 1) = SP * \left\{ \sum_{D=Q_o}^{\infty} \text{Prob}(D) - UC/SP \right\}$$

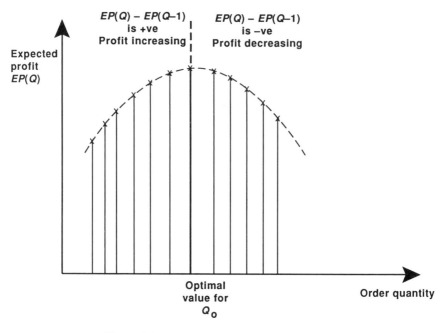

Figure 4.3 Expected profits for order quantity Q

Then replacing Q by $Q + 1$ gives the relationship we want:

$$SP * \left\{ \sum_{D=Q_o+1}^{\infty} \text{Prob}(D) - UC/SP \right\} < 0 < SP * \left\{ \sum_{D=Q_o}^{\infty} P(D) - UC/SP \right\}$$

$$\sum_{D=Q_o+1}^{\infty} \text{Prob}(D) < UC/SP < \sum_{D=Q_o}^{\infty} \text{Prob}(D)$$

$$\text{Prob}(D \geq Q_o + 1) < UC/SP < \text{Prob}(D \geq Q_o)$$

This is the result found by the marginal analysis when the scrap value, SV, is set to zero. If we included SV in this analysis we would get the final result:

$$\text{Prob}(D \geq Q_o + 1) < \frac{UC - SV}{SP - SV} < \text{Prob}(D \geq Q_o)$$

Worked Example 4.3

In recent years the demand for a seasonal product has shown the following pattern:

Units:	1	2	3	4	5	6	7	8
Probability:	0.05	0.1	0.15	0.2	0.2	0.15	0.1	0.05

It costs £80 to buy each unit of the product and the selling price is £120. How many units should be bought for the season? What is the expected profit? Would this decision change if the product has a scrap value of £20?

Solution

In this example UC = £80, SP = £120 and there is no scrap value. Then $UC/SP = 80/120 = 0.67$.

Substituting values for Q gives the results shown in Table 4.3.

Table 4.3

Q	Prob(D)	Prob($D \geq Q$)
1	0.05	1.00
2	0.10	0.95
3	0.15	0.85
4	0.20	0.70
5	0.20	0.50
6	0.15	0.30
7	0.10	0.15
8	0.05	0.05

The rule derived above says we choose Q_0 so that:

$$\text{Prob}(D \geq Q_0 + 1) < UC/SP < \text{Prob}(D \geq Q_0)$$

This happens when Q equals 4 and:

$$\text{Prob}(D \geq 5) < UC/SP < \text{Prob}(D \geq 4)$$

$$0.5 < 0.67 < 0.7$$

The optimal policy is to buy four products. Then the expected profit is:

$$EP(Q) = SP * \left\{ \sum_{D=0}^{Q} D * \text{Prob}(D) + Q * \sum_{D=Q+1}^{\infty} \text{Prob}(D) \right\} - Q * UC$$

$$EP(4) = 120 * \left\{ \sum_{D=0}^{4} D * \text{Prob}(D) + 4 * \sum_{D=5}^{\infty} \text{Prob}(D) \right\} - 4 * 80$$

$$= 120 * \{1.5 + 4 * 0.5\} - 320$$

$$= \pounds 100$$

If each unit has a scrap value, SV, of £20, we want:

$$\text{Prob}(D \geq Q_o + 1) < \frac{UC - SV}{SP - SV} < \text{Prob}(D \geq Q_o)$$

$$(UC - SV)/(SP - SV) = (80 - 20)/(120 - 20) = 0.6$$

Then the optimal order quantity is still four, which gives:

$$\text{Prob}(D \geq 5) < UC/SP < \text{Prob}(D \geq 4)$$

$$0.5 < 0.6 < 0.7$$

Worked Example 4.4

A package holiday company is about to block book hotel rooms for the coming season. The number of holidays actually booked is equally likely to be any number between 0 and 99 (for simplicity rather than reality). Each room booked costs the company £250 and they can sell them for £350. How many rooms should the company book if unsold rooms have no value? How many rooms should it book if unsold rooms can be sold as last-minute bookings for £100 each?

Solution

The variables given are:

UC = £250 a room
SP = £350 a room

Then $UC/SP = 0.71$.

As each number of bookings between 0 and 99 is equally likely, the probability of each number is 0.01. When unsold rooms have no value, Q_o has:

$$\sum_{D=Q_o+1}^{\infty} \text{Prob}(D) < 0.71 < \sum_{D=Q_o}^{\infty} \text{Prob}(D)$$

This occurs when $Q = 29$ and the optimal policy is to book 29 rooms.

When last-minute bookings allow rooms to be sold for £100, there is a "scrap value", $SV = £100$. Then

$$\frac{UC - SV}{SP - SV} = \frac{250 - 100}{350 - 100} = 0.6$$

Now we want:

$$\sum_{D=Q_0+1}^{\infty} \text{Prob}(D) < 0.60 < \sum_{D=Q_0}^{\infty} \text{Prob}(D)$$

This happens when $Q_0 = 40$ and the optimal policy is to book 40 rooms.

In Summary

The marginal analysis for single periods can be extended to the general Newsboy Problem. Then expected profit can be maximised by ordering the number of units, Q_0, which ensures:

$$\sum_{D=Q_0+1}^{\infty} \text{Prob}(D) < \frac{UC - SV}{SP - SV} < \sum_{D=Q_0}^{\infty} \text{Prob}(D)$$

SELF-ASSESSMENT QUESTIONS

4.4   What is meant by a single period model?

4.5   Give some examples of situations where single period models might be used.

4.6   What happens if a marginal analysis suggests an order size Q, but $Q + 1$ units are actually bought?

4.3.3   Discrete Demand with Shortages

We can extend the Newsboy Problem by looking at models for discrete demand over several periods. Then we could balance the long-term expected profit from selling a unit with the potential loss of having to scrap it. A more useful approach, however, incorporates the scrap value in a general shortage cost, SC. This would include all costs incurred when customer demand is not met.

We will illustrate this kind of analysis by a model which describes a stock of spare parts. In particular we assume the system has:

- discrete demand for an item which follows a known probability distribution
- relatively small demands and low stock levels
- a policy of replacing a unit of the item every time one is used
- an objective of finding the optimal number of units to stock

In this analysis our objective is to find, explicitly, an optimal stock level rather than calculate an optimal order quantity. In these circumstances we need a model which balances the cost of units that are bought but never used, against the cost of shortages. We can start by defining the following relationships.

- When an amount of stock, A, is held and demand, D, is less than this, there is a cost for holding units which are not used. This is $(A - D) * HC$ per unit of time.
- When demand is greater than A there is a shortage cost for demand not met. This is $(D - A) * SC$ per unit of time.

Then the total expected cost of holding A units, $TEC(A)$, is:

$$TEC(A) = HC * \sum_{D=0}^{A} \text{Prob}(D) * (A - D) + SC * \sum_{D=A+1}^{\infty} \text{Prob}(D) * (D - A)$$

If amount of stock held is $A + 1$ instead of A the cost is:

$$TEC(A + 1) = HC * \sum_{D=0}^{A+1} \text{Prob}(D) * (A + 1 - D)$$

$$+ SC * \sum_{D=A+2}^{\infty} \text{Prob}(D) * (D - A - 1)$$

Similarly if the stock level is $A - 1$ instead of A the cost is:

$$TEC(A - 1) = HC * \sum_{D=0}^{A-1} \text{Prob}(D) * (A - 1 - D)$$

$$+ SC * \sum_{D=A}^{\infty} \text{Prob}(D) * (D - A + 1)$$

Now for an optimal stock level of A_o:

$$TEC(A_o) \leq TEC(A_o + 1) \qquad \text{and} \qquad TEC(A_o) \leq TEC(A_o - 1)$$

If we substitute the values found above and do some manipulation we get the result:

$$\sum_{D=0}^{A_o - 1} \text{Prob}(D) \leq \frac{SC}{HC + SC} \leq \sum_{D=0}^{A_o} \text{Prob}(D)$$

$$\text{Prob}(D \leq A_o - 1) \leq \frac{SC}{HC + SC} \leq \text{Prob}(D \leq A_o)$$

This result is obviously similar to that found above for the single period model.

Worked Example 4.5

A store of spare parts estimates the cost of holding one unit of an item in stock for a month to be £50. When there is a shortage of the item production is disrupted with estimated costs of £1000 a unit a month. Over the past few months the following figures have been collected.

Demand for the item:	0	1	2	3	4	5
Proportion of months:	0.8	0.1	0.05	0.03	0.015	0.005

What is the optimal stock level for the part?

Solution

We are given:

$SC = 1000$ a unit a month
$HC = £50$ a unit a month

From the demand figures we can form the table:

Stock level, A:	0	1	2	3	4	5
$\text{Prob}(D = A)$:	0.8	0.1	0.05	0.03	0.015	0.005
$\text{Prob}(D \leq A)$:	0.8	0.9	0.95	0.98	0.995	1.00

We are looking for an optimal stock level, A_o, when:

$$\text{Prob}(D \leq A_o - 1) \leq \frac{SC}{HC + SC} \leq \text{Prob}(D \leq A_o)$$

$SC/(HC + SC) = 1000/(1000 + 50) = 0.952$, so we are looking for the two adjacent values of cumulative probability which enclose 0.952. In this case A_o equals 3, giving:

$$\text{Prob}(D \leq 2) \leq \frac{1000}{1050} \leq \text{Prob}(D \leq 3)$$

$$0.95 \leq 0.952 \leq 0.98$$

This analysis relies on a value for the shortage cost SC. It is often difficult to find reliable values for this, but one interesting approach is to calculate the shortage cost implied by current practice. Suppose, for example, the store in Worked Example 4.5 actually held stocks of 4. Then we could work backwards and calculate an implied shortage cost.

We know that actual stock, A, is set to equal 4, so substitution gives:

$$\text{Prob}(D \leq A - 1) \leq \frac{SC}{HC + SC} \leq \text{Prob}(D \leq A)$$

$$\text{Prob}(D \leq 3) \leq \frac{SC}{50 + SC} \leq \text{Prob}(D \leq 4)$$

or

$$0.98 \leq SC/(SC + 50) \leq 0.995$$

$$49 + 0.98 * SC \leq SC \leq 49.75 + 0.995 * SC$$

$$2450 \leq SC \leq 9950$$

This suggests the shortage cost is in the range £2450 to £9950 a unit a month. Although this is quite a wide range, the values can be used as the basis for further discussions to agree a more reliable figure.

In Summary

Some problems, such as stocks of spare parts, have discrete, probabilistic demand and shortage costs. These problems look for an optimal stock level, A_o, which can be found from:

$$\text{Prob}(D \leq A_o - 1) \leq \frac{SC}{HC + SC} \leq \text{Prob}(D \leq A_o)$$

4.3.4   Joint Calculation of Order Quantity and Reorder Level

Since calculating the economic order quantity, we have assumed that this is the best order size in a variety of circumstances. However, the original derivation assumed that shortages were not allowed. It would seem reasonable to ask whether uncertain demand and the possibility of shortages affect the calculation. This section looks at an alternative derivation for an optimal order quantity when demand is uncertain.

We will assume all shortages are met by back-orders and the number of back-orders is relatively small. Then, if the lead time is shorter than the stock cycle, we get the pattern shown in Figure 4.4.

The average amount of stock left at the end of a cycle depends on demand in the lead time and equals $(ROL - LT * D)$. Orders of size Q are placed, so the average stock level is $Q/2$ plus the amount left at the end of the cycle.

$$\text{average stock level} = (ROL - LT * D) + Q/2$$

There is a shortage whenever demand in the lead time is greater than the reorder level. Then the expected shortage is:

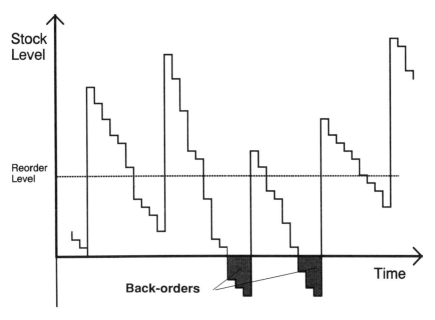

Figure 4.4 Variable demand with back-orders

$$\sum_{D=ROL}^{\infty} (D - ROL) * \text{Prob}(D)$$

The different components of variable cost per cycle can now be found, and dividing by the cycle length gives the following costs per unit time:

- reorder cost component   = number of orders $(D/Q)*$ reorder cost (RC)
  $$= RC * D/Q$$
- holding cost component   = average stock $(ROL - LT * D + Q/2)*$ holding cost (HC)
  $$= HC * (ROL - LT * D + Q/2)$$
- shortage cost component = expected shortage per cycle

$$\left(\sum_{D=ROL}^{\infty} (D - ROL) * \text{Prob}(D) \right) *$$

number of cycles (D/Q) $*$ shortage cost (SC)

$$= \frac{SC * D}{Q} \sum_{D=ROL}^{\infty} (D - ROL) * \text{Prob}(D)$$

The expected variable cost per unit time is found by adding these three components.

$$\frac{RC * D}{Q} + HC * \left(ROL - LT * D + \frac{Q}{2} \right) + \frac{SC * D}{Q} * \sum_{D=ROL}^{\infty} (D - ROL) * \text{Prob}(D)$$

This equation contains two unknowns, Q and ROL. Differentiating with respect to both of these and setting the derivatives to zero, gives two simultaneous equations which can be used to find optimal values. We will not do the arithmetic for this, but will simply quote the final results as:

$$Q = \sqrt{\frac{2 * D}{HC} * \left[RC + SC * \sum_{D=ROL}^{\infty} (D - ROL) * \text{Prob}(D) \right]}$$

$$\frac{HC * Q}{SC * D} = \sum_{D=ROL}^{\infty} \text{Prob}(D)$$

We can make the following points about these results.

- Firstly, the optimal order quantity is never less than the economic order quantity. The EOQ calculation underestimates the best order quantity as it balances only ordering and holding costs but makes no allowance for shortages. By increasing the amount ordered the number of shortages, and hence costs, are reduced.
- Secondly, the equations are only valid if $HC * Q$ is less than $SC * D$.

Unfortunately, the equations are not in a form which is easy to solve. The best approach uses an iterative procedure with the following four steps:

(1) calculate the economic order quantity and use this as an initial estimate of Q
(2) substitute this value for Q into the second equation and solve this to find a value for ROL
(3) substitute this value for ROL into the first equation to give a revised value for Q
(4) repeat steps (2) and (3) until the values converge to their optimal values.

We can illustrate this approach in the following worked example.

Worked Example 4.6

The demand for an item follows a Poisson distribution with mean 4 units a month. The lead time is one week, shortage cost is £200 a unit a month, reorder cost is £40, and holding cost is £4 a unit a month. Calculate optimal values for the order quantity and reorder level.

Solution

The values given, in consistent units, are:

D = 4 units a month
LT = 0.25 months
RC = £40 an order
HC = £4 a unit a month
SC = £200 a unit a month

Following the steps of the procedure above:

Step 1
The economic order quantity is:

$$Q_o = \sqrt{(2 * RC * D / HC)} = \sqrt{(2 * 40 * 4 / 4)} = 8.944 \text{ units}$$

Step 2
Substituting this value into the second equation above gives:

$$\frac{HC * Q}{SC * D} = \sum_{D=ROL}^{\infty} \text{Prob}(D) = \frac{4 * 8.944}{200 * 4} = 0.045$$

Now we want the probability that demand is greater then the reorder level to be 0.045. As demand follows a Poisson distribution, this cumulative probability can be found from Table 4.4. This table gives discrete values from the Poisson distribution with mean 4, so we want the cumulative probability nearest to 0.045. This is 0.051 which corresponds to a value of 8, which is an initial estimate for the reorder level.

Step 3
Taking this initial reorder level and substituting it into the first equation above allows a revised value for Q.

$$Q = \sqrt{\frac{2 * D}{HC} * \left[RC + SC * \sum_{D=ROL}^{\infty} (D - ROL) * \text{Prob}(D) \right]}$$

Table 4.4

Value	Probability	Prob($D \geq$ Value)
0	0.018	0.999
1	0.073	0.981
2	0.147	0.908
3	0.195	0.761
4	0.195	0.566
5	0.156	0.371
6	0.104	0.215
7	0.060	0.111
8	0.030	0.051
9	0.013	0.021
10	0.005	0.008
11	0.002	0.003
12	0.001	0.001

Table 4.5

D	Prob(D)	$D-ROL$	$(D-ROL) * \text{Prob}(D)$
8	0.030	0	0
9	0.013	1	0.013
10	0.005	2	0.010
11	0.002	3	0.006
12	0.001	4	0.004
Total			0.033

The summation here is calculated in Table 4.5. Then substitution gives:

$$Q = \sqrt{[(2 * 4/4) * (40 + 200 * 0.033)]}$$

$$= 9.654$$

Step 4
This repeats steps 2 and 3 until convergent values are found.

The new value for Q can be substituted into the second equation to give a new value for ROL:

$$(HC * Q)/(SC * D) = (4 * 9.654)/(200 * 4) = 0.048$$

From the table above this again corresponds to a reorder level of 8, so we should accept this as the final solution.

- reorder quantity, $Q = 9.654$ (rounded to 10)
- reorder level, $ROL = 8$

Ordinarily, fractional values for the reorder level will mean that more iterations are needed to find optimal values.

As we might expect, the savings in costs of using the joint calculation for Q and ROL rather than separate calculations are usually small. In this example, substitution in the cost equation shows the variable cost is:

$$VC = \frac{RC * D}{Q} + HC * \left(ROL - LT * D + \frac{Q}{2}\right) + \frac{SC * D}{Q} *$$

$$\left[\sum_{D=ROL}^{\infty} (D - ROL) * \text{Prob}(D)\right]$$

$$= \frac{40 * 4}{10} + 4 * \left(8 - 0.25 * 4 + \frac{10}{2}\right) + \frac{200 * 4 * 0.033}{10}$$

$$= \text{£66.64 a month}$$

If the rounded economic order quantity of 9 units had been used, variable cost would be:

$$VC = \frac{RC * D}{Q} + HC * \left(ROL - LT * D + \frac{Q}{2}\right) + \frac{SC * D}{Q} *$$

$$\left[\sum_{D=ROL}^{\infty} (D - ROL) * \text{Prob}(D)\right]$$

$$= \frac{40 * 4}{9} + 4 * \left(8 - 0.25 * 4 + \frac{9}{2}\right) + \frac{200 * 4 * 0.033}{9}$$

$$= \text{£66.71 a month}$$

In Worked Example 4.6 the savings from jointly calculating reorder quantity and reorder level were small. Sometimes, however, there are significant differences, particularly when demand and lead times vary widely, and when the shortage cost is small compared with the holding cost. Some organisations have found saving of 5–7% of variable costs when using the joint optimisation. To achieve this saving they have, of course, put considerably more effort into the computation of results.

In Summary

The EOQ makes no allowance for shortages and tends to underestimate the optimal order quantity. In some circumstances a joint calculation of order quantity and reorder level gives a more reliable result.

SELF-ASSESSMENT QUESTIONS

4.7 What values are most difficult to find in the analyses presented in this section?

4.8 With stocks of spare parts, why is an optimal order quantity not calculated?

4.9 Why is the economic order quantity not necessarily optimal?

4.10 What are the main problems with jointly calculating optimal reorder quantities and reorder levels?

4.4 SERVICE LEVEL MODELS

4.4.1 Introduction

In the last section we described some models for discrete demand with uncertainty. In this section we will extend these models to describe continuous demand with uncertainty and will then consider uncertainty in the lead time.

We can start by saying again that shortage costs are usually high in relation to holding costs. Then organisations are willing to incur the costs of holding stock, in order to avoid the cost of shortages. We can go further than this and suggest that organisations are willing to hold additional stocks, above their perceived needs, to add a margin of safety. In other words, a section of stock is held in reserve and will only be used when deliveries are late or demand is higher than expected (see Figure 4.5). This stock is called the "safety stock", so we have:

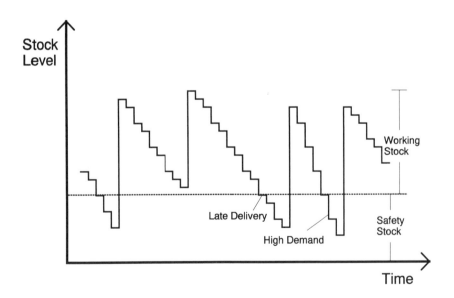

Figure 4.5 Safety stock is used for late deliveries and high demand

- working stock to meet normal demand
- safety stock to cover unexpectedly high demand or late deliveries

Earlier in the chapter we showed how mean values for lead time demand would give shortages in 50% of cycles when lead time demand is above the mean. Now we can use the safety stock to avoid shortages in these cycles. The larger the quantity of safety stock, the higher the probability of meeting demand in a cycle and the lower the probability of shortages.

The obvious question is, "How much safety stock should be held?". In principle, it is possible to calculate the cost of shortages and balance this with the cost of holding stock. In practice this is difficult as shortage costs are notoriously difficult to find and are often little more than informed guesses. Some people suggest that any analysis based on shortage costs is too unreliable to give useful results.

An alternative relies more directly on the judgement of management and allows a "service level" to be specified. This requires a positive decision to specify the desired probability that a demand is met directly from stock (or, conversely, the maximum acceptable probability that a demand cannot be met from stock). Typically a company will specify a service level of 95%, implying a probability of 0.05 that a demand cannot be met.

Higher safety stocks give higher service levels, but the actual service depends on the variation of lead time demand. If demand varies widely, very high safety stocks would be needed to ensure a high service level. In principle, widely varying demand would need an infinite safety stock to ensure a service level of 100%. Large stocks can become prohibitively expensive, and organisations usually settle for a figure around 95%. Often, items are given service levels related to their importance, so that very important items may have levels set at 98%, while less important ones are set around 85%. The choice of service level is a positive decision made by management. They must assess all the information available and choose suitable levels for all items.

Although we have suggested that service level is the proportion of customer demand met from stock, there are several ways in which this can be measured. They include:

- percentage of orders completely satisfied from stock
- percentage of units demanded which are met from stock
- percentage of units demanded which are delivered on time
- percentage of time there is stock available
- percentage of stock cycles without shortages
- percentage of item-months there is stock available
- and so on

The percentage of units demanded which are met from stock is the most obvious measure of service level. This is particularly useful in organisations like retail shops, where it represents the percentage of customers satisfied. Unfortunately, it has the disadvantage of not taking into account the frequency of stock-outs. So a 90% service level could mean a shortage once a day or once a year.

In this chapter we will use "cycle service level", which sets the probability that all demand in a single stock cycle is met. Again, a problem with this definition is that it does not take into account the frequency of ordering. A 90% cycle service level means there is a shortage once in ten days for an item which is ordered daily, but only once in ten years for an item which is ordered annually. Despite this problem the definition allows the most straightforward analyses.

Before looking in detail at some analyses, we should remember that lead time demand is a key factor. It does not matter how the demand varies outside the lead time, as this is allowed for by the timing and size of the next order. Any changes during the lead time, however, cannot be allowed for. With this in mind we can demonstrate a service level calculation in Worked Example 4.7.

Worked Example 4.7

In the last 50 stock cycles demand in the lead time has been as follows.

Demand:	10	20	30	40	50	60	70	80
Frequency:	1	5	10	14	9	6	4	1

What reorder level would give a service level of 95%?

Solution

At this point we are really discussing continuous distributions of demand, but this example shows how the same reasoning can be applied to discrete distributions. The starting point is to find the cumulative distribution of lead time demand (Table 4.6). To achieve a service level of 95%, the lead time demand must be less than the reorder level in 95% of cycles. This means that the reorder level must be set at 70 units.

If a lower reorder level is used, say 60 units, this will cover lead time demand in 90% of cycles, but will fall short of the required 95%.

Table 4.6

Lead time demand	Frequency	Percentage	Cumulative percentage
10	1	2	2
20	5	10	12
30	10	20	32
40	14	28	60
50	9	18	78
60	6	12	90
70	4	8	98
80	1	2	100

In Summary

Stock can be classified as working stock (which is used normally) and safety stock (which is used when deliveries are delayed or lead time demand is higher than usual). The amount of safety stock determines the service level. We will measure service by the cycle service level, which is the probability there are no shortages during a stock cycle.

SELF-ASSESSMENT QUESTIONS

4.11 What is safety stock and when is it used?

4.12 What is meant by "service level"?

4.13 How might the service level be improved?

4.14 Why is it usually impossible to guarantee a service level of 100%?

4.4.2 Uncertainty in Demand

Aggregate demand for an item is usually formed from a large number of smaller demands from individual customers. Then it is reasonable to assume the resulting demand is continuous and Normally distributed. We will also assume, for the moment, that lead time is constant.

With deterministic models the reorder level is equal to lead time demand:

$$ROL = LT * D$$

If, however, demand in the lead time is Normally distributed, it will be greater than the mean on half of occasions and there will be stock-outs in 50% of stock cycles (see Figure 4.6). To give a cycle-service level which is greater than 50% we must add a safety stock. The size of this safety stock can be calculated from the following argument.

Consider an item where demand is known to be Normally distributed with a mean of D per unit time and a standard deviation of σ. If the lead time is constant at LT, the mean lead time demand is $LT * D$, variance of lead time demand is $\sigma^2 * LT$ and standard deviation is $\sigma * \sqrt{LT}$. This is a standard result which comes from the observation that variances can be added, but standard deviations cannot. Thus:

- during 1 period demand has mean D and variance of σ^2
- during 2 periods demand has mean $2 * D$ and variance $2 * \sigma^2$
- during 3 periods demand has mean $3 * D$ and variance $3 * \sigma^2$, and
- during LT periods demand has mean $LT * D$ and variance $LT * \sigma^2$

The service level gives the required probability that lead time demand is below the reorder level. Thus we can use Normal distribution tables to give:

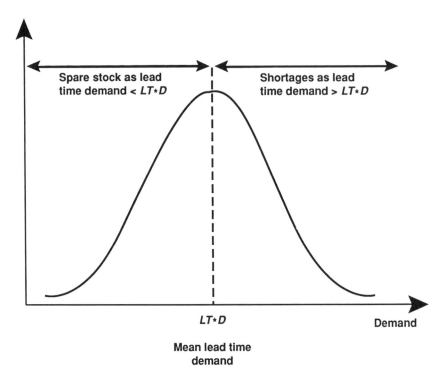

Figure 4.6 Showing the need for safety stock with Normally distributed demands

safety stock $= Z *$ standard deviation of lead time demand
$$= Z * \sigma * \sqrt{LT}$$

where Z is the number of standard deviations from the mean corresponding to the probability specified by the service level. This value for Z can be found in Normal distribution tables. A 95% service level, for example, has a probability of 0.05 that lead time demand is higher than safety stock. Normal tables can then be used to find that a probability of 0.05 corresponds to Z equal to 1.65. Thus the safety stock, SS, for a 95% service level is calculated from:

$$\text{safety stock} = SS = 1.65 * \sigma * \sqrt{LT}$$

An extract of Normal tables (see Table 4.7) shows how higher values of Z give higher safety stocks and lower probabilities of shortages (see Figure 4.7).

The main consequence of the safety stock calculation is that the reorder level is increased by the amount of the safety stock. Then:

<table>
<tr><td colspan="3" align="center">**Table 4.7**</td></tr>
</table>

Z	Percentage of cycles with shortages	Cycle service level (%)
0	50.0	50
0.84	20.0	80
1	15.9	84.1
1.04	15.0	85
1.28	10.0	90
1.48	7.0	93
1.64	5.0	95
1.88	3.0	97
2	2.3	97.7
2.33	1.0	99
2.58	0.5	99.5
3	0.1	99.9

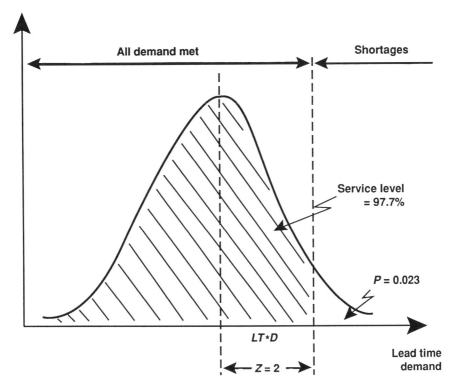

Figure 4.7 Typical service level calculation with Normally distributed lead time demand

> reorder level = lead time demand + safety stock
> $$= LT * D + Z * \sigma * \sqrt{LT}$$

This assumes that the lead time is shorter than the stock cycle so we do not need to consider stock already on order (Figure 4.8).

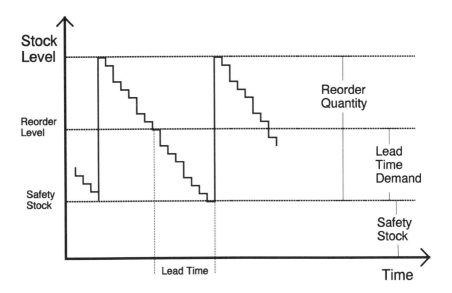

Figure 4.8 Safety stock with uncertain demand

Worked Example 4.8

A retailer guarantees a 95% service level for all stock items. Stock is replenished from a single wholesaler who has a fixed lead time of 4 weeks. What reorder level should the retailer adopt for an item which has Normally distributed demand with a mean of 100 units a week and a standard deviation of 10 units? What would the reorder level be if a 98% service level were used?

Solution

The reorder level is found from:

$$ROL = \text{lead time demand} + \text{safety stock}$$
$$= LT * D + SS$$
$$= 4 * 100 + SS$$

For a service level of 95%, the number of standard deviations from the mean, Z, is found from Normal tables to equal 1.64. Then:

$$\text{safety stock} = Z * \sigma * \sqrt{LT}$$
$$= 1.64 * 10 * \sqrt{4}$$
$$= 33 \text{ (when rounded)}$$

The reorder level becomes:

$$ROL = 400 + SS$$
$$= 400 + 33$$
$$= 433 \text{ units}$$

If the service level is increased to 98%, $Z = 2.05$ and

$$\text{safety stock} = 2.05 * 10 * \sqrt{4}$$
$$= 41 \text{ units}$$
$$\text{and reorder level} = 400 + 41$$
$$= 441 \text{ units}$$

Worked Example 4.9

Demand for an item is Normally distributed with a mean of 1000 units a week and standard deviation of 200 units. Unit cost is £10 and reorder cost is £100. Holding costs are 30% of value a year and lead time is fixed at 3 weeks. Describe an ordering policy which gives a 95% service level. What is the cost of the safety stock in this case?

Solution

Listing the values we know:

D = 1000 a week ($\sigma = 200$)
UC = £10 a unit
RC = £100 an order
HC = 0.3 of value held a year = £3 a unit a year
LT = 3 weeks

Substituting these gives:

$$Q_0 = \sqrt{2 * RC * D / HC}$$
$$= \sqrt{2 * 100 * 1000 * 52 / 3}$$
$$= 1862 \text{ (rounded to the nearest integer)}$$

$ROL = LT * D$ + safety stock

$= 3 * 1000$ + safety stock

For a 95% service level $Z = 1.64$ standard deviations from the mean. Then:

safety stock $= Z * \sigma * \sqrt{LT}$

$= 1.64 * 200 * \sqrt{3}$

$= 568$

The ordering policy is to order 1862 units whenever stock declines to 3568 units. Orders should arrive, on average, when there are 568 units remaining.
The expected cost of the safety stock is:

$=$ safety stock $*$ holding cost
$= 568 * 3$
$= £1704$ a year

In Chapter 2 we described a two-bin system which is useful for the control of some stocks. This has one bin which holds the reorder level while a second bin holds the remainder of the stock. Stock is withdrawn from the second bin until it is empty, at which point the reorder level has been reached and it is time to place an order.

When demand is more variable, this idea can be extended to a three-bin system. This has:

- the first bin filled with the reorder level
- the second with the remainder of the working stock
- the third with the safety stock

Stock is withdrawn from the second bin until it is exhausted. At this point it is time to place an order and start withdrawing from the first bin. When the first bin is emptied, the safety stock remains, and it may be time to start expediting procedures.

In Summary

When a continuous demand is uncertain, the lead time demand is important. When lead time demand is Normally distributed, the reorder level is given by:

$ROL =$ lead time demand + safety stock

$= LT * D + Z * \sigma * \sqrt{LT}$

where Z determines the cycle service level.

SELF-ASSESSMENT QUESTIONS

4.15 Why is the lead time demand particularly important for uncertain demand?
4.16 Should the safety stock increase or decrease with increasingly variable demand?
4.17 How is the reorder level calculated when demand is Normally distributed?
4.18 A company keeps three weeks' average demand as a safety stock. Does this seem reasonable?

4.4.3   Uncertainty in Lead Time

In the last section we developed a service level model which assumed that demand was uncertain, but lead time was constant. In this section we will change these assumptions and look at uncertain lead time, but constant demand.

In most circumstances the delay between placing an order and having goods arrive in stock ready for use is to some extent uncertain. Some suppliers are totally reliable, but there are many causes of uncertainty which are outside their control. These range from simple delays, due to heavy traffic, to a shortage of raw materials interrupting production.

If we base inventory control on the mean lead time and do not allow any safety stocks, there are three possible outcomes.

- Lead time is the expected length, in which case we get the ideal stock pattern shown in Figure 4.9(a).

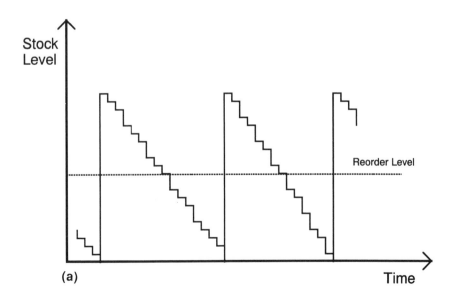

Figure 4.9 Effects of varying lead time. (a) Expected lead time presents no problem

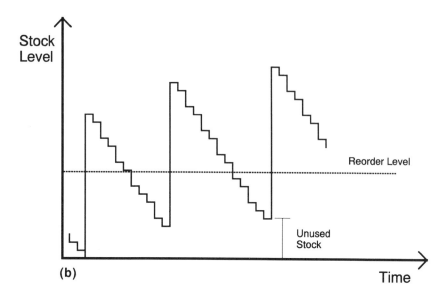

(b)

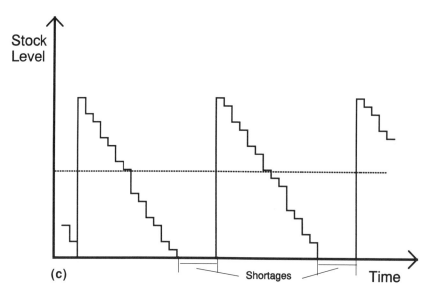

(c)

Figure 4.9 (continued)   (b) Lead time shorter than expected gives unused stock. (c) Lead time greater than expected gives shortages

- Lead time is shorter than expected, in which case there is some unused stock, as shown in Figure 4.9(b).
- Lead time is longer than expected, in which case stock runs out and there are shortages, as shown in Figure 4.9(c).

These patterns are very similar to those for variable demand, and we can approach the problem in the same way. If the lead time demand is Normally distributed with mean $LT * D$, we can set the reorder level to give any required cycle service level. In particular, the probability of a shortage is the probability that lead time demand is greater than the reorder level. This gives a simple calculation:

$$\text{service level} = \text{Prob}(LT * D < ROL)$$
$$= \text{Prob}(LT < ROL/D)$$

Worked Example 4.10

Lead time for a product is Normally distributed with mean 8 weeks and standard deviation 2 weeks. If demand is constant at 100 units a week, what ordering policy gives a 95% cycle service level?

Solution

For a 95% service level we want:

$$\text{Prob}(LT < ROL/D) = 0.95$$

From Normal tables, a probability of 0.95 corresponds to 1.64 standard deviations. On 95% of occasions lead time is less than $8 + 1.64 * 2 = 11.3$ weeks. This corresponds to a demand of 1130 which is the required reorder level.

In Summary

Lead time may vary for a variety of reasons. The reorder level which gives a desired service level can be calculated when lead time varies and demand is constant.

4.4.4   Uncertainty in Both Lead Time and Demand

In the last two analyses we have looked at models with:

- uncertain demand but constant lead time, and
- uncertain lead time but constant demand.

In the final analysis of this section we will see what happens when both lead time and demand are uncertain. In particular, we will assume that both are Normally distributed.

This analysis is similar to the last two, but we need to make some adjustment. This is based on the standard result:

If   demand has mean D and standard deviation σ_D
and lead time has mean LT and standard deviation σ_{LT}
then lead time demand has mean $LT * D$ and standard deviation

$$\sqrt{LT * \sigma_D{}^2 + D^2 * \sigma_{LT}{}^2}$$

The use of these calculations is illustrated in Worked Example 4.11.

Worked Example 4.11

Demand for a product is Normally distributed with mean 400 units a month and standard deviation 30 units a month. Lead time is Normally distributed with mean 2 months and standard deviation 0.5 months. What reorder level gives a 95% cycle service level? What is the best reorder quantity if reorder cost is £400 and holding cost is £10 a unit a month?

Solution

Listing the variables given:

D = 400 units a month
σ_D = 30 units
LT = 2 months
σ_{LT} = 0.5 months

Then mean lead time demand is $LT * D = 2 * 400 = 800$ units and standard deviation of lead time demand is:

$$\sqrt{LT * \sigma_D{}^2 + D^2 * \sigma_{LT}{}^2}$$

$$= \sqrt{(2 * 30^2 + 400^2 * 0.5^2)}$$

$$= 204.45 \text{ units}$$

For a 95% cycle service level:

safety stock = 1.64 * 204.45
           = 335 units

Then reorder level = $LT * D + SS$
                = 800 + 335
                = 1135 units

The economic order quantity gives the best order size of:

$$Q_o = \sqrt{(2 * RC * D / HC)} = \sqrt{(2 * 400 * 400 / 10)} = 179 \text{ units.}$$

In Summary

A simple extension to the previous analyses has both lead time and demand varying Normally.

SELF-ASSESSMENT QUESTIONS

4.19 Why might the lead time vary?

4.20 What factors should affect the amount of safety stock?

4.21 In practice, lead time demand is always Normally distributed. Is this statement true or false?

4.22 What is the optimal order quantity when demand is Normally distributed?

4.5   PERIODIC REVIEW SYSTEMS

4.5.1   Target Stock Level

In Chapter 1 we said there are two fundamentally different ordering policies (see Figure 4.10):

- *fixed order quantity system*, where an order of fixed size is placed whenever stock falls to a certain level
- *periodic review system*, where orders of varying size are placed at regular intervals to raise the stock to a specified level (the target stock level).

Fixed order quantity systems allow for uncertainty by placing orders of fixed size at different time intervals; periodic review systems allow for uncertainty by placing orders of different sizes at fixed time intervals. If demand is constant these two systems are identical, so differences only appear when the demand is uncertain.

With a periodic review system we are looking for answers to two questions:

- How long should the interval between orders be?
- What should the target stock level be?

The order interval, T, can really be any convenient period. It might, for example, be convenient to place an order at the end of every week, or every morning, or at the end of a month. If there is no obvious cycle we might aim for a certain number of orders a year or some average order size. One approach would be to calculate an economic order quantity, and then find the period which gave orders of about this size. The final decision is largely a matter for management judgement.

Whatever interval is chosen we need to find a suitable target stock level, TSL. The system then works by examining the amount of stock on hand when an order is placed and ordering the amount which brings this up to TSL.

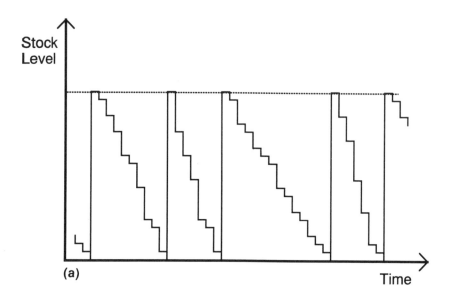

(a)   Time

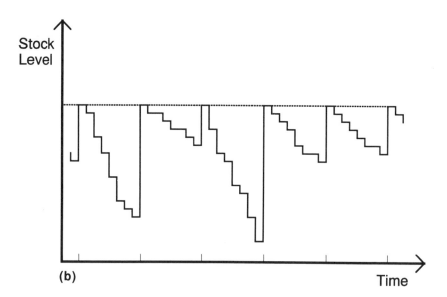

(b)   Time

Figure 4.10 Alternative ordering policies. (a) Fixed order quantity system. (b) Periodic review system

> order quantity = target stock level − stock on hand

A common example of this can be seen in supermarkets. Every evening they examine the shelves and replace items which were sold during the day. The order period is a day, and the target stock level is the amount of shelf space allocated to the item.

In the following analysis we will assume that the lead time for an item is constant at LT and the demand is Normally distributed. The stock level for a periodic review system shown in Figure 4.10 assumes that lead time is zero, so that stock actually rises to the target stock level. In practice there is time for the stock to decline before a delivery arrives, so the actual stock level never reaches the target. A more accurate picture of the stock level is given in Figure 4.11. The size of order A is determined by the stock level at point A_1, but when this actually arrives at time A_2 stock has declined. This order has to satisfy all demand until the next order arrives at point B_2. Thus, the target stock level has to satisfy all demand over the period A_1 to B_2, which is $T + LT$.

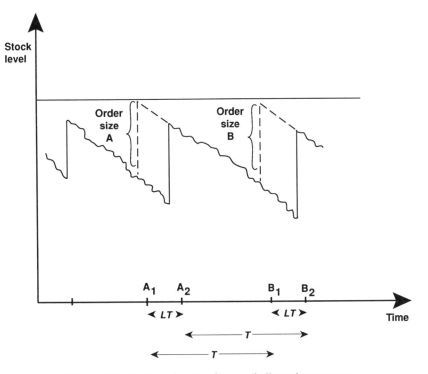

Figure 4.11 Timing of orders for a periodic review system

The demand over $T + LT$ is Normally distributed with mean of $(T + LT) * D$, variance of $\sigma^2 * (T + LT)$ and standard deviation of $\sigma * \sqrt{(T + LT)}$. A safety stock can then be defined as:

$$
\begin{aligned}
\text{safety stock} &= Z * \text{standard deviation of demand over } T + LT \\
&= Z * \sigma * \sqrt{(T + LT)}
\end{aligned}
$$

where Z is the number of standard deviations from the mean corresponding to the selected service level. Then:

$$
\begin{aligned}
\text{target stock level} &= \text{demand over } T + LT + \text{safety stock} \\
&= D * (T + LT) + Z * \sigma * \sqrt{(T + LT)}
\end{aligned}
$$

This argument assumes that the lead time is less than the cycle length. If this is not true, the order placed must also take into account the stock already on order, so that:

$$
\text{order quantity} = \text{target stock level} - \text{stock on hand} - \text{stock on order}
$$

Worked Example 4.12

Demand for an item is Normally distributed with a mean of 1000 units a month and standard deviation of 100 units. Stock is checked every three months and lead time is constant at one month. Describe an ordering policy which gives a 95% service level. If the holding cost is £20 a unit a month, what is the cost of the safety stock with this policy? What would be the effect of using a 98% service level?

Solution

Listing the variables in consistent units:

D = 1000 units a month
σ = 100 units
HC = £20 a unit a month
T = 3 months
LT = 1 month

For a 95% safety stock Z can be found from Normal distribution tables to be 1.64. Then:

$$
\begin{aligned}
\text{safety stock} &= Z * \sigma * \sqrt{(T + LT)} \\
&= 1.64 * 100 * \sqrt{(3 + 1)} \\
&= 328 \\
\text{target stock level} &= D * (T + LT) + \text{safety stock} \\
&= 1000 * (3 + 1) + 328 \\
&= 4328
\end{aligned}
$$

Every three months, when it is time to place an order, the stock on hand should be found and an order placed for:

$$
\text{order size} = 4328 - \text{stock on hand}
$$

If, for example, there were 1200 units in stock the order would be for $4328 - 1200 = 3128$ units.

$$
\begin{aligned}
\text{The cost of holding this safety stock} &= SS * HC \\
&= 328 * 20 \\
&= £6560 \text{ a month}
\end{aligned}
$$

If the service level is increased to 98%, $Z = 2.05$ and:

$$
\text{safety stock} = 2.05 * 100 * \sqrt{4} = 410
$$

The target stock level is then 4410 units and the cost of the safety stock is $410 * 20 = £8200$ a month.

In Summary

A periodic review system places orders of variable size at regular intervals. The quantity ordered is enough to raise stock on hand plus stock on order to a target level, TSL, where:

$$
TSL = D * (T + LT) + Z * \sigma * \sqrt{(T + LT)}
$$

4.5.2 Advantages of Each System

Both fixed order quantity systems and periodic review systems have advantages in different circumstances. It is certainly not possible to say that one is always superior to the other, and the choice of the most appropriate must largely be a management decision.

The main benefit of a periodic review system is that it is simple and convenient to administer. There is a routine where stock is checked at regular times, orders are placed, delivery is arranged, goods arriving are checked, and so on. This is particularly useful for cheap items with high demand. The routine also means that the stock level is only checked at specific intervals and does not have to be monitored continuously. Fixed order quantity systems require the stock to be checked continuously so that a message is given when stock falls to the reorder level.

Another advantage of periodic review systems is the ease of combining orders for several items into a single order. This gives larger orders which might encourage suppliers to give price discounts.

Conversely a major advantage of fixed order quantity systems is that orders of constant size are easier to regulate than variable ones. Suppliers know how much to send and the administration and transport can be tailored to specific needs (perhaps supplying a truck load at a time). Another advantage is that the system can cater for specific characteristics of each item. In a periodic review system it is common to use the same period for many items. This means that items with low demands are ordered as frequently as those with high demands. A fixed order quantity system has more flexibility to suit order frequency to demand.

The last advantage of fixed order quantity systems is that they give lower stocks. The safety stock has to cover uncertainty in LT, rather than $T+LT$ in periodic review systems. This allows smaller safety stock and hence lower overall stocks.

Some benefits of both systems might be found by using hybrid systems. Two common types of hybrid system are as follows.

- *Periodic review with reorder level.* This is similar to the standard periodic review system, but this time an order is only placed if stock on hand is below a specified reorder level. If the stock on hand is above the reorder level no order is placed this period.

- *Reorder level and target stock.* This is a variation of the fixed order quantity systems which can be used when individual orders take the stock level well below the reorder level. Then, instead of ordering the economic order quantity, an order is placed which will raise current stock to a target level. This is sometimes called the min–max system as gross stock will generally vary between a minimum (the reorder level) and a maximum (the target stock level).

In Summary

Both fixed order quantity systems and periodic review systems have advantages in different circumstances. Any choice between the two must be a positive decision by management. They may also consider hybrid systems.

SELF-ASSESSMENT QUESTIONS

4.23 How is the order size calculated for a periodic review system?
4.24 Will the safety stock be higher for:
  (a) a fixed order quantity system?
  (b) a periodic review system?
  (c) both the same?
  (d) could be either?
4.25 Why might a company decide to use a periodic review system?

SUMMARY OF CHAPTER

This chapter has described some probabilistic models for inventory control. In particular it has:

- discussed the type of uncertainty met in inventory systems, particularly uncertain demand and lead time
- described a marginal analysis for single period models
- used a more formal approach to the Newsboy Problem
- solved problems with discrete demand and shortages
- calculated optimal stock levels for spare parts
- calculated jointly the optimal reorder quantity and reorder level with shortages
- discussed service levels
- determined the best policy for Normally distributed demands
- determined policies with uncertain lead time
- described periodic review systems and related calculations

Based on these discussions we can suggest the following approach to inventory control.

Demand and lead time	Suggested approach
Known with certainty	Variations on deterministic quantitative models
With some uncertainty	Variations on probabilistic models with safety stocks or shortage costs

ADDITIONAL PROBLEMS

4.1 In a particular period demand for an item is equally likely to be any value between 100 and 199 units. Each unit of the item costs £75 and can be sold for £100. At the end of the period all unsold stock is scrapped, with a return of £25 a unit. How many units should be bought for the period?

4.2 At the beginning of December the owner of a conifer plantation employs a contractor to cut enough trees to meet the expected demand for Christmas trees. He supplies these to a local wholesaler in batches of 100. Over the past few years the demand has been as follows:

Batches:	1	2	3	4	5	6	7	8	9
Probability:	0.05	0.1	0.15	0.2	0.2	0.15	0.1	0.05	0

If it costs £16 to cut and trim a tree which sells for £25, how many trees should be cut down?

4.3 A store for spare parts estimates the cost of holding one unit of a replacement part in stock for a month to be £30. Any shortage of the part is estimated to cost £500 a unit a month. Over the past few months the following figures have been collected:

Demand for the part:	1	2	3	4	5	6	7	8	9	10
Percentage of months:	50	20	10	5	5	3	3	2	1	1

What is the optimal stock level for the part? If the store currently holds 7 units of the part in stock, what is the implied shortage cost?

4.4 The demand for an item follows a Normal distribution with mean 40 units and standard deviation 4 units a month. The lead time is one week, shortage cost is £200, reorder cost is £40, and holding cost is £4. Calculate the joint optimal values for order quantity and reorder size.

4.5 Demand for an item is Normally distributed with a mean of 400 units a week and a standard deviation of 40 units. Reorder cost (including delivery) is £300, holding cost is £12 a unit a year and lead time is constant at 3 weeks. Describe an ordering policy which gives a 95% cycleservice level. What is the cost of holding the safety stock in this case? By how much would the costs rise if the service level is raised to 98%?

4.6 Demand for an item is constant at 10 units a week and the economic order quantity has been calculated at 100 units. The lead time varies as follows:

Percentage of orders:	5	10	15	40	15	10	5
Lead time (weeks):	1	2	3	4	5	6	7

What ordering policy would give a cycle service level of 95%?

4.7 Demand for an item is 100 units a week with a standard deviation of 10 units. Lead time is one week and the reorder level used is 115 units. What is the probability of running out of stock?

4.8 Demand for an item has a mean of 200 units a week and standard deviation of 40 units. Stock is checked every four weeks and lead time is constant at two weeks. Describe a policy which will give a 95% service level. If the holding cost is £2 a unit a week, what is the cost of the safety stock with this policy? What would be the effect of a 98% service level?

REFERENCES FOR FURTHER READING

- Many operations management and management science books describe a range of inventory models. Some useful references are listed below.

Aft, L.S. (1987) *Production and Inventory Control*, Harcourt, Orlando, FL.
Buffa, E.S. and Miller, J.G. (1979) *Production-Inventory Systems: Planning and Control* (3rd edn), Irwin, Homewood, IL.
Buffa, E.S. and Sarin, R.K. (1987) *Modern Production/Operations Management*, John Wiley, New York.
Chase, R.B. and Aquilano, N.J. (1989) *Production and Operations Management* (5th edn), Irwin, Homewood, IL.
Fogarty, D.W. and Hoffman, T.R. (1983) *Production and Inventory Management*, South-Western Publishing, Dallas, TX.
Greene, J.H. (1970) *Production and Inventory Control Handbook*, McGraw-Hill, New York.
Hadley, G. and Whitin, T.M. (1963) *Analysis of Inventory Systems*, Prentice Hall, Englewood Cliffs, NJ.
Hax, A.C. and Candea, D. (1984) *Production and Inventory Management*, Prentice Hall, Englewood Cliffs, NJ.
Lewis, C.D. (1970) *Scientific Inventory Control*, Butterworth, London.
Love, S.F. (1979) *Inventory Control*, McGraw-Hill, New York.
McLeavy, D.W. and Seetharama, L.N. (1985) *Production Planning and Inventory Control*, Allyn and Bacon, Boston, MA.
Silver, E.A. and Peterson, R. (1985) *Decision Systems for Inventory Management and Production Planning* (2nd edn), John Wiley, New York.
Tersine, R.J. (1987) *Principles of Inventory and Materials Management* (2nd edn), North-Holland, New York.
Thomas, A.B. (1980) *Stock Control in Manufacturing Industries* (2nd edn), Gower Press, London.
Waters, C.D.J. (1991) *Introduction to Operations Management*, Addison-Wesley, Wokingham.

5
FORECASTING DEMAND

SYNOPSIS

The previous three chapters of this book have described a number of models for independent demand inventory systems. To give useful results these models need reliable information about demand, costs and suppliers. In the next two chapters we are going to discuss how this information can be supplied. This chapter describes methods of forecasting demand, while the following chapter outlines other information needs.

The future demand for an item is generally the most important input to an inventory control model. It is the factor which has most impact on the stocks held. With independent demand inventory systems this demand is forecast, usually by projecting past demand patterns into the future.

In addition to its role in stock control, forecasting is important for many other aspects of business. Organisations make plans which become effective at some point in the future, so they need information about prevailing circumstances. This information must be forecast. Unfortunately, forecasting can be difficult and, despite its importance, progress in many areas has been limited.

There are a number of forecasting methods, but no one of them is best in all circumstances. We will describe a range of methods and suggest the circumstances in which each is useful.

One classification of forecasting methods has the types: judgemental, causal and projective. Judgemental forecasting, which relies on subjective views and opinions, is illustrated by personal insight, panel consensus, Delphi method, historic analogy and market surveys. Judgemental methods often have problems with reliability and more formal quantitative methods are usually preferred.

Causal forecasting looks for relationships between variables. Then the demand for soft drinks, for example, can be related to the average daily temperature. Causal forecasting is illustrated by linear regression, which draws the line of best fit through a set of data. The quality of results is measured by the coefficients of determination and correlation.

Most quantitative forecasts are concerned with time series, where demand is measured at regular intervals of time. Then demand can be described by an underlying pattern with superimposed random noise. The underlying pattern can be projected into the future, but the noise cannot be forecast so some error is almost inevitable.

In contrast to causal forecasting, demand can also be forecast by ignoring external influences and simply projecting patterns in historic data to the future. These projective methods are illustrated by simple averages, moving averages, exponential smoothing and models for seasonality and trend.

OBJECTIVES

After reading this chapter and completing the exercises you should be able to:

- appreciate the requirements of forecasts for inventory control systems
- categorise different approaches to forecasting
- discuss the characteristics of judgemental forecasting
- describe a variety of judgemental forecasting methods
- define "time series" and appreciate their importance
- calculate forecast errors using mean error, mean absolute deviation and mean squared error
- describe the characteristics of causal forecasting
- use linear regression for forecasting
- calculate coefficients of determination and correlation and appreciate their importance
- describe the characteristics of projective forecasting
- forecast demand using simple averages, moving averages and exponential smoothing
- forecasts demands with seasonality and trend

5.1   BACKGROUND TO FORECASTING

5.1.1   Introduction

The last three chapters have described how quantitative models can be used for independent demand inventory systems. These models rely on the availability of information about demand, costs and suppliers. In this chapter we will examine methods of forecasting demand, while the following chapter discusses other information needs.

The most important factor in an inventory control model is usually the expected demand. This has most direct effect on the stocks held, and determines the effectiveness of the inventory system. With independent demand systems the expected demand is found from forecasts. The problem of forecasting values for the future is not, of course, unique to inventory control. All business plans become effective at some point in the future, so they must be based on forecasts of expected conditions. In this sense, forecasting is a central part of any organisation.

There are many methods of forecasting and our intuition might suggest that those which give best results are the most complex and expensive. In practice this is not necessarily true. Simple forecasting methods often give very good results, while complex ones can give very poor ones. It is also important to remember that inventory models are relatively insensitive to errors in data. It might be suggested, therefore, that inventory systems need *simple* forecasting methods which give reasonable results. These are generally preferable to more sophisticated methods, even if the results are slightly inferior. This suggestion is reinforced by the observation that inventories often contain thousands of items, and using complex models to make regular forecasts soon becomes prohibitively expensive.

We are now looking for simple forecasting methods, but there are still many alternatives. Unfortunately, no one of these is consistently better than the others. The range of things to be forecast, different patterns of demand and different circumstances in which forecasts are needed, mean the best we can do is describe a range of methods and say which is most appropriate in different circumstances.

In Summary

Independent demand inventory systems rely on forecast demand. Simple forecasting methods which give reasonable results are most useful. There are several methods available, but no one of them is always the best.

5.1.2 Classifications of Forecasting Methods

A useful classification of forecasting methods concerns the time in the future which is considered. In particular:

- short-term forecasts cover the next few months (the continuing demand for a product, for example)
- medium-term forecasts look ahead between a few months and two or three years (say, the time needed to replace an old product by a new one)
- long-term forecasts might look ahead several years (the time needed to build a new factory)

The time horizon affects the choice of forecasting method, because of the availability and relevance of historic data, the time available to do the forecasting, the cost involved and the effort considered worthwhile. In essence, long-term forecasts are concerned with strategic decisions, medium-term forecasts with tactical decisions, and short-term forecasts with operational decisions.

Inventory control is primarily concerned with short-term forecasting. This means there usually enough relevant data to allow good forecasts. Sometimes, however, data is not available when, for example, a new item is added to the inventory. Forecasting demand for a new item, for which there is no historic data, must use a qualitative approach. Such methods are generally referred to as judgemental, and they rely on subjective assessments and opinions.

Items which have been in stock for some time will have records of past demand and the factors which affect this. Then more reliable quantitative forecasts can be used. There are two distinct approaches to quantitative forecasting:

- *causal methods* which analyse the effects of outside influences and use these to produce forecasts. Sales of an item might, for example, depend directly on the price charged, so that future sales can be forecast from the planned future price.
- *projective methods* which examine the pattern of past demand and extends this into the future. If demand in the past four months has been 20, 25, 30 and 35, it would be reasonable to project this pattern and suggest that demand in the next month will be around 40.

Thus we have three distinct approaches to forecasting:

- *judgemental methods*, which rely on subjective assessment
- *causal methods*, which look at external factors and use these to forecast demand
- *projective methods*, which project past demand for an item into the future

---

Most inventory systems use projective forecasts. Managers are, however, ultimately responsible for any decisions and they must consider all available information. This implies that forecasts should have some subjective review before they are adopted. The rest of this chapter looks in more detail at a number of different forecasting methods, starting with judgemental methods.

In Summary

Forecasting methods can be classified in several ways, with two useful ones describing the time they look ahead (short-, medium- or long-term), and the overall approach (judgement, causal or projective).

SELF-ASSESSMENT QUESTIONS

5.1 Why is forecasting important to an organisation?
5.2 List three fundamentally different approaches to forecasting.

5.3 What factors should be considered when choosing a forecasting method?

5.4 Most forecasting for inventory control is short-term using quantitative methods. Is this statement true?

5.2 JUDGEMENTAL FORECASTS FOR NEW STOCK ITEMS

Judgemental forecasting methods are subjective assessments, usually based on the opinions of experts. They are not usually as reliable as quantitative forecasts, but they are very flexible and can be used in a wide range of circumstances. If, for example, an organisation is about to stock an entirely new item there is no appropriate historic data and it must use a judgemental forecast. Sometimes, even when there is data, it is unreliable, out of date, or irrelevant to the future. In these cases quantitative forecasts cannot be used and judgemental methods are the only alternative.

Judgemental forecasts collect opinions from various experts in the field. For inventory systems these experts might include suppliers, purchasing departments, store keepers, salesmen, customers, organisations supplying similar or related items, trade reviews, government publications, and so on.

Here we will outline five widely used methods of judgemental forecasting:

- personal insight
- panel consensus
- Delphi method
- historic analogy
- market surveys

Personal Insight

This uses a single expert who is familiar with the situation to produce a forecast based on his or her own judgement. This is the most widely used forecasting method, and is the one which managers should try to avoid. It relies entirely on one person's judgement (opinions, prejudices and ignorance).

Personal insight can give good forecasts, but often gives very bad ones and there are countless examples of experts being totally wrong. Perhaps the major weakness of the method is its unreliability. This may not matter for minor decisions, but when the consequences of errors are large some more reliable method should be used.

Comparisons of forecasting methods clearly show that someone who is familiar with a situation and uses experience and subjective opinions to forecast will consistently produce *worse* forecasts than someone who knows nothing about the situation but uses a more formal method.

Panel Consensus

As unreliability is the main problem with personal insight, collecting together several experts and allowing them to talk freely to each other should lead to a consensus which is more reliable. When there is no secrecy and the panel are encouraged to talk openly, a genuine consensus can be found. Conversely, there may be difficulties getting the panel to talk openly, and in combining the views of different experts when a consensus is not found.

Although it is more reliable than personal insight, panel consensus still has the major weakness that all experts can make mistakes. There are also problems of group working, where "he who shouts loudest gets his way", everyone tries to please the boss, some people do not speak well in groups, and so on.

Overall, panel consensus is an improvement on personal insight, but results from either method should be viewed with caution.

Delphi Method

This method is an improvement on panel consensus as it overcomes the problems with face-to-face discussions. A number of experts are contacted by post and each is given a questionnaire to complete. The replies from these questionnaires are analysed and summaries are passed back to the experts. Each expert is then asked to reconsider his or her original reply in the light of the summarised replies from others. Each reply is anonymous so that undue influences of status and the pressures of face-to-face discussions are avoided.

This process of modifying responses in the light of replies made by the rest of the group is repeated several times (often between three and six). By this time, the range of opinions should have narrowed enough to help with decisions.

Historic Analogy

The demand for most products follows a common pattern through their lifetime. In particular, sales go through periods of:

- introduction
- growth
- maturation
- decline
- withdrawal

as illustrated in Figure 5.1.

Historic analogy uses the demand of a similar item which was introduced in the past to judge the demand for a new item. When a new item is to be introduced an organisation can look for a comparable item which was launched recently and assume that demand for the new item will follow a similar pattern. If, for example, a television retailer is ordering a new type of set, it could forecast demand by reviewing demand for the last set it stocked.

The main problems with historic analogy are finding a recently introduced product with enough similarities, and fitting the characteristic life-cycle curve to actual demand.

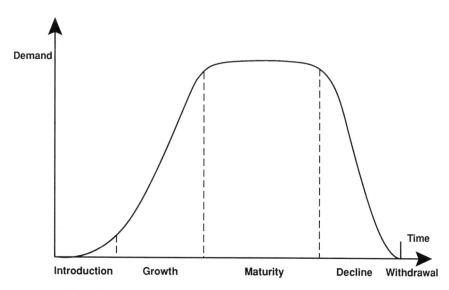

Figure 5.1 Demand at different stages in a typical product life cycle

Market Surveys

Sometimes, particularly with the launch of a new product, the opinions of experts are not reliable enough to make a satisfactory forecast. Then more useful information can be found by talking directly to potential customers. Market surveys collect data from a representative sample of customers. Their views are analysed, with inferences drawn about the population at large.

Market surveys can give useful information but they tend to be expensive and time-consuming. They are also prone to errors as they rely on:

- a sample of customers which is representative
- useful, unbiased questions
- reliable analyses of the replies
- valid conclusions drawn from the analyses

Each of the judgemental methods is appropriate in different circumstances. If a quick reply is needed, personal insight is the fastest and cheapest method. For many inventories, suppliers provide the best source of information. They have contact with similar organisations and can give useful advice. This does, however, need a supplier who is objective and is not trying to make short-term gains. If more reliable forecasts are needed it may be worth organising a market survey or Delphi method.

We should always bear in mind that inventory systems are insensitive to small errors. The implication is that simpler methods should be used whenever they give reasonable results.

In Summary

Judgemental forecasts can be used when there is no relevant historic data. They rely on subjective views and opinions, as demonstrated by personal insight, panel consensus, Delphi method, historic analogy and market surveys.

SELF-ASSESSMENT QUESTIONS

5.5 When are judgemental forecasts most likely to be used?
5.6 List five types of judgemental forecast.
5.7 What are the main problems with judgemental forecasts?

5.3 ERRORS IN FORECAST DEMAND

Forecasts almost inevitably contain errors. In other words, there is a difference between forecast and actual demand. The quality of a forecast is determined by the size of these errors. Before discussing quantitative forecasts in more detail it would be sensible to describe some appropriate measures for these errors. This is most easily done in the context of time series.

5.3.1 Time Series

Most quantitative forecasting is based on "time series", which are series of observations taken at regular intervals of time. Thus, weekly demand for a product, monthly unemployment figures, daily rainfall and annual population statistics are examples of time series.

If we are presented with a time series, the best way to start analysing it is to draw a graph. This allows us to recognise very quickly any underlying patterns. Three patterns commonly found in time series (see Figure 5.2) are:

- *constant series*, where demand continues at roughly the same level over time (such as demand for bread)
- *series with a trend*, where demand either rises or falls steadily (such as demand for computers)
- *seasonal series*, where demand has a cyclical component (such as demand for ice cream)

Forecasting would be easy if demand followed such simple patterns. Unfortunately, there is almost always a random variation, or "noise", superimposed on the underlying pattern. Then a constant series, for example, does not always take exactly the same value, but is somewhere close. Thus:

$$101 \quad 105 \quad 93 \quad 96 \quad 108 \quad 103 \quad 98 \quad 101 \quad 91 \quad 95 \quad 109$$

is a constant series of 100 with superimposed noise.

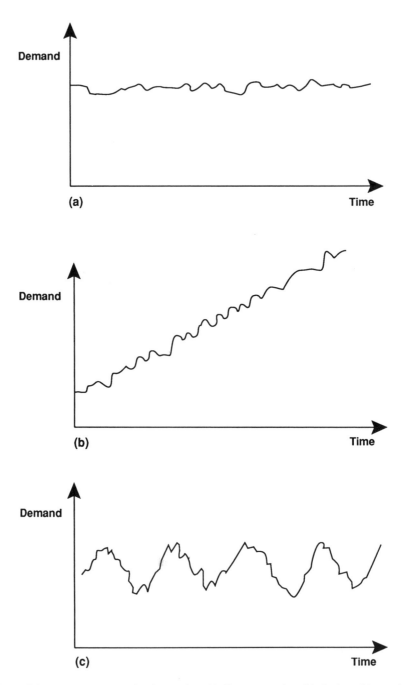

Figure 5.2 Common patterns in time series. (a) Constant series. (b) Series with trend. (c) Seasonal series

actual demand = underlying pattern + random noise

The random noise cannot be forecast, and is the reason why forecasting is so difficult. If there is little noise, forecasts can be good, but if there is a lot of noise it obscures the underlying pattern and it becomes difficult to get accurate results. To judge the quality of forecasts we need some way of measuring the errors. This measure could then be used to:

- give a measure for the accuracy of the forecast
- minimise the errors in future forecasts
- show how confident we are in the forecast
- monitor forecasts to see if they are maintaining reliability
- recognise when a forecast is seriously wrong
- compare different forecasting methods

There are several ways of describing these errors, with three common measures outlined below.

In Summary

Many forecasts are concerned with time series, which are demand figures taken at regular periods. These often have underlying patterns, with superimposed random noise. This noise cannot be forecast and is the reason why forecasts usually contain errors.

5.3.2 Measures of Error

If a forecast, $F(t)$, is made for the demand in period t, and the actual demand turns out to be $D(t)$, there is an error of:

error = actual demand − forecast demand

$$E(t) = D(t) - F(t)$$

If we collect data for a number of periods, N, an obvious measure of forecast error is the mean error per period.

$$\text{mean error} = \frac{1}{N} * \sum_{t=1}^{N} E(t)$$

$$= \frac{1}{N} * \sum_{t=1}^{N} [D(t) - F(t)]$$

The drawback with this calculation is that positive and negative errors cancel each other, and very poor forecasts can have small mean error. Consider, for example, the following values.

t:	1	2	3	4
$D(t)$:	200	400	600	800
$F(t)$:	2000	0	0	0

The forecasts are obviously very poor, but if we calculate the mean error we get:

mean error $= (200 - 2000) + (400 - 0) + (600 - 0) + (800 - 0)$
$= 0$

In practice the mean error is not a reliable measure of forecast accuracy, but it measures bias.

- If the mean error has a positive value, the forecast is consistently too low.
- If the mean error has a negative value, the forecast is consistently too high.

The mean error allows positive and negative errors to cancel each other, so we need alternative measures which avoid this. Two options use the absolute values of errors (calculating the mean absolute deviation), and the square of errors (calculating the mean squared error).

$$\text{Mean absolute deviation} = \frac{1}{N} * \sum_{t=1}^{N} ABS[E(t)]$$

$$= \frac{1}{N} * \sum_{t=1}^{N} ABS[D(t) - F(t)]$$

$$\text{Mean squared error} = \frac{1}{N} * \sum_{t=1}^{N} [E(t)]^2$$

$$= \frac{1}{N} * \sum_{t=1}^{N} [D(t) - F(t)]^2$$

The mean absolute deviation has an obvious meaning; when it takes a value of 6 the forecast is on average 6 away from actual demand. The mean squared error has a less clear meaning, but is useful for some statistical analyses (we will use it in the next section on linear regression). Whichever measure is used, smaller values mean better forecasts.

Worked Example 5.1

Demand for an item over the past six months has been forecast using two alternative methods, with the results shown below.

Period:	1	2	3	4	5	6
Demand:	101	121	110	98	114	126
Forecast 1:	107	117	112	104	112	120
Forecast 2:	98	116	105	105	110	120

Which forecasting method gives the better results?

Solution

The better method of forecasting is the one which gives the smaller errors. The errors for each method are calculated as follows.

Forecasting method 1

Period:	1	2	3	4	5	6
Demand:	101	121	110	98	114	126
Forecast 1:	107	117	112	104	112	120
$E(t)$:	−6	4	−2	−6	2	6
$ABS[E(t)]$:	6	4	2	6	2	6
$[E(t)]^2$:	36	16	4	36	4	36

- mean error = $(-6+4-2-6+2+6)/6 = -0.33$ (so each forecast is slightly biased, being an average of 0.33 too high)
- mean absolute deviation = $(6+4+2+6+2+6)/6 = 4.33$ (so each forecast is, on average, 4.33 away from actual demand)
- mean squared error = $(36 + 16 + 4 + 36 + 4 + 36)/6 = 22$

Forecasting Method 2

Period:	1	2	3	4	5	6
Demand:	101	121	110	98	114	126
Forecast 2:	98	116	105	105	110	120
$E(t)$:	3	5	5	−7	4	6
$ABS[E(t)]$:	3	5	5	7	4	6
$[E(t)]^2$:	9	25	25	49	16	36

- mean error = $(3 + 5 + 5 - 7 + 4 + 6)/6 = 2.67$ (so each forecast is slightly biased, being an average of 2.67 too low)
- mean absolute deviation = $(3 + 5 + 5 + 7 + 4 + 6)/6 = 5.0$ (so each forecast is, on average, 5.0 away from actual demand)
- mean squared error = $(9 + 25 + 25 + 49 + 16 + 36)/6 = 26.67$

All measures of error are lower for the first method, so this is giving better forecasts.

In Summary

Forecast errors are commonly measured by mean error (which gives bias), mean absolute deviation and mean squared error.

SELF-ASSESSMENT QUESTIONS

5.8   What is a time series?
5.9   Why do forecasts almost always contain errors?
5.10 Why is the mean error of a forecast of limited use?
5.11 How would you compare different forecasting methods?

5.4   CAUSAL FORECASTING

Causal forecasts look for a cause or relationship which can be used to forecast demand for an item. The demand might, for example, depend on the price being charged. Then we could find the relationship between price and demand, and use this to forecast likely demand at a planned price. This is an example of a true relationship, where changes in price (an independent variable which can take any value) cause changes in demand (a dependent variable which is fixed for any particular value of price).

We will illustrate the principles of causal forecasting through linear regression.

5.4.1   Linear Regression

Linear regression assumes a dependent variable is linearly related to an independent one, as shown in Figure 5.3. Then it finds the equation of the line of best fit through the data. Even the best line will not fit the data perfectly, but there will be an error at each point, $E(i)$. In other words, at each point, i:

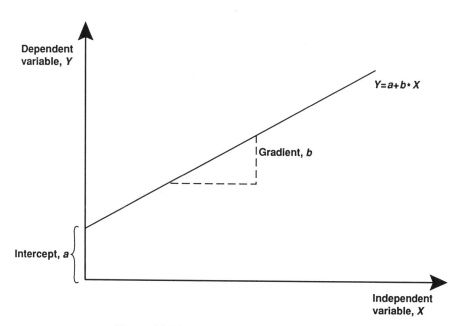

Figure 5.3 Linear relationship used in regression

$$Y(i) = a + b * X(i) + E(i)$$

where $X(i)$ = ith value of the independent variable
$Y(i)$ = corresponding ith value of the dependent variable
$E(i)$ = ith value of the error
a = point at which the regression line intersects the Y axis
b = gradient of the regression line

Linear regression finds the values of a and b which minimise some measure of the error. We saw earlier that simply adding the errors and finding the mean allows positive and negative errors cancel. Better alternatives would be to minimise the mean absolute deviation or the mean squared error. Because it allows other statistical analyses, the mean squared error is preferred for regression.

Deriving the equation for the line of best fit is quite straightforward, but we are more interested in the result than the derivation. We will simply quote the standard results (the derivation of which is given in the references at the end of the chapter). Using the abbreviations:

$$\sum X = \sum_{i=1}^{N} X(i)$$

Mean(X) = mean value of X

N = number of observations

the line of best fit is given by:

$$Y = a + b * X$$

$$b = \frac{N * \sum(X * Y) - \sum X * \sum Y}{N * \sum X^2 - (\sum X)^2}$$

$$a = \text{Mean}(Y) - b * \text{Mean}(X)$$

Use of these equations can be demonstrated most easily by an example.

Worked Example 5.2

Demand for a product over the past 10 periods has been as follows:

Period:	0	1	2	3	4	5	6	7	8	9
Demand:	3	4	8	10	15	18	20	22	27	28

Use linear regression to forecast demand for the next three periods.

Solution

The independent variable, X, is the period and the dependent variable, Y, is the demand. Then the easiest way of doing the calculations is to draw a table (see Table 5.1). (Actually, the easiest way to do this arithmetic is with a computer, either with special software or a spreadsheet.)

Table 5.1

Period, X	Demand, Y	$X*Y$	X^2
0	3	0	0
1	4	4	1
2	8	16	4
3	10	30	9
4	15	60	16
5	18	90	25
6	20	120	36
7	22	154	49
8	27	216	64
9	28	252	81
Totals 45	155	942	285

With $N = 10$, substitution leads to:

$$b = \frac{N * \sum(X * Y) - \sum X * \sum Y}{N * \sum X^2 - (\sum X)^2}$$

$$= \frac{10 * 942 - 45 * 155}{10 * 285 - 45 * 45}$$

$$= 2.96$$

$$a = \text{Mean}(Y) - b * \text{Mean}(X)$$

$$= 155/10 - 2.96 * 45/10$$

$$= 2.18$$

The line of best fit is:

$$Y = a + b * X$$
$$= 2.18 + 2.96 * X$$

The next three periods are numbers 10, 11 and 12, so substitution gives:

$$Y = a + b * X$$
$$Y = 2.18 + 2.96 * 10 = 31.78$$
$$Y = 2.18 + 2.96 * 11 = 34.74$$
$$Y = 2.18 + 2.96 * 12 = 37.70$$

In Summary

Causal forecasts look for relationships between variables. This is illustrated by linear regression which finds the line of best fit through a set of data, and allows a dependent variable to be forecast by examining a related independent variable.

5.4.2   Coefficient of Determination

We can now calculate the line of best fit through a set of data, but have not found how good this line is. It may be a perfect fit, with all points on the line, or it may be a poor fit with points widely dispersed around the line. We really need some measure which says how good the line is. For this we use the coefficient of determination.

If we look in more detail at the error in the regression equation, we can separate it into different components. Suppose we take a number of observations of $Y(i)$ and calculate the mean, $\text{Mean}(Y)$. Actual values will vary around this mean, and we can define the total sum of squared errors as:

$$\text{total SSE} = \sum \left[Y(i) - \text{Mean}(Y) \right]^2$$

When we build a regression model, we estimate values, $\widehat{Y}(i)$, which show what the observations would be if all noise is eliminated. Thus, the regression model explains some of the variation from the mean.

$$\text{explained SSE} = \sum \left[\widehat{Y}(i) - \text{Mean}(Y) \right]^2$$

Because of random noise, the regression model does not explain all the variation, and there is some residual left unexplained.

$$\text{unexplained SSE} = \sum \left[Y(i) - \widehat{Y}(i) \right]^2$$

With a little algebra it can be shown that:

$$\text{total SSE} = \text{explained SSE} + \text{unexplained SSE}$$

as shown in Figure 5.4.

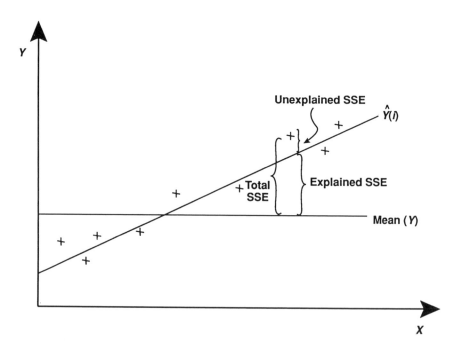

Figure 5.4 Sum of squared errors in a regression line

When the regression line is a good fit, most of the error is explained by the regression. Conversely, when the line is not a good fit, only a small amount of the error is explained by the regression. Thus the proportion of total SSE explained by the regression model gives a measure of how well the line fits the data. This ratio is defined as the coefficient of determination.

$$\text{coefficient of determination} = \frac{\text{explained SSE}}{\text{total SSE}}$$

This measure has a value between zero and one. If it is near to one, most of the variation is explained by the regression and the line is a good fit. Conversely, if the value is near to zero, most of the variation is unexplained and the line is not a good fit.

The easiest way of calculating the coefficient of determination is the equation:

$$\text{coefficient of determination} = \left[\frac{N * \sum (X * Y) - \sum X * \sum Y}{\sqrt{\left[N * \sum X^2 - (\sum X)^2 \right] * \left[N * \sum Y^2 - (\sum Y)^2 \right]}} \right]^2$$

Although this looks rather messy, we should make two points:

- all the values, except $\sum Y^2$, have already been calculated to find the regression line
- such calculations are well suited to computer spreadsheets or specialised programs

Worked Example 5.3

Calculate the coefficient of determination for the data in Worked Example 5.2.

Solution

Drawing the table of results as before, and adding values for $\sum Y^2$ gives Table 5.2. We already know the line of best fit through this data is $Y = 2.18 + 2.96 * X$, and are now checking to see how good this line is. The coefficient of determination is calculated as:

Table 5.2

Period, X	Demand, Y	$X*Y$	X^2	Y^2
0	3	0	0	9
1	4	4	1	16
2	8	16	4	64
3	10	30	9	100
4	15	60	16	225
5	18	90	25	324
6	20	120	36	400
7	22	154	49	484
8	27	216	64	729
9	28	252	81	784
$\sum$ 45	155	942	285	3135

coefficient of determination

$$= \left[\frac{N * \sum(X*Y) - \sum X * \sum Y}{\sqrt{\left[N * \sum X^2 - (\sum X)^2\right] * \left[N * \sum Y^2 - (\sum Y)^2\right]}} \right]^2$$

$$= \left[\frac{10 * 942 - 45 * 155}{\sqrt{[10*285 - 45*45] * [10*3135 - 155*155]}} \right]^2$$

$$= \left[\frac{9420 - 6975}{\sqrt{825 * 7325}} \right]^2$$

$$= 0.989$$

This shows that 99% of the variation can be explained by the regression model and only 1% is unexplained. This is evidence of a very good fit. Normally any value for the coefficient of determination above about 0.5 is considered a good fit.

In Summary

The coefficient of determination shows how well a regression line fits the data. Generally, any value over about 0.5 is considered a good fit.

5.4.3   Coefficient of Correlation

A second useful measure in regression is the coefficient of correlation which asks the question "are X and Y linearly related?". The coefficients of correlation and determination answer very similar questions, and a fuller analysis shows:

coefficient of correlation = $\sqrt{\text{coefficient of determination}}$

The coefficient of determination is usually referred to as r^2 and the coefficient of correlation as r.

The coefficient of correlation has a value between $+1$ and -1.

- a value of $r = 0$ shows there is no correlation at all between the two variables and no linear relationship
- a value of $r = 1$ shows the two variables have a perfect linear relationship with no noise at all, and as one increases so does the other
- a value of $r = -1$ shows the two variables have a perfect linear relationship and as one increases the other decreases

With correlation coefficients near to $+1$ or -1 there is a strong linear relationship between the two variables. When r is between 0.7 and -0.7 the coefficient of determination is less than 0.49 and less than half the sum of squared errors is explained by the regression model. Thus, values of r between 0.7 and -0.7 show a weak linear relationship (Figure 5.5).

Worked Example 5.4

The following table shows corresponding values for two variables. What conclusions can be drawn from these?

X:	25	23	4	12	30	15	36
Y:	92	63	28	44	51	42	98

Solution

The first thing we should do is calculate the coefficients of correlation and determination. We use Table 5.3 for the data. Now we can calculate the coefficient of correlation to see if there is a linear relationship.

$$r = \frac{N * \sum(X * Y) - \sum X * \sum Y}{\sqrt{[N * \sum X^2 - (\sum X)^2] * [N * \sum Y^2 - (\sum Y)^2]}}$$

$$= \frac{7 * 10\,077 - 145 * 418}{[7 * 3735 - 145 * 145] * [7 * 29\,122 - 418 * 418]}$$

$$= 0.81$$

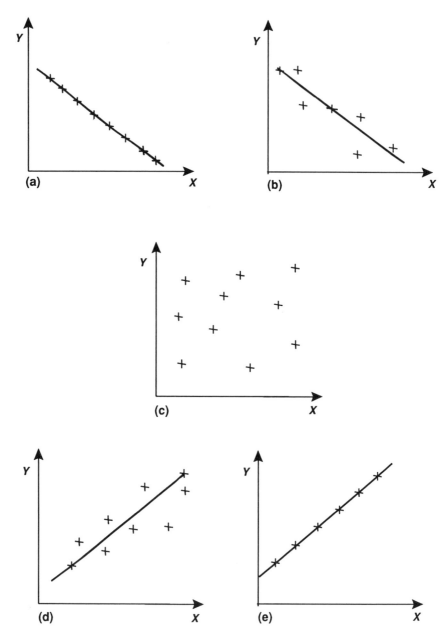

Figure 5.5 Effects of different coefficients of correlation. (a) $r = -1.0$ perfect negative correlation. (b) $r = -0.7$ good negative correlation. (c) $r = 0$ random points. (d) $r = 0.7$ good positive correlation. (e) $r = 1.0$ perfect positive correlation

Table 5.3

	X	Y	$X*Y$	X^2	Y^2
	25	92	2 300	625	8 464
	23	63	1 449	529	3 969
	4	28	112	16	784
	12	44	528	144	1 936
	30	51	1 530	900	2 601
	15	42	630	225	1 764
	36	98	3 528	1 296	9 604
Totals	145	418	10 077	3 735	29 122

This indicates a reasonably strong linear relationship. If we square this we get the coefficient of determination:

$$r^2 = 0.66$$

This shows that 66% of the variation is explained by the linear relationship, and only 34% is unexplained.

As there is a fairly strong linear relationship, it is worth calculating the line of best fit.

$$Y = a + b * X$$

with:

$$b = \frac{N * \sum(X * Y) - \sum X * \sum Y}{N * \sum X^2 - (\sum X)^2}$$

$$= \frac{7 * 10\,077 - 145 * 418}{7 * 3735 - 145 * 145}$$

$$= 1.94$$

$$a = \text{Mean}(Y) - b * \text{Mean}(X)$$

$$= 418/7 - 1.94 * 145/7$$

$$= 19.53$$

Then:

$$Y = 19.53 + 1.94 * X$$

There are several extensions to the basic linear regression model. One of these uses multiple linear regression to find a linear relationship between a dependent variable and several independent ones.

$$Y = a + b_1 * X_1 + b_2 * X_2 + b_3 * X_3 + b_4 * X_4 \dots$$

The sales of a product, for example, might depend on its price, the advertising budget, number of suppliers, local unemployment rate, and so on. The arithmetic in multiple regression is very tedious by hand, and it should really only be tackled with a computer, using one of the many standard packages.

Another extension would consider non-linear regression. This fits a more complex curve to the data. Again this is simple with a computer, but is usually too complicated to do by hand.

In Summary

The coefficient of correlation shows how strong a linear relationship is. Generally any value in the range 0.7 to 1 or −0.7 to −1 shows a strong linear relationship.

SELF-ASSESSMENT QUESTIONS

5.12 What is meant by "causal forecasting"?
5.13 What does linear regression do?
5.14 What is measured by the coefficient of determination?
5.15 What values can be taken by the coefficient of correlation and how is this related to the coefficient of determination?

5.5   PROJECTIVE FORECASTING

Causal forecasting is extrinsic, in that it forecasts demand for an item by looking at values taken by other variables. Projective forecasting is intrinsic, in that it uses only historic values for demand to forecast future demand. Any external influences are ignored. We will describe four methods of this type:

- simple averages
- moving averages
- exponential smoothing
- models for seasonality and trend

5.5.1   Simple Averages

An obvious method of projective forecasting is to look at records for previous demand and take the average of these. This is the principle of forecasting using simple averages.

$$\text{simple averages forecasting} \quad F(t + 1) = \frac{1}{N} * \sum_{t=1}^{N} D(t)$$

where: N = number of periods of historic data
t = time period
$D(t)$ = demand at time t
$F(t + 1)$ = forecast for time $t + 1$

Worked Example 5.5

Use simple averages to forecast demand for period six of the following two time series. How accurate are the forecasts? What are the forecasts for period 50?

Period:	t	1	2	3	4	5
Series 1:	$D(t)$	49	50	49	52	50
Series 2:	$D(t)$	70	33	76	29	42

Solution

- Series 1 $\quad F(6) = \dfrac{1}{N} * \sum_{t=1}^{N} D(t) = 1/5 * 250 = 50$

- Series 2 $\quad F(6) = 1/5 * 250 = 50$

Although the forecasts are the same, there is clearly less noise in the first series than the second. Consequently we would be more confident in the first forecast and expect the error to be less.

Simple averages assume the demand to be constant. Therefore, the forecasts for period 50 are the same as the forecasts for period 6 (i.e. 50).

Using simple averages to forecast demand is easy and can give good results when demand is constant (or at least relatively stable). Unfortunately, it does not work well if the demand pattern changes. Then older data tends to swamp the latest figures and the forecast is very unresponsive to the change. Suppose, for example, demand for an item has been constant at 50 units a week for the past year. Simple averages would give a forecast demand for week 53 of 50 units. If the demand in week 53 suddenly rises to 100 units, simple averages would give a forecast for week 54 of:

$$F(54) = (52 * 50 + 100)/53 = 50.94$$

A doubling of demand has increased the forecast by less than 2%. If demand continued at 100 units a week subsequent forecasts are:

$$F(55) = 51.85 \qquad F(56) = 52.73 \qquad F(57) = 53.57$$

and so on. The forecasts are rising but the response is very slow.

The implication is that simple averages can only be used for demand which is stable over long periods. Few demands are this stable, and the restriction makes simple averages of limited value. One way around this is to ignore old data, as discussed in the following section.

In Summary

Forecasting with simple averages can give good results if demand is constant. For any other pattern some alternative method should be used.

5.5.2   Moving Averages

The problem with simple averages is that old data, which may be out of date, tends to swamp newer, more relevant data. One way around this is to ignore old data and only use the most recent values in forecasts. This is the principle of moving averages.

The demand for most items changes over time, so that only a certain amount of historic data is relevant to future forecasts. The implication is that all observations older than some specified value can be ignored. This suggests an approach where the average demand over, say, the past ten periods is used in forecasting, and any data older than this is ignored. This is the basis of moving averages.

Moving average forecasts are found from:

$F(t + 1)$ = average of N most recent pieces of data
= [latest demand + next latest + ... + Nth latest]$/N$
= $[D(t) + D(t - 1) + ... + D(t - N + 1)]/N$

Worked Example 5.6

Demand for an item over the past six periods has been as follows:

t:	1	2	3	4	5	6
$D(t)$:	203	194	188	206	173	119

If data over three periods old is no longer considered relevant, use a moving average to forecast demand for the item.

Solution

Only data more recent than three periods is relevant, so we can use a three-period moving average for the forecast. If we consider the situation at the end of period 3, the forecast for period 4 is:

$$F(4) = [D(1) + D(2) + D(3)]/3 = (203 + 194 + 188)/3 = 195$$

At the end of period 4, when demand is known to be 206, this forecast is updated to give:

$$F(5) = [D(2) + D(3) + D(4)]/3 = (194 + 188 + 206)/3 = 196$$

Similarly:

$$F(6) = [D(3) + D(4) + D(5)]/3 = (188 + 206 + 173)/3 = 189$$
$$F(7) = [D(4) + D(5) + D(6)]/3 = (206 + 173 + 119)/3 = 166$$

Worked Example 5.6 shows how moving average forecasts respond to changing demand, with a high demand moving the forecast upwards and vice versa. At the same time the forecast is smoothing out variations, so that it does not blindly follow variations in the random noise. The rate at which a moving average forecast responds to changing demand can be adjusted by using an appropriate value of N.

- A large value for N takes the average of many observations and the forecast is unresponsive. The forecast will smoothe out random variations, but will be slow to follow genuine changes in demand.
- A small value for N gives a responsive forecast which quickly follows genuine changes in demand, but may be too sensitive to random fluctuations.

A compromise value of N is needed to give reasonable results and typically a value around six is used.

Worked Example 5.7

Demand for an item over the past 9 months is as follows. Use moving averages with $N = 2$, $N = 4$ and $N = 6$ to produce one-period ahead forecasts.

Month:	1	2	3	4	5	6	7	8	9
Demand:	48	42	36	45	54	63	69	72	75

Solution

The earliest forecast which can be made using a three-period moving average is $F(4) = [D(1)+D(2)+D(3)]/3$. Similarly the earliest forecasts for a four- and six-period moving average are $F(5)$ and $F(7)$ respectively. Then the forecasts are given in Table 5.4. Plotting a graph (Figure 5.6) of these shows how the three-month moving average is most responsive to change and the six-month moving average is least responsive.

Table 5.4

Month	Demand	Forecasts		
		$N=3$	$N=4$	$N=6$
1	48	—	—	—
2	42	—	—	—
3	36	—	—	—
4	45	42	—	—
5	54	41	42.75	—
6	63	45	44.25	—
7	69	54	49.5	48.0
8	72	62	57.75	51.5
9	75	68	64.5	56.5
10	—	72	69.75	63.0

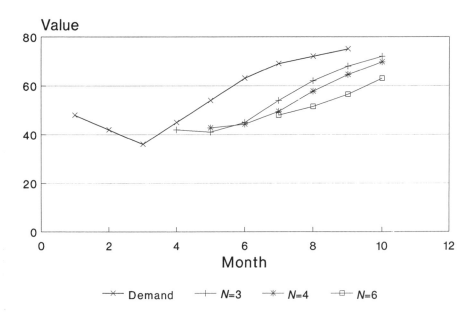

Figure 5.6 Forecasts for Worked Example 5.7

A particularly useful property of moving averages is the way they smoothe out demands which have strong seasonal variations. If N is chosen to equal the number of periods in a season, a moving average will completely deseasonalise data. This is illustrated in the following example.

Worked Example 5.8

Use moving averages with 2, 4 and 6 periods to calculate the one-month ahead forecasts for the following data.

Month:	1	2	3	4	5	6	7	8	9	10	11	12
$D(t)$:	20	10	4	30	22	11	5	28	19	9	6	29

Solution

This data has a clear seasonal pattern, with a peak every fourth month. Calculating the moving averages gives the results shown in Table 5.5. The patterns can be seen clearly in a graph, shown in Figure 5.7. The moving average with both $N=2$ and $N=6$ respond to the peaks and troughs of demand, but neither has got the timing right. As expected, the two-period moving average is much more responsive than the six-period one. The most interesting result is the four-period moving average which has completely deseasonalised the data.

Although moving averages overcome some of the problems with simple averages, the method still has three major defects:

- all data used are given the same weight regardless of age
- the method only works well with constant demand
- a large amount of historic data must be stored

The first of these defects can be overcome by assigning different weights to observations. A four-period moving average, for example, gives equal weight to the last four observations, so each is given a weight of 0.25. These weights could be changed to put more emphasis on later results, perhaps using:

$$F(t) = 0.1 * D(t-4) + 0.2 * D(t-3) + 0.3 * D(t-2) + 0.4 * D(t-1)$$

In practice, a more convenient way of changing the weights is to use exponential smoothing, which is described in the following section.

In Summary

Moving averages use average demand over the latest N periods as a forecast. The responsiveness can be changed by altering the value of N. Time series can be deseasonalised by setting N to the number of periods in the season.

Table 5.5

Month	Demand	Forecasts		
		$N=2$	$N=4$	$N=6$
1	20	—	—	—
2	10	—	—	—
3	4	15	—	—
4	30	7	—	—
5	22	17	16	—
6	11	26	16.5	—
7	5	16.5	16.75	16.2
8	28	8	17	13.7
9	19	16.5	16.5	16.7
10	9	23.5	15.75	19.2
11	6	14	15.25	15.7
12	29	7.5	15.5	13
13	—	17.5	15.75	16

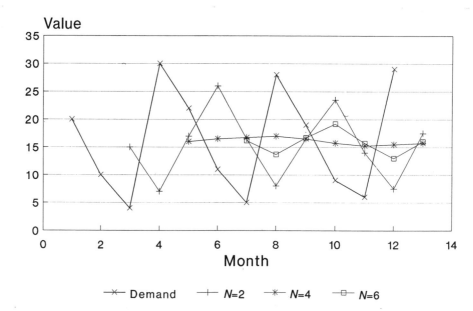

Figure 5.7 Forecasts for Worked Example 5.8

SELF-ASSESSMENT QUESTIONS

5.16 Why are simple averages of limited use for forecasting?
5.17 What is the main benefit of moving average forecasts?
5.18 How can forecasts by moving averages be made more responsive?
5.19 How can data be deseasonalised?

5.5.3 Exponential Smoothing

Exponential smoothing is based on the idea that as data gets older it becomes less relevant and should be given less weight. The method, then, gives high weight to most recent data, but the weight declines exponentially with the age of data, as shown in Figure 5.8. This declining weight can be achieved using only the latest demand figure and the previous forecast. In particular, a new forecast is calculated by taking a proportion, α, of the latest demand and adding a proportion, $1 - \alpha$, of the previous forecast.

---

new forecast = $\alpha *$ latest demand + $(1 - \alpha) *$ last forecast

$$F(t + 1) = \alpha * D(t) + (1 - \alpha) * F(t)$$

In this equation, α is the smoothing constant which is usually given a value between 0.1 and 0.2.

We can illustrate the way exponential smoothing adapts to changing demand by rearranging the formula:

$$F(t + 1) = \alpha * D(t) + (1 - \alpha) * F(t)$$

$$= F(t) + \alpha * [D(t) - F(t)]$$

But

$$E(t) = D(t) - F(t)$$

so

$$F(t + 1) = F(t) + \alpha * E(t)$$

Thus the error in each forecast is noted and a proportion is added to adjust the next forecast. This gives a continuously self-correcting method where larger errors in the last forecast lead to larger adjustments in the next forecast.

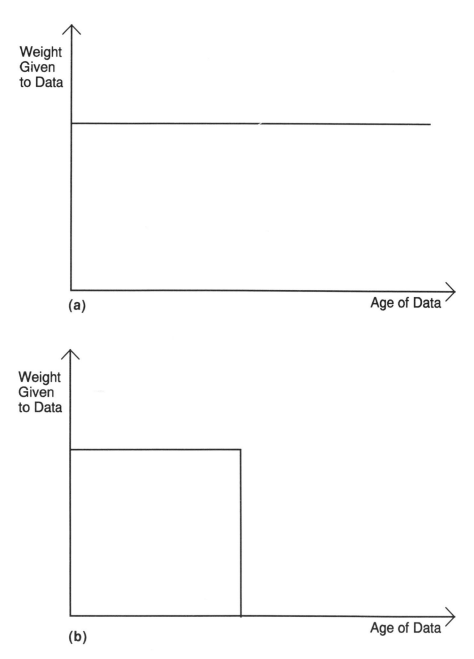

Figure 5.8 Weight given to data by different forecasting methods. (a) Actual averages give equal weight to all data. (b) Moving averages ignore all data beyond a certain age

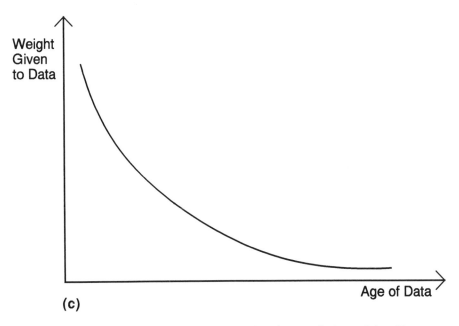

Figure 5.8 (continued) (c) Exponential smoothing gives a reducing weight with age

Worked Example 5.9

Use exponential smoothing with $\alpha = 0.2$ and an initial value of $F(1) = 102$ to produce one-period ahead forecasts for the following demands.

Week:	1	2	3	4	5	6
Demand:	107	115	94	89	98	91

Solution

We know the $F(1) = 102$ and $\alpha = 0.2$. Substitution then gives:

$$F(2) = \alpha * D(1) + (1 - \alpha) * F(1) = 0.2 * 107 + 0.8 * 102 = 103$$
$$F(3) = \alpha * D(2) + (1 - \alpha) * F(2) = 0.2 * 115 + 0.8 * 103 = 105.4$$

and so on, as shown in the following table:

t:	1	2	3	4	5	6	7
$D(t)$:	107	115	94	89	98	91	—
$F(t)$:	102	103	105.4	103.1	100.3	99.8	98.0

It may not be obvious that exponential smoothing actually does give less weight to data as it gets older. We can demonstrate this by taking an arbitrary value for α, say 0.2. Then:

$$F(t + 1) = 0.2 * D(t) + 0.8 * F(t)$$

But substituting $t - 1$ for t gives:

$$F(t) = 0.2 * D(t - 1) + 0.8 * F(t - 1)$$

and using this in the equation above gives:

$$F(t + 1) = 0.2 * D(t) + 0.8 * [0.2 * D(t - 1) + 0.8 * F(t - 1)]$$
$$= 0.2 * D(t) + 0.16 * D(t - 1) + 0.64 * F(t - 1)$$

But

$$F(t - 1) = 0.2 * D(t - 2) + 0.8 * F(t - 2)$$

so

$$F(t + 1) = 0.2 * D(t) + 0.16 * D(t - 1) + 0.64 * [0.2 * D(t - 2) + 0.8 * F(t - 2)]$$
$$= 0.2 * D(t) + 0.16 * D(t - 1) + 0.128 * D(t - 2) + 0.512 * F(t - 2)$$

The weight put on older data is getting progressively less, and the above calculation could be continued to give weights shown in Table 5.6. In this calculation we took an arbitrary value of $\alpha = 0.2$, but repeating the calculations with other values would lead to similar results.

Table 5.6

Age of data	Weight
0	0.2
1	0.16
2	0.128
3	0.102 4
4	0.081 92
5	0.065 536
6	0.052 428 8
etc.	etc.

The value given to the smoothing constant, α, is important in setting the responsiveness of the forecasts.

- A high value of α, perhaps around 0.3, puts more emphasis on the latest demands and gives a responsive forecast.
- A low value of α, perhaps around 0.1, puts more emphasis on previous forecasts and gives a less responsive forecast.

A compromise is needed between having a responsive forecast (which might follow random fluctuations) and an unresponsive one (which is slow to follow real changes).

Worked Example 5.10

The following time series has a clear step upwards in demand in month 3. Use an initial forecast of 50 to compare exponential smoothing forecasts with varying values of α.

Period:	1	2	3	4	5	6	7	8	9	10	11
Demand:	48	50	150	145	155	150	148	152	150	149	150

Solution

Taking values of $\alpha = 0.1$, 0.2 and 0.3 gives the results shown in Table 5.7. All these forecasts would eventually follow the sharp step and raise forecasts to around 150. Higher values of α make this adjustment more quickly and give a more responsive forecast, as shown in Figure 5.9.

Although higher values of α give more responsive forecasts, they do not necessarily give more accurate ones. Demand always contains random noise, and very sensitive forecasts tend to follow these random fluctuations. One way of selecting an appropriate value for α is to test several values over a trial period and select the one which gives smallest errors. This value is then used for all future forecasts.

An alternative to using a fixed value for α would be to change the value depending on circumstances. If, for example, forecast errors begin to rise, the forecast may be adapting to a real change in demand and a more sensitive forecast would give better results. Thus, a check could be kept on errors and if these get too big the value of α may be increased. We could use any of the errors defined previously to keep a check on forecast performance, but a simpler way is to use a tracking signal. Many of these have been suggested, with a popular one calculated from:

$$\text{tracking signal} = \frac{\text{sum of forecast errors}}{\text{mean absolute deviation}}$$

If the forecast error remains small, this tracking signal has a value close to zero. If, however, the error gets bigger the value of the tracking signal increases. When it reaches some predefined limit around, say, 2.5, remedial action is needed. This might be a small adjustment like increasing the value of α by 0.1, or it may include major changes to the forecasting method.

In Summary

Exponential smoothing is based on the calculation:

$$F(t + 1) = \alpha * D(t) + (1 - \alpha) * F(t)$$

This gives a reducing weight to data as its age increases. The responsiveness of forecasts can be adjusted by changing the value given to the smoothing constant, α. A tracking signal may be useful for checking performance.

Table 5.7

Period	Demand	Forecast		
		$\alpha = 0.1$	$\alpha = 0.2$	$\alpha = 0.3$
1	48	50.00	50.00	50.00
2	50	49.80	49.60	49.40
3	150	49.82	49.68	49.58
4	145	59.84	69.74	79.71
5	155	68.35	84.80	99.29
6	150	77.02	98.84	116.01
7	148	84.32	109.07	126.20
8	152	90.69	116.86	132.74
9	150	96.82	123.88	138.52
10	149	102.14	129.11	141.96
11	150	106.82	133.09	144.08
12	—	111.14	136.47	145.85

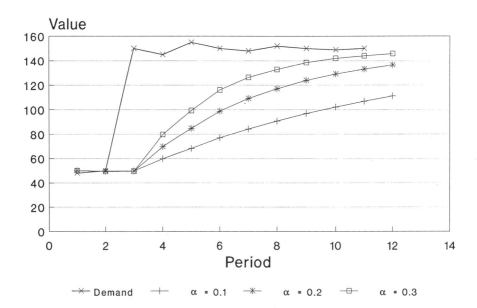

Figure 5.9 Forecasts for Worked Example 5.14

SELF-ASSESSMENT QUESTIONS

5.20 Why is the forecasting method called "exponential smoothing"?
5.21 How can an exponential smoothing forecast be made more responsive?
5.22 What is a tracking signal?

5.5.4   Models for Seasonality and Trend

Exponential smoothing is currently the most widely used forecasting method for inventory control. In its standard form, however, it does not cope well with demand which is either seasonal or has a trend. In this section we will extend the idea of exponential smoothing to deal with seasonality and trend.

We will start by defining "trend" as the amount by which demand grows between two consecutive periods. If two consecutive periods have demands of 50 and 60 the trend is 10: if two consecutive periods have demands of 110 and 100 the trend is -10.

Seasonality is a regular cyclical pattern, which is not necessarily annual. It is measured by seasonal indices, which are defined as the amounts deseasonalised values must be multiplied by to get seasonal values. Then:

$$\text{seasonal index} = \frac{\text{seasonal value}}{\text{deseasonalised value}}$$

If a newspaper has average daily sales of 100 copies in a particular area, but this rises to 200 copies on Saturday and falls to 50 copies on Monday and Tuesday. The deseasonalised value is 100, the seasonal index for Saturday is 2.0, the seasonal indices for Monday and Tuesday are 0.5, and seasonal indices for other days are 1.0.

Now we can look at the details of forecasting demand with seasonality and trend. The easiest way of doing this is to split the demand into separate components and then forecast each component separately. The final forecast is found by recombining the separate components. To be more specific, the demand is split into four components (see Figure 5.10):

- underlying value (which is the basic value of demand)
- adjustment for trend (which is an addition or subtraction to allow for steady increases or decreases)
- seasonal index (which allows for regular cyclical variation)
- random noise (which cannot be forecast)

Then:

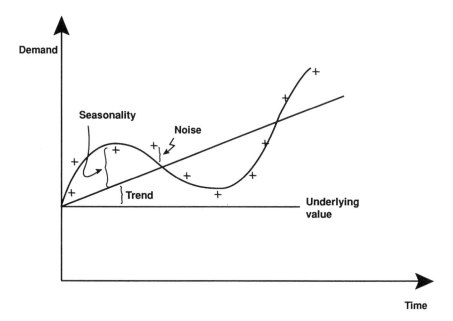

Figure 5.10 Components in a time series with seasonality and trend

$$D(t) = \left[\begin{array}{c} \text{underlying} \\ \text{value} \end{array} + \begin{array}{c} \text{adjustment} \\ \text{for trend} \end{array} \right] * \begin{array}{c} \text{seasonal} \\ \text{index} \end{array} + \text{noise}$$

The steps in forecasting are then:

(1) deseasonalise demand and use exponential smoothing to give the smoothed underlying value
(2) use exponential smoothing on the trend to give a smoothed adjustment for trend
(3) use exponential smoothing on the seasonal index to give the smoothed index for the period
(4) add the smoothed underlying value to the smoothed trend adjustment and multiply by the seasonal index to give the forecast

$$F(t+1) = \left[\begin{array}{c} \text{smoothed} \\ \text{underlying} \\ \text{value} \end{array} + \begin{array}{c} \text{smoothed} \\ \text{adjustment} \\ \text{for trend} \end{array} \right] * \begin{array}{c} \text{smoothed} \\ \text{seasonal} \\ \text{index} \end{array}$$

$$F(t+1) = [U(t) + T(t)] * I(n)$$

where $U(t)$ = smoothed underlying value for period t
$\quad T(t)$ = smoothed trend for period t
$\quad I(n)$ = smoothed seasonal index for period t, which is the nth period of a
$\qquad$ cycle

Although this procedure is quite straightforward, the amount of arithmetic can be tedious. Here we will illustrate the approach, and bear in mind that such procedures will inevitably be computerised in practice.

Worked Example 5.11

Over the past 12 periods demand for an item has been as follows:

t	1	2	3	4	5	6	7	8	9	10	11	12
$D(t)$	602	620	304	396	798	804	602	630	941	896	664	736

Forecast demand for the next five periods.

Solution

Exponential smoothing is an updating process, so we must start with initial values. We will use the first two-thirds of the data to find these initial values and then do some fine tuning over the last third.

If we take the first eight values we can draw a linear regression line through them, and the usual calculations give $a = 486.92$ and $b = 23.90$. This regression line effectively gives deseasonalised values. Then by taking the ratio of actual demand to deseasonalised demand we can calculate seasonal indices as shown in Table 5.8.

Table 5.8

t	Deseasonalised value	Seasonal value, $D(t)$	Seasonal index
1	510.82	602	1.18
2	534.72	620	1.16
3	558.62	304	0.54
4	582.52	396	0.68
5	606.42	798	1.32
6	630.32	804	1.28
7	654.22	602	0.92
8	678.12	630	0.93

The data, shown in Figure 5.11, shows a clear season which is four periods long. The eight periods of data used to find initial values give two complete cycles, so the seasonal index for each period in a cycle can be found by averaging values in the two cycles.

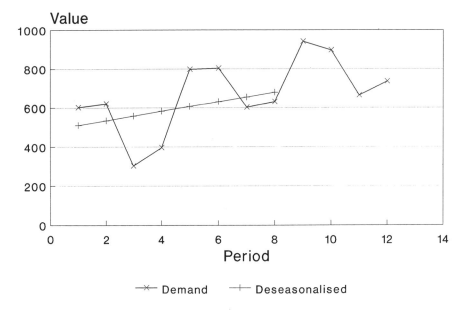

Figure 5.11 Demand for Worked Example 5.11

- for first period in cycle, $I(1) = (1.18 + 1.32)/2 = 1.25$
- for second period in cycle, $I(2) = (1.16 + 1.28)/2 = 1.22$
- for third period in cycle, $I(3) = (0.54 + 0.92)/2 = 0.73$
- for fourth period in cycle, $I(4) = (0.68 + 0.93)/2 = 0.81$

The initial value for the trend is $T(8)$, which is the value of b in the regression equation (23.90). The initial underlying value is the deseasonalised value at period 8, $U(8)$, which is $486.92 + 8 * 23.90 = 678.12$. The only other value we need is a smoothing constant, α, and we will set this to 0.2.

Having found initial values, the next stage is to tune these over the last third of the data. We know that:

$$F(t+1) = \left[\begin{array}{c} \text{underlying} \\ \text{value} \end{array} + \begin{array}{c} \text{adjustment} \\ \text{for trend} \end{array} \right] * \begin{array}{c} \text{seasonal} \\ \text{index} \end{array}$$

Substituting the initial values of $U(8) = 678.12$, $T(8) = 23.90$ and $I(1) = 1.25$, gives:

$$F(9) = [U(8) + T(8)] * I(1)$$
$$= (678.12 + 23.90) * 1.25$$
$$= 877.53$$

This compares with the actual demand of 941. The forecast for period 10 can now be found by updating values using the procedure described above.

1. Deseasonalise the latest demand and use exponential smoothing to find the smoothed underlying value

- The last underlying value is $U(8) = 678.12$, but the trend, $T(8)$, has to be added to give the underlying value for the next period ($678.12 + 23.90 = 702.02$).
- The latest demand is $D(9) = 941$ and the seasonal index for the first period of the cycle is $I(1) = 1.25$, so the latest deseasonalised demand is $941/1.25 = 752.8$.
- Exponential smoothing is used to give the smoothed underlying value.

$$U(9) = \alpha * [D(9)/I(1)] + (1 - \alpha) * [U(8) + T(8)]$$
$$= 0.2 * 752.8 + 0.8 * 702.02$$
$$= 712.18$$

In general this calculation is:

$$U(t) = \alpha * [D(t)/I(n)] + (1 - \alpha) * [U(t - 1) + T(t - 1)]$$

2. Use exponential smoothing on the trend to give a smoothed adjustment for trend

- The latest value for trend is the difference between the last two underlying values. These are $U(8) = 678.12$ and $U(9) = 712.18$, so the latest trend figure is $712.18 - 678.12 = 34.06$.
- The last value for trend was $T(8) = 23.90$, so a smoothed value is found using exponential smoothing:

$$T(9) = \alpha * [U(9) - U(8)] + (1 - \alpha) * T(8)$$
$$= 0.2 * [712.18 - 678.12] + 0.8 * 23.90$$
$$= 25.93$$

In general this calculation is:

$$T(t) = \alpha * [U(t) - U(t - 1)] + (1 - \alpha) * T(t - 1)$$

3. Use exponential smoothing on the seasonal index to find the smoothed index for the period

- The latest figure for the underlying value is $U(9) = 712.18$. The latest actual demand for period 9 is 941, so the latest seasonal index for the first period in the cycle is $941/712.18 = 1.32$.

- The last value was 1.25, so a smoothed seasonal index is calculated using exponential smoothing:

$$I(1) = \alpha * [D(9)/U(9)] + (1 - \alpha) * \text{last value for } I(1)$$
$$= 0.2 * 1.32 + 0.8 * 1.25$$
$$= 1.26$$

In general this calculation is:

$$I(n) = \alpha * [D(t)/U(t)] + (1 - \alpha) * I'(n)$$

where $I'(n)$ is the previous value of the seasonal index.

4. Add the underlying value to the trend adjustment and multiply by the seasonal index to give the forecast

Now we can substitute values and produce a forecast for the next period, but have to be careful with the seasonal index. Although we have just updated a value for $I(1)$, the next forecast is for period 10 which is the second period in the cycle and the latest value for $I(2)$ must be used.

$$F(t+1) = \left[\begin{array}{c} \text{underlying} \\ \text{value} \end{array} + \begin{array}{c} \text{adjustment} \\ \text{for trend} \end{array} \right] * \begin{array}{c} \text{seasonal} \\ \text{index} \end{array}$$
$$= [U(t) + T(t)] * I(n)$$

$$F(10) = [U(9) + T(9)] * I(2)$$
$$= [712.18 + 25.93] * 1.22$$
$$= 900.49$$

This compares with the actual demand of 896.
This tuning procedure can be repeated as follows.

1. Latest figure for deseasonalised, underlying value:

$$U(t) = \alpha * [D(t)/I(n)] + (1 - \alpha) * [U(t-1) + T(t-1)]$$
$$U(10) = \alpha * [D(10)/I(2)] + (1 - \alpha) * [U(9) + T(9)]$$
$$= 0.2 * [896/1.22] + 0.8 * [712.18 + 25.93]$$
$$= 737.37$$

2. Latest figure for trend:

$$T(t) = \alpha * [U(t) - U(t-1)] + (1 - \alpha) * T(t-1)$$
$$T(10) = \alpha * [U(10) - U(9)] + (1 - \alpha) * T(9)$$
$$= 0.2 * [737.37 - 712.18] + 0.8 * 25.93$$
$$= 25.78$$

3. Latest figure for seasonal index for the second period of the cycle:

$$I(n) = \alpha * [D(t)/U(t)] + (1 - \alpha) * I'(n)$$
$$I(2) = \alpha * [D(10)/U(10)] + (1 - \alpha) * I'(2)$$
$$= 0.2 * [896/737.37] + 0.8 * 1.22$$
$$= 1.22$$

4. Next forecast:

$$F(t + 1) = [U(t) + T(t)] * I(n)$$
$$F(11) = [U(10) + T(10)] * I(3)$$
$$= [737.37 + 25.78] * 0.73$$
$$= 557.10$$

We now continue this updating for as long as there are demand figures.

$$U(11) = 0.2 * [664/0.73] + 0.8 * [737.37 + 25.78] = 792.44$$
$$T(11) = 0.2 * [792.44 - 737.37] + 0.8 * 25.78 = 31.64$$
$$I(3) = 0.2 * [664/792.44] + 0.8 * 0.73 = 0.75$$
$$F(12) = [792.44 + 31.64] * 0.81 = 667.50$$

$$U(12) = 0.2 * [736/0.81] + 0.8 * [792.44 + 31.64] = 840.99$$
$$T(12) = 0.2 * [840.99 - 792.44] + 0.8 * 31.64 = 35.02$$
$$I(4) = 0.2 * [736/840.99] + 0.8 * 0.81 = 0.82$$

This finishes the fine tuning of the variables, as there is no more historic data. Forecasts can now be found for any period in the future.

$$F(13) = [U(12) + T(12)] * I(1) \quad = [840.99 + 35.02] * 1.26 \quad = 1103.77$$
$$F(14) = [U(12) + 2 * T(12)] * I(2) = [840.99 + 2 * 35.02] * 1.22 = 1111.46$$
$$F(15) = [U(12) + 3 * T(12)] * I(3) = [840.99 + 3 * 35.02] * 0.75 = 709.54$$
$$F(16) = [U(12) + 4 * T(12)] * I(4) = [840.99 + 4 * 35.02] * 0.82 = 804.48$$
$$F(17) = [U(12) + 5 * T(12)] * I(1) = [840.99 + 5 * 35.02] * 1.26 = 1280.27$$

and so on (see Figure 5.12).

There are three main problems with this approach to forecasting.

- Firstly, there is the amount of computation, but this can easily be overcome with a specialised computer program or a spreadsheet.
- Secondly, there is the need to initialise variables. As exponential smoothing reacts to errors, the initial values are not so important, provided the process is tuned over a suitable period. In the example above, better forecasts could have been obtained if the method was tuned using more demand figures.

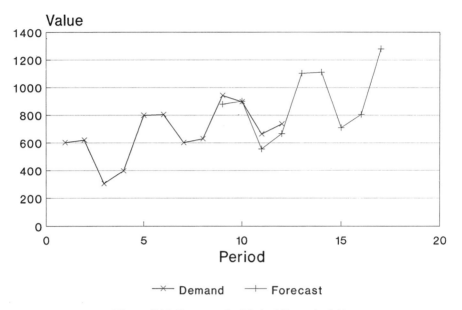

Figure 5.12 Forecasts for Worked Example 5.11

- Thirdly, there is the selection of smoothing constants. Sometimes values for α are arbitrarily set around 0.15, but these forecasts tend to be sensitive to the values given to smoothing constants. It is worthwhile putting some effort into their selection. The best way of doing this is to have trial runs using historic data to compare errors with various values of α. In the example above, we used the same α for all components, but there is no need for this. The forecast could, for example, be made more responsive to changes in underlying values than to trend.

In Summary

Data with seasonality and trend can be split into four components of underlying value, trend, seasonal index and noise. The first three of these can be forecast separately and combined to give overall forecasts.

SELF-ASSESSMENT QUESTIONS

5.23 Why is ordinary exponential smoothing not used for demand figures with seasonality and trend?

5.24 Define all terms in the equation

$$F(t + 1) = [U(t) + T(t)] * I(n)$$

5.25 How can demand which has trend but no seasonality be forecast?

SUMMARY OF CHAPTER

This chapter has described various aspects of forecasting demand. In particular it:

- discussed some features of forecasts
- classified approaches to forecasting according to judgemental, causal or projective
- described a range of judgemental forecasting methods including personal insight, panel consensus, Delphi method, historic analogy and market survey
- discussed the causes of forecast errors and appropriate measures of these
- discussed the approach of causal forecasting and illustrated this by linear regression
- discussed the approach of projective forecasting and illustrated this by simple averages, moving averages and exponential smoothing
- used projective forecasts for demand patterns with seasonality and trend

ADDITIONAL PROBLEMS

5.1 Two forecasting methods have been used to give the following estimates for demand. Which method is better?

t:	1	2	3	4	5	6
$D(t)$:	40	44	52	38	28	30
$F(t)$ method 1:	34	46	48	44	34	32
$F(t)$ method 2:	30	40	44	48	38	34

5.2 Production of an item depends on the number of shifts worked in a month. Data for the past 9 months is shown below. If 400 units are needed next month, how many shifts should be planned? How reliable is this result?

Month:	1	2	3	4	5	6	7	8	9
Shifts worked:	50	70	25	55	20	60	40	25	35
Units made:	352	555	207	508	48	498	310	153	264

5.3 Sales of a product for the past 10 weeks are shown below. Use linear regression to forecast sales for the next 3 weeks. How reliable are these figures?

Week:	1	2	3	4	5	6	7	8	9	10
Sales:	12	20	81	150	201	262	299	364	422	485

5.4 Calculate the coefficients of correlation and determination for the following data. What conclusions can be drawn from these? What is the line of best fit?

X:	4	17	3	21	10	8	4	9	13	12	2	6	15	8	19
Y:	13	47	24	41	29	33	28	38	46	32	14	22	26	21	50

5.5 The following data show monthly demand for a product over the past year. Use moving averages with $N = 3$, $N = 4$ and $N = 6$ to produce one-period ahead forecasts. Calculate the errors and say which gives the best results.

Month:	1	2	3	4	5	6	7	8	9	10	11	12
Demand:	32	28	24	30	36	42	46	48	50	52	64	76

5.6 Find deseasonalised forecasts for the following time series and hence identify the underlying trend.

t:	1	2	3	4	5	6	7	8	9	10
$D(t)$:	188	75	130	220	80	133	225	75	140	240

5.7 Use exponential smoothing with smoothing constant equal to 0.1, 0.2 and 0.3 to produce one-period ahead forecasts for the following time series. Use an initial value of $F(1) = 69$ and say which value of α is best.

t:	1	2	3	4	5	6	7	8
$D(t)$:	71	72	141	162	71	69	69	68

5.8 Quarterly demand for a product has been recorded over the past three years as follows.

Quarter:	1	2	3	4	5	6	7	8	9	10	11	12
Demand:	190	143	101	168	228	184	138	213	270	210	150	255

Use a constant value of $\alpha = 0.2$ to produce forecasts for the next two years.

REFERENCES FOR FURTHER READING

Armstrong, J.C. (1978) *Long Range Forecasting: From Crystal Ball to Computer*, John Wiley, New York.

Benton, W.K. (1972) *Forecasting for Managers*, Addison-Wesley, Reading, MA.

Bowerman, B.L. and O'Connell, R.T. (1979) *Forecasting and Time Series*, Duxbury Press, MA.

Box, G.E.P. and Jenkins, G.M. (1976) *Time Series Analysis: Forecasting and Control* (revised edn), Holden Day, San Francisco.

Croxton, F.E. *et al.* (1967) *Applied General Statistics* (3rd edn) Prentice Hall, Englewood Cliffs, NJ.

Gilchrist, W. (1976) *Statistical Forecasting*, John Wiley, Chichester.

Granger, C.W.J. (1980) *Forecasting in Business and Economics*, Academic Press, New York.

Gross, C.W. and Peterson, R.T. (1983) *Business Forecasting* (2nd edn), Houghton Mifflin, Boston, MA.

Hanke, J.E. and Reitsch, A.G. (1986) *Business Forecasting* (2nd edn), Allyn and Bacon, Boston, MA.

Linstone, H.A. and Turoff, M. (1975) *The Delphi Method: Techniques and Applications*, Addison-Wesley, Reading, MA.

Makridakis, S., Wheelwright, S.C. and McGee, V.E. (1983) *Forecasting: Methods and Applications* (2nd edn), John Wiley, New York.

Thomopoulos, N.T. (1980) *Applied Forecasting Methods*, Prentice Hall, Englewood Cliffs, NJ.

Wheelwright, S.C. and Makridakis, S. (1985) *Forecasting Models for Management* (4th edn), John Wiley, New York.

Willis, R.E. (1987) *A Guide to Forecasting for Planners and Managers*, Prentice Hall, Englewood Cliffs, NJ.

Younger, M.S. (1979) *A Handbook for Linear Regression*, Duxbury Press, MA.

6
INFORMATION FOR INDEPENDENT DEMAND INVENTORY SYSTEMS

SYNOPSIS

Independent demand inventory systems rely on several types of information. Chapter 5 showed how demand forecasts could provide some of this. Here we continue the theme by discussing other aspects of information.

Within an organisation there are two major flows: materials and information. This chapter starts by outlining the flow of information found in demand forecasting. This, together with other information flows, is coordinated by an organisation's management information system.

The discussion is then extended to other types of information needed for inventory control. The large amount of data manipulation, calculation and transaction recording makes it difficult for a manual system to work efficiently. Most organisations use computerised stock control, often with centralised databases. This chapter outlines the inputs required by these systems and the way information is stored. Then it describes some of the transactions in a typical system.

Stocks are a key element in an organisation's operations, and most functions have some contact with them. The links between stocks and other functions are illustrated by reference to accounting, logistics, warehousing and purchasing.

All inventory control involves a lot of effort. Sometimes, particularly with cheap items, this effort would not be worthwhile. A useful piece of information, then, is the amount of effort worth putting into the control of each item. This information can be supplied by an ABC analysis, which identifies items which need no control, as well as those which need special attention.

The last topic discussed in this chapter is the use of simulation. This dynamic representation of systems has proved particularly useful for stock control. It allows realistic experiments to be done on a model rather than the actual system.

OBJECTIVES

After reading this chapter and completing the exercises you should be able to:

- discuss the flow of information in demand forecasting
- appreciate the amount of information needed for inventory control and the limitations of manual systems
- list typical inputs to an inventory control system
- discuss the files in a database which are of primary interest to inventory control
- list some reasons for errors in stock records
- describe the transactions in a typical inventory control system
- discuss the links between inventory and other functions, particularly accounting, logistics, warehousing and purchasing
- do an ABC analysis of inventories
- appreciate the use of simulation in inventory systems

6.1 INFORMATION FROM FORECASTS

The last chapter described some methods of forecasting demand. These forecasts provide one of the main inputs to an independent demand inventory system. We should remember, however, that organisations forecast many things, not just demand for stock items. All plans and decisions in an organisation become effective at some point in the future. They should, therefore, be based on prevailing conditions which will, almost inevitably, be known from forecasts. It follows that forecasting is done throughout an organisation and should not be the work of an isolated group of specialists. It should also be clear that forecasting is never finished. Figure 6.1 shows how forecasts, objectives and past performance are passed to decision makers who use them for planning. Later, details of actual performance must be monitored, errors noted, future forecasts updated and fed back as an input for future plans, and so the cycle continues.

Decisions in an organisation are made by managers, but they can delegate some of these decisions to computers or automatic systems. Then the "decision making system" in Figure 6.1 consists of management and all related procedures and mechanisms.

In effect, Figure 6.1 shows a flow of information needed to support one part of decision making. All decisions rely on the availability of timely and relevant information. This is supplied by a management information system, whose purpose is to control information flows and to ensure that everyone in an organisation has the information they need to function properly. Such systems range from very informal ones (based on meetings in corridors and coffee lounges) to very formal ones (based on computer systems providing reports to a rigid process for making decisions).

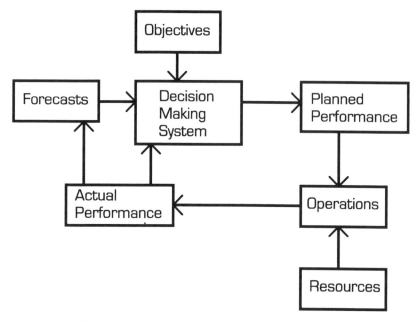

Figure 6.1 Forecasting as an input to decision making

Now we can consider two distinct flows in an organisation:

- a flow of materials
- a flow of information

Sometimes this distinction is not clear. Computer software, for example, is transferred on disks: moving these disks from one location to another represents a flow of materials, but the value of the disks is negligible compared with the value of the information they contain. Inventory control is an area where the flow of material and information can be unclear. Although it is a rather artificial distinction, it is usually suggested that:

- inventory control is the management function which makes decisions about stocks (and is, therefore, concerned with information flows)
- warehousing is the operational function which implements these decisions (and is, therefore, concerned with material flows)

The links between inventory control and warehousing are discussed again later in the chapter.

Forecasts provide an important input to an organisation's decision making but, in turn, they need information from other sources. This information includes the type of forecasting model to be used, values for parameters, historic data, subjective inputs, and so on. Then the flow of information needed to produce demand forecasts is summarised in Figure 6.2.

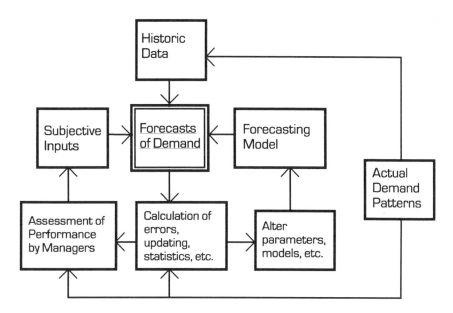

Figure 6.2 Information flow for producing forecasts of demand

Even small inventories involve a lot of data manipulation for forecasting, calculating reorder quantities, recording transactions, and so on. This cannot be done efficiently by hand, so most inventory control systems are computerised. Surveys suggest that over 90% of commercial stocks are now controlled by computer.

The fact that inventory control is largely computerised makes us look again at Figure 6.2. Most of the process illustrated can be automated. This means that forecasts of demand are normally produced automatically and presented to managers, who can make any adjustments they feel necessary. These adjustments are often based on information (sometimes called "meta information") which is not available to the computer or which cannot be encoded in its instructions.

Even a modest inventory contains several thousand items. This usually means there is not enough time for managers to adjust many of the computer's forecasts. The automated systems should, therefore, be programmed to give the results preferred by managers, even if these are not the theoretical "optimum". A reasonable computer system should, then, automatically produce the kind of forecasts which managers want and pass them directly to other parts of the system. It should also recognise those specific areas where management input might be needed and print these in an "exception report". This might include forecasts for items which:

- are particularly important or expensive
- have large or erratic forecasting errors
- have demand which suddenly changes
- have a major change of some other type, perhaps cost
- have no recent demand and which may be obsolete
- have recently been introduced to stock
- and so on

Having looked at information flows in forecasts, the following section discusses some other types of information needed for inventory control.

In Summary

Forecasts provide an important input to inventory control systems. These, together with other information, flow through an organisation under the control of a management information system. Most demand forecasting and inventory control is automated.

SELF-ASSESSMENT QUESTIONS

6.1 What is a management information system?

6.2 Most inventory control systems are computerised. Is this statement true or false?

6.3 When, particularly, is subjective management input needed in forecasting?

6.2   INFORMATION NEEDED FOR INVENTORY CONTROL

Effective planning and control of inventories depends on a variety of information in addition to forecasts. In this section we will outline some of the information flows, illustrating them with a very simple inventory system.

6.2.1   Manual Control Systems

It is only since the 1960s that computers have been widely available to business. Their introduction for inventory control has brought much greater efficiency, whether this is measured by operating costs, stock turnover, investment, customer service, loss through obsolescence, or any other measure. Before computers, however, stocks were controlled manually or with some mechanical assistance. For very small inventories this may still be the most efficient type of control.

The simplest inventory control system would need records of:

• current stocks by item
• reorder levels and quantities
• goods on order (with quantities, due dates, etc.)

Then, provided an order is placed of the specified size whenever stock levels fall to the reorder level, the system should run smoothly. One problem, however, would be the difficulty of measuring performance. Presumably, any major failings would be noted and adjustments made by, for example, increasing the reorder level if there were frequent shortages. Other measures, such as the operating cost, forecast error, total investment and reaction to changes would be difficult to find.

The simplicity of the basic control system is somewhat misleading. In reality it also uses a range of other information. The reorder levels and quantities, for example, should be based on forecast demand. A more complete picture of the information needed for even a simple system would include:

• details of current stocks on hand
• allowed variation in stock on hand, often expressed as acceptable maximum and minimum levels
• lists of goods in transit (coming from suppliers and other stores, or going to customers and other stores) with quantities, due dates, etc.
• forecast demand for each time period, including variation and uncertainty
• current reorder level and quantity
• desired service level, including measures of past performance to allow control
• age of inventory, to identify obsolescent and slow-moving stock
• and so on

Manual control systems keep this information on a series of record cards. An example of a stock record card is shown in Figure 6.3. For the system to work properly the stock record card must be updated with every transaction. The card illustrated does not give all the information listed above, so it must be used in conjunction with other records. The order number, for example, can be used to cross-reference entries in an order book which records details of every order in terms of quantity, date, expected delivery date, supplier, and so on. The order book can, in turn, be cross-referenced to supplier records which give details of addresses, costs, reliability, and so on. Similarly, a customer issue book is needed to give details of demands for the item, customers, addresses, timing of orders, when deliveries were made, delivery details, payment details, and so on.

At this point we can begin to appreciate the amount of information needed for even a simple inventory system. In practice this complexity means that most inventories of any size are computerised. Then routine decisions are automated and a manager would not intervene in decisions about, say, whether the reorder level for an unimportant item needs to be adjusted.

STOCK RECORD						
Description:			Maximum Stock:			
Location:			Minimum Stock:			
Item Number:			Reorder Level:			
Unit of issue:			Reorder Quantity:			
Comments:						
RECEIVED:			ISSUED:			BALANCE
Date	Order Number	Quantity	Date	Requisition Number	Quantity	

Figure 6.3 Typical stock record card

In Summary

Small inventories can be controlled manually by using stock cards to record transactions. With a reasonably sized inventory there is a considerable amount of information to be recorded. This means that most stock control is computerised.

6.2.2 Inputs to an Inventory System

We have begun to describe in more detail the information needed by an inventory control system, and at this stage we should look at where this information comes from. There are a number of sources which we will classify according to:

- general inputs (including operating plans, forecasts, current stocks, etc.)
- constraints (including service level, space, maximum investment, etc.)
- cost information

These inputs are processed to give the system outputs, which are a variety of reports and information. These are either given to management, or are passed directly to other systems (see Figure 6.4).

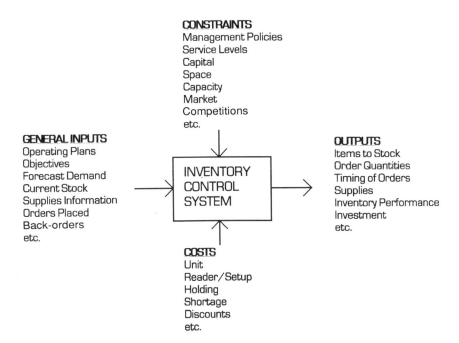

Figure 6.4 Main inputs and outputs for an inventory control system

Now we can look in more detail at the inputs. We can notice, for example, that some of them come from a purchasing function, others from warehousing, and so on. Similarly, the outputs are sent back to warehousing, sales and other functions. We could, therefore, illustrate some typical inputs and outputs as shown in Figure 6.5. The links between inventory control and other functions are discussed more fully later in the chapter.

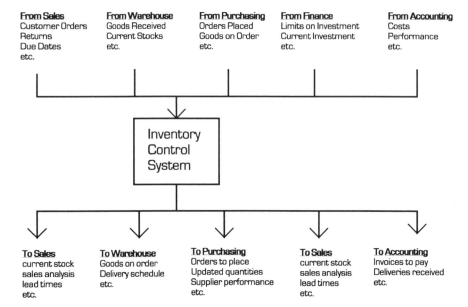

Figure 6.5 Some sources and destinations for information

Because stocks are so diverse in character, it is difficult to go beyond these general comments. The following list gives an idea of the inputs which may be used in a system, but this can only illustrate the possible range and is certainly not exhaustive.

- *Management policies*: service levels, planned investment in stocks, aggregate costs, aggregate sales forecasts, competitive environment, organisational objectives and strategy, current performance (return on inventory, service levels, etc.)
- *Procurement information*:
  - Suppliers (preferred list, addresses, items, location, reliability)
  - Purchasing (unit costs, quantity discounts, minimum quantities, credit terms, lead times, quality of goods, order restrictions, returns)
  - Environment (tariffs, duty, quotas, taxes, licences, exchange rates, shortages)
  - Production (processes, design, make/buy decisions, materials and components needed)
  - Delivery (alternative channels, speed, reliability, frequency, costs, insurance)
- *Warehousing information*: locations, space, conditions, material handling equipment, restrictions, security, stocks in each location
- *Logistics information*: alternative modes of transport, speed, frequency, reliability, quality, capacities, costs, returned materials

- *Accounting and finance information*: cost information, inventory levels and turnover, financing charges, investment in stock, projected inventory levels, opportunity costs
- *Marketing information*: cost of shortages, service levels demanded by customers, competitors' policies, back-orders, stock levels, location of stock, planned marketing campaigns, trends, new product demands
- *Sales information*: on-hand stocks at each branch, due dates and quantities of goods on order, allocation of stocks to orders, cost/sales prices, transportation schedules (between stores and customers), product characteristics, cancellations and returns, commissions earned by sales force
- *Customer information*: identification, location, forecast demands, service demanded, preferred delivery modes, sensitivity to prices, returns, complaints
- *Cost information*: all procurement, storage and supply costs, including internal distribution, customer delivery, storage, handling, insurance, obsolescence, capital, production set-up, shortages
- *Environmental factors*: cost of shortages, impending shortages, competition, government policies, employment rates, exchange rates

In Summary

Inputs of many types are needed to support an inventory control system. An overall classification of these has constraints, costs and general inputs.

SELF-ASSESSMENT QUESTIONS

6.4 What are the main problems with manual inventory control systems?
6.5 What is the minimum amount of information needed by an inventory control system?
6.6 The more information a system can supply, the better will be the decisions made by management. Is this statement:
  (a) true?
  (b) false?

6.2.3 Inventory Databases

The last section listed some of the inputs to an inventory control system. Much of this information is used by other parts of the organisation, so it is common to set up a centralised database which can be accessed by all interested parties. This has the main advantage of removing duplicated information. Then the effort needed to maintain data is reduced and errors cannot be caused by conflicting information held in different parts of the organisation.

Some of the database is of primary concern to inventory control (such as current stock levels, forecast demand, etc.). If we concentrate on this primary information, some is "soft", like customer goodwill and reputation. This is clearly difficult to store in a database and forms part of the subjective input. Generally, however, it is fairly straightforward to develop a database capable of receiving, storing, processing and reporting the relevant "hard" information. Typically, the information which is of primary concern to inventory control is held in four related files:

- *Product file*, stores product features, such description, identification code, price, weight, size, packaging, storage requirements, and so on
- *Sales file*, stores a complete sales history by item, shop or salesperson, and time period (including date sold, size of order, payment method, customer, delivery point, and so on)
- *Stock file*, contains current stock levels by item and location (including units reserved for known orders)
- *Goods on order file*, which contains details of all deliveries due from suppliers, including supplier, items, quantities, due dates, destinations, delivery method, and so on.

An important issue is the method of updating these files. Essentially there are three alternatives:

- *Manual updating*. As we have already seen, small inventories can be controlled manually, but this is impracticable for large stocks. When manual updating can be used it has the advantages of being cheap and convenient. Generally it is labour-intensive, prone to errors and slow.
- *Batch updating* has all records updated in a batch at regular intervals, typically overnight. This has a moderate cost, but the delays between transactions and updating runs mean there are always discrepancies between reported and actual stock levels.
- *On-line updating*, where transactions are recorded and files updated in real time. This is most expensive to operate, but it gives an accurate view of the position at any time.

The choice between these three depends largely on the computer resources available. As the cost of computer processing declines, more companies are moving to on-line systems which update files at the time of a transaction. Then, when a sale is made to a customer the sales file is updated and simultaneously the amount of stock recorded in the stock file is decreased. Similarly, when an order is delivered from a supplier the goods on order file and the stock file are updated simultaneously.

A common example of on-line updating is found in supermarkets. At check-out desks a cashier uses a laser reader to identify items bought by a customer. Item descriptions are then printed and given to the customer as a receipt. At the same time the shop's inventory system records the withdrawal of the items from stock and the accounting system is updated with the income generated.

It should, perhaps, be emphasised that even a real-time control system does not eliminate the need for periodic manual counts of stock (generally referred to as "stock-taking"). Such audits are needed to find differences between recorded and actual stock levels. These errors can be important when, say, a customer is promised delivery of an item which records show to be in stock, but actually there are no stocks and the order cannot be met.

There are several reasons why actual stock may differ from recorded stock:

- records may not have been updated for recent transactions
- hurried withdrawals from stock may not have been recorded
- stock is mislaid (particularly if the item is kept in several locations) and will turn up later
- deliveries or withdrawals are recorded twice by mistake
- cancelled orders or withdrawals are not recorded
- stock becomes obsolete and is discarded
- stock is stolen
- stock is damaged or deteriorates while in store

Obviously, it is desirable to have the match between actual and recorded stock as close as possible. There are several ways of encouraging this, and perhaps the most important is to restrict access to stores. Allowing only designated people into a store should ensure there is no unauthorised use of the stock, and all transactions are properly recorded. The implication is that stores should be kept locked and secure.

Another way of improving accuracy of records is to do regular manual stock checks. Many organisations feel that stock taking is an expensive and inconvenient formality, and only do one check at the end of their financial year. This means that discrepancies can go for long periods without being found. A more appropriate method is to use "cycle counting" where stock is checked at regular intervals. Typically, a small proportion of items is checked every week, with high-usage items checked every month and less widely used items every three months. This counting can be expensive, so checks may be triggered by specific conditions such as:

- a reported discrepancy in stock
- an item with zero or low stock
- an item with very high stock
- a back-order placed for an item which is recorded as being in stock
- a specified period without a movement
- some other specific condition.

The question of how much error is acceptable depends entirely on the situation. One common suggestion is that important items should have discrepancies of less than 0.2% in stock levels, while other items should be within 1%.

In Summary

Many organisations with computerised inventory control systems link these to a centralised database. Ideally, the files of primary interest to inventory control are updated in real time. This does not avoid the need for manual checks to detect errors.

6.2.4 Transactions in an Inventory Control System

In this section we will give some more details of the operations performed by an inventory control system. In a typical system, the main functions would include:

- maintaining accurate records of current stocks
- updating these records after each delivery and withdrawal
- extensive validation of all data
- automatic control of selected items involving:
  — forecasting demand and delivery lead time
  — calculation of reorder level to meet a specified service level
  — calculation of reorder quantity
- automatic reordering when stocks decline to reorder levels
- order follow-up for overdue orders
- clearing of invoices and printing cheques
- on-line display of any information on request
- exception reporting of conditions needing management action
- summarising data to give management reports
- updating all parameters used by the system

These operations can be combined in a large and sophisticated system which can perform millions of separate operations a day. We can, therefore, only give a general idea of a working system, which we will give the structure shown in Figure 6.6. Such a system would perform most functions routinely, with specific operations as follows.

- *Data validation.* As we have seen, inventory control systems rely on a considerable amount of information. Stringent checks are needed to ensure that this remains accurate and valid. These checks are done on all inputs, transactions and calculations.
- *Stock transaction recording.* Once the data has been validated, it can be passed on to the rest of the system. Stock transaction recording maintains records of the current situation by noting each stock transaction and updating appropriate files. It maintains files of stock levels, calculates additional requirements, issues regular management reports, highlights exceptional conditions, and so on.

  Stock transaction recording must maintain links with the accounting system. Issues from stock are chargeable to customer or internal accounts, and the details of charges are forwarded to the accounting system to raise invoices.

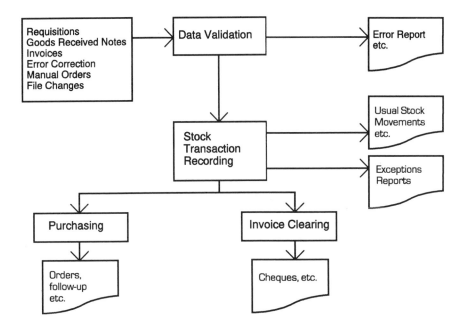

Figure 6.6 Some elements in a computerised inventory control system

Conversely, each receipt of goods into stock represents an outstanding financial commitment. These are used by invoice clearing to match invoices with goods received and arrange payment details.

- *Purchasing.* This part of the system forecasts demand and calculates the reorder quantity and reorder level. When the pattern of demand for an item becomes unpredictable a report is given to management who decide whether the item should be removed from automatic control, the reorder level changed, or no further action taken.

    As decisions about when to order an item and how much to order are automated, there is no reason why the computer system cannot also generate and transmit the orders. Stock transaction records identify items which need more stock, then the purchasing routines select suppliers, print orders and transmit them. The choice of supplier may be based on price, delivery performance, quality, availability of goods, and so on. A check is also kept on overdue orders, with appropriate letters and reminders sent to offending suppliers.

- *Invoice clearing.* Goods received notes are matched with invoices and deletions made where necessary. Any supplier price discrepancies are noted, the value of goods received calculated and invoices which can be paid immediately are identified. Then cheques are printed and information is prepared for the costing system.

In Summary

Some guidelines can be given for the operations of a typical inventory control system. There are so many variations in stock holdings that only general guidelines are possible.

SELF-ASSESSMENT QUESTIONS

6.7 What four files in a database are likely to be of primary interest to inventory control?

6.8 What is the main advantage of on-line updating of inventory files?

6.9 What are the main transactions in an inventory control system?

6.10 Where do the outputs from an inventory control system go?

6.3 LINKS BETWEEN INVENTORY AND OTHER FUNCTIONS

Figure 6.5 showed how some functions within an organisation provided inputs and received outputs from the inventory control system. We could go through other functions and say how they are affected by stock holdings, and would eventually come to the conclusion that almost every part of an organisation has some contact with stocks. In this section we will illustrate some of these contacts by reference to the four areas of accounting, logistics, warehousing and purchasing.

6.3.1 Accounting

Accounting has the obvious link with stocks that it provides the cost data used in control models. It also has connections through the payment of customer accounts and supplier invoices. In a wider sense, accounting uses the value of stocks held to assess the performance of an organisation as a whole. We can demonstrate this by looking at the standard organisational objective of maximising return on assets For this, return on assets is defined as:

$$\text{return on assets} = \frac{\text{net profit}}{\text{total assets}}$$

Stock holdings affects this equation twice:

- firstly, profit depends on the cost of goods sold and delivered from stock
- secondly, some of the assets of an organisation are its stocks

This is illustrated in Figure 6.7.

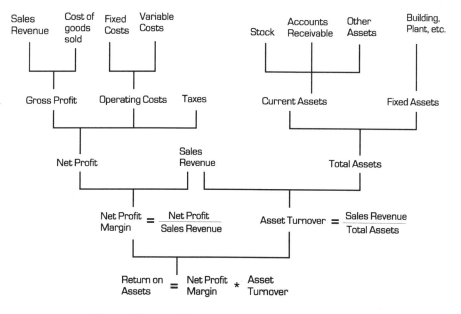

Figure 6.7 Role of stock in an organisation's profitability

The role of stocks in determining profit starts with the definition:

> gross profit = sales revenue − cost of goods sold

The cost of goods sold is the total price paid to acquire the units which were later sold. This kind of transaction appears in trading accounts, with a typical entry shown in Table 6.1.

The second role of stocks is seen in the evaluation of assets. Accounting considers stock as a current asset which is transformed into cash or debtors. Hence it forms a link in the cycle generating cash, as shown in Figure 6.8.

The accurate evaluation of assets is important in any organisation, as it directly affects the performance reported in accounts. Any errors may bring serious consequences. At times of high inflation, for example, the valuation of stocks is often too low and the company appears to have fewer assets than it really has. This may give an artificially high return on assets, but in extreme cases it may also allow the company to be bought at a fraction of its true value.

We should bear in mind the view that the value of stocks is really an accounting convention, as they have no real value until actually sold or used. The usual practice is to value stock at the lesser of unit cost or realisable value. However, this still does not completely solve the problem of stock evaluation. Suppose an

Table 6.1

Trading account for month ending 31st January

	£	£		£
Opening stock		2 500	Sales	22 100
Purchases	13 000		Less returns	600
Less returns	500			
			Net sales	21 500
Net purchases		12 500		
Total stock		15 000		
Less closing stock		3 000		
Cost of stock sold		12 000		
Gross profit		9 500		
		21 500		21 500

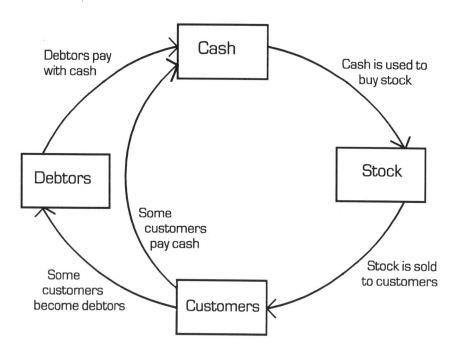

Figure 6.8 Stock as a link in the generation of cash

item is bought by an organisation. If all units of the item currently in stock were bought at the same price, it is easy to find the investment in stock as the number of units held multiplied by the unit cost. A major complication is that in reality both the number of units held and the unit cost will vary.

The number of units held varies according to the point in the stock cycle. The way around this is to count the number of units of all items held at a specific time, usually the end of the financial year. Then, if enough items are combined, the total investment found is a reasonable average. This assumes that items are more or less independent and that they do not all follow some strong seasonal variation.

Another problem with valuing stock arises from changing unit cost. Inflation usually makes prices rise, and there are other factors such as quantity discounts, different suppliers, variations in quality, different options or features, and so on. How then do we put a reasonable value on the stock? There are four main options for this:

- *Specific identification.* This identifies each unit in stock with the price actually paid for it. This method can only be used for expensive items which have low demand. A car retailer, for example, can identify the individual cars in stock and know how much was paid for each one. Then it can give an exact valuation of stock.

  This system has the advantage of being accurate and flexible. If the value of a unit changes, this can be reported precisely in the stock evaluation. The disadvantage is that it can only be used for small stocks of expensive items.
- *Average cost.* An alternative for valuing stock is to use the average unit cost over a typical period (perhaps a year):

$$\text{average cost} = \frac{\text{total cost of purchases}}{\text{number of units purchased}}$$

  This calculation need be done only once in an accounting period, when final accounts are being prepared. It has the advantage of being easy to use, and gives a reasonable value of the cost of stock. Unfortunately, if costs are rising with inflation, it could undervalue stock, as units bought some time ago will reduce the average below current values.
- *First-in-first-out (FIFO).* This works on the principle that the first units arriving in stock are the first to be sold. Then the value of stock is determined by the amount paid for the units actually remaining in stock. Sometimes, this does not give a fair representation. When, for example, there has been a sudden price rise the stock will be valued at the higher price, but there is no guarantee that customers will buy it. On occasions, then, FIFO systems can over-value stocks.
- *Last-in-first-out (LIFO).* This works on exactly the reverse basis of the FIFO system and assumes that the last units added to stock will be used first. This might be realistic for stocks of coal, for example, where the latest arrival

on a tip is used first. It has the disadvantage of possibly undervaluing stock, by using historic rather than current values. However, this may reduce tax liabilities for some organisations and is often an attractive alternative.

Surveys suggest that FIFO is the most widely used method of evaluation. Sometimes, LIFO evaluation is expressly prohibited, particularly when its use would artificially reduce tax liabilities. A general rule is that the method used should give the fairest matching of costs to revenues. One other consideration is that accounting conventions should be used consistently, so that short-term gains cannot be made by rapidly changing the basis of calculations.

Worked Example 6.1

A company's accounts note the transactions shown in Table 6.2 for an item. What is the value of stock at the end of June? What is the gross profit from sales?

Table 6.2

Date	Purchases		Sales	
	Number	Unit Cost	Number	Unit Price
Jan 1—Opening stock	80	£2		
Jan			20	£3
Feb			40	£4
Mar	60	£3		
Apr			50	£5
May	80	£4		
Jun			20	£6

Solution

At the end of June the stock level is:

$$\text{closing stock} = \text{opening stock} + \text{purchases} - \text{sales}$$
$$= 80 + (60 + 80) - (20 + 40 + 50 + 20)$$
$$= 90 \text{ units}$$

The value of these units depends on the assumption used. Specific identification could give the actual amount paid for the stock, but with reasonably large sales of inexpensive items this system would be too expensive to administer. Alternatives give:

- *Average cost*
  The average cost of purchases is:

$$\frac{\text{total cost}}{\text{units purchased}} = \frac{80 * 2 + 60 * 3 + 80 * 4}{80 + 60 + 80} = \pounds 3 \text{ a unit}$$

This values stock at $90 * 3 = \pounds 270$.

- *First-in-first-out*
This assumes the 90 units remaining in stock are the last 90 bought. This values stock at:

$$80 * 4 + 10 * 3 = \pounds 350 \text{ or } \pounds 3.89 \text{ a unit}$$

- *Last-in-first-out*
This assumes the 90 units remaining in stock were the first units bought. This values stock at:

$$80 * 2 + 10 * 3 = \pounds 190 \text{ or } \pounds 2.11 \text{ a unit}$$

The gross profit from sales is the total revenue minus the cost of units sold.

- revenue from sales $= 20 * 3 + 40 * 4 + 50 * 5 + 20 * 6 = \pounds 590$

The cost of units sold is the total cost of buying all units, minus the present value of stock.

- total cost of buying all units $= 80 * 2 + 60 * 3 + 80 * 4 = \pounds 660$

This give the gross profit from sales as:

$$\text{gross profit} = \frac{\text{revenue}}{\text{from sales}} - \left[\frac{\text{total cost of}}{\text{buying units}} - \frac{\text{value of}}{\text{remaining stock}} \right]$$

Average cost: $= 590 - [660 - 270] = \pounds 200$
FIFO: $= 590 - [660 - 350] = \pounds 280$
LIFO: $= 590 - [660 - 190] = \pounds 120$

Worked Example 6.2

An oil company buys crude oil on the open market, transports and refines it, and sells petrol at a chain of filling stations. The price of crude oil fluctuates quite widely. What policy could the company use for maximising its profits?

Solution

When the price of oil rises, the company could adopt a LIFO system and raise prices at the filling stations immediately. When the price of oil falls, the company could adopt a FIFO system and only lower prices at the filling station when all its old stock is exhausted. In practice, two factors limit this approach:

- there is some competition in petrol retailing which affects the price which can be charged
- accounting practices prohibit rapid changes from one set of conventions to another.

In Summary

Inventory control is closely linked to accounting. This link supplies cost data to inventory models, pays suppliers, invoices customers, and so on. Accounting also evaluates stocks, and shows their direct effect on organisational performance.

6.3.2   Logistics

Logistics is concerned with the physical movement and storage of goods on their journey from suppliers, through all operations in an organisation, and on to final customers. It is usual to describe logistics as consisting of a number of separate functions:

Logistics
- facility location
- transport
- inventory control
- warehousing
- associated communications

Thus, inventory control is commonly viewed as a function of logistics. There is, however, some disagreement about this and many organisations locate inventory control in other operational areas. Stocks of raw materials and work in progress are often managed by the manufacturing or operations areas, while stocks of finished goods are managed by marketing.

Even when it is accepted as a part of logistics its position may be unclear. Some people draw a distinction between materials management (which considers the movement of goods from suppliers into an organisation) and physical distribution (which considers the movement of goods out from the organisation to customers). The sum of these two is then called logistics (as shown in Figure 6.9). This artificial separation encourages the fragmentation of inventory control. It is only when an organisation develops an integrated view of its logistics that all (or most) inventory control can be coordinated by one function.

However it is organised or located in an organisation, there are clear links between inventory control and the other logistics functions. The links with warehousing are so strong that these are considered separately in the following

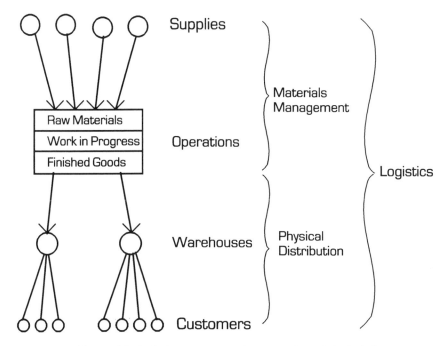

Figure 6.9 Typical movements and storage of goods in logistics

section. In this section we will outline some links with other logistics functions. Consider, for example, transport. Raw materials are brought into an organisation by delivery vehicles, and the type of vehicle used has direct effects on stock holdings. Some of these effects are outlined below.

Mode of transport
The "mode of transport" describes the overall type of delivery vehicle used. The alternatives are:

Modes of transport
- road
- rail
- air
- inland waterway
- ocean shipping
- pipeline

The choice of transport mode depends on a number of factors, such as location, infrastructure, weight and volume carried, value of goods, customer service offered, and so on. Whichever mode is chosen, there are direct effects on the order quantity and reorder costs. There are obvious differences in delivery costs with air travel being very expensive (but fast) compared with the alternatives. There are, however, other considerations. Suppose, for example, raw materials are delivered in containers. Transport costs will usually be minimised if an order is placed for a full container load. Conversely, transport (and hence reorder) costs rise if part container loads are ordered. Depending on the type of delivery vehicle, there may be advantages in ordering quantities which correspond to a pallet load, a truck full, a barge load, or some other discrete amount.

At the other end of operations, stocks of finished goods are passed to customers. By similar reasoning it is preferable to keep these stocks until a suitable quantity is ready for shipping in a single delivery. Unfortunately, this is one area of disagreement between suppliers (who usually want to make large, infrequent deliveries) and customers (who usually want small, frequent deliveries).

Pipeline stock
The mode of transport also affects the amount of stock which is in transit from suppliers and to customers. Transporting materials from overseas locations by air might take two days, while equivalent journeys by ship might take four weeks. This means that air freight will give considerably less pipeline stocks (which are the goods in transit between locations). Sometimes this cost reduction will justify a more expensive, but faster transport mode.

The cost of pipeline stock is not necessarily borne directly by the customer, but it may be included in an overall delivered price. This depends on the conditions of purchase. Goods are supplied FOB (free on board) a specific location where ownership changes. Historically this change often occurred when goods were delivered safely onto a ship for transport (hence "on board"). Sometimes deliveries were specified as FAS (free along side) which meant the supplier would take goods to a dock, but would not be responsible for loading them onto the ship. Over time, the terms have become more generally used to describe any point where ownership changes. If goods are bought "FOB factory gate" it means that purchasers assume responsibility and costs for the journey to their premises. Conversely "FOB destination" means the supplier has ownership (and costs) up to the point of delivery to customers.

Order quantities
Whatever mode of transport is chosen, the cost of transport per unit delivered will usually decline with increasing order quantity. In other words there is an incentive to order larger quantities to take advantage of lower transport costs. In principle these costs are contained in the reorder cost, but it is often difficult to include all possible cost combinations.

Location of warehouses
Logistics is responsible for finding the best location of warehouses. This raises the question of how many warehouses are operated, and hence the location and

amount of stock being held. Often, sites for warehouses are chosen so they are near to customers and allow good service with relatively low delivery costs. Unfortunately, this means that stocks are duplicated at a number of locations. Consider, for example, supermarkets. These are located near to customers, but the total amount of stock is high as each store carries a stock of every item.

An empirical observation suggests the aggregate amount of stock held in a number of locations can be found from:

$$AS(N_1) = AS(N_2) * \sqrt{\frac{N_2}{N_1}}$$

where N_2 = number of planned future facilities
        N_1 = number of existing facilities
    $AS(N_i)$ = aggregate stock with N_i facilities

In Summary

Inventory control is sometimes considered a part of logistics. There are certainly clear links between stock holdings and other logistics functions.

Worked Example 6.3

(a) A distribution system currently has 12 depots with aggregate stock valued at £12 million. If it plans to expand to 16 depots what is the likely value of its future aggregate stock?
(b) These new depots are likely to reduce the amount of stock in transit by 5% of total holdings. If the carrying cost is 20% of value a year, what will be the overall cost of this change?

Solution

(a) Listing the variables given:

$N_1 = 12$
$N_2 = 16$
$AS(N_1) = £12$ million

Then substitution gives:

$$AS(N_1) = AS(N_2) * \sqrt{\frac{N_2}{N_1}}$$

$$= 12\,000\,000 * \sqrt{(16/12)}$$

$$= £13.9 \text{ million}$$

(b) The additional depots will raise stock holding costs by:

$$(13\,900\,000 - 12\,000\,000) * 0.2 = \pounds380\,000$$

Some of this is recovered by reducing the stock in transit. By introducing more depots the company will reduce stocks by 5% of £13.9 million, giving annual savings of:

$$0.2 * 0.05 * 13\,900\,000 = \pounds139\,000$$

There is a net cost of £241 000 which must be recovered from other savings or higher sales due to improved customer service.

6.3.3 Warehousing

Warehousing and inventory control are so closely linked that they are sometimes considered to be the same function. In essence, inventory control is the management function associated with decisions about stock, while warehousing is the operational function which physically looks after the stock. Thus, inventory control might decide that 100 units of an item should be stocked, while warehousing physically receives the goods from suppliers, looks after them while they are being stored, and then ships them to customers.

We will outline the main functions of warehousing and show how they are related to inventory control. These functions are:

Warehouse functions
- setting warehouse objectives
- warehouse design and layout
- receiving goods
- storing goods
- shipping of materials
- monitoring and control
- managing warehouse personnel
- other functions

- *Setting warehouse objectives.* This sets the overall aims of the warehouse and the performance standards it tries to achieve. Measures of performance are specified so that efficiency can be maintained in the receipt of items from suppliers, their storage and release to customers. These decisions must be made after liaison with customers and other interested people.
- *Warehouse design and layout.* There are many factors to consider in the way storage is arranged in a warehouse, and the way items are assigned to storage areas. Some decisions are obvious, such as the location of frequently used

items near to delivery areas, and storage of heavy items at ground level. Other decisions are more complex, such as the choice between an automated warehouse and a manually controlled one, or the choice between automatic cranes and fork-lift trucks.

- *Receiving goods.* The receipt of goods into a warehouse consists of several distinct jobs. A typical delivery might entail identification of the material delivered, directing the delivery to the correct unloading area, unloading goods, comparing delivered items with the order list, checking for superficial damage, opening boxes to check for internal damage, photographing any visible damage, checking material delivered against packing slips, making out a material received report (including a note of shortages, overages, damage or unsatisfactory units), noting the proposed location and marking the materials with their codes, order numbers, etc. After this the paperwork for orders received is passed to accounting, while the goods are passed on for storage.

- *Storing goods.* This involves everything necessary to make sure the item remains in good condition while it is held in stock. This might include maintaining a proper climate (such as temperature or humidity control), rotating equipment (some items such as engines have to be rotated to avoid uneven wear on bearings), keeping a tidy warehouse and minimising breakages.

- *Shipping of materials.* This is essentially the reverse of receiving goods from suppliers, and involves sending goods out to customers. It might start when an inventory clerk receives a request for materials. He or she checks that the request is in order with the correct authorisation, and then verifies that the materials are available. Typically a "materials transfer report" is written and passed to warehousemen who locate the materials and arrange its movement.

- *Monitoring and control.* These are the procedures which ensure a warehouse continues to operate efficiently (or is preferably improving its performance). They involve frequent comparisons of actual performance with stated objectives, with discrepancies noted and remedial action taken. This needs continuous liaison with customers and other interested people.

- *Managing warehouse personnel.* Traditionally the staff of a warehouse consist of a hierarchy which can be described as manager, warehouseman, inventory clerk and handler. The manager is in overall control. Under the manager are warehousemen who are in charge of day-to-day operations in the warehouse. They have inventory clerks who check stock, record transactions, and so on. The handlers actually fetch goods and deliver them as necessary. There are obviously many variations on this basic hierarchy.

- *Other functions.* Depending on the circumstances, warehousing might also include quality inspection and assurance, organising spare parts, returning containers where deposits have been charged, identification and collection of scrap, disposal of surplus stock, issuing permits for the removal of stock, and so on.

In Summary

Warehousing is the function which physically receives stock, stores it and ships it to customers. Subsidiary functions include setting warehouse objectives, layout and design, and receiving, storing and shipping goods.

6.3.4 Purchasing

It is the function of purchasing to ensure that items arrive in stock when requested. Purchasing is closely connected to logistics, and some organisations combine the two. Other organisations put purchasing in different areas, commonly in finance. Sometimes purchasing is part of a wider procurement function which includes transport, quality checks on delivered material, looking for alternative products, recognising changes in the market place, checking financial arrangements, and so on.

The basic functions of purchasing are to:

- determine the quantity and quality of items needed by the organisation
- identify possible suppliers
- maintain information about suppliers and select the best for each item (or order)
- negotiate contracts with suppliers to obtain the best price and conditions for items
- maintain relations with suppliers and liaise between the organisation and suppliers
- be knowledgeable about existing items and any conditions which may change (new items, services, etc.)
- expedite deliveries from suppliers when necessary

Each of these functions can be quite complex. Selecting a supplier, for example, is often quoted as the most important function of the purchasing department. This itself can be considered in four stages of:

- surveying all possible suppliers of an item
- examining each of these possible suppliers in detail
- negotiating and selecting the best supplier, then issuing an order
- maintaining relations while items are being supplied

Purchasing usually works in a cycle as shown in Figure 6.10. This cycle consists of the following stages.

- *Requisition request*. The cycle starts when a requisition request is received by purchasing. This request might be triggered by the inventory control system or warehouse noting that stock of an item has fallen to its reorder level. The requisition contains all relevant details, such as the item required, the quantity, quality, delivery date needed, who is requisitioning, and so on.

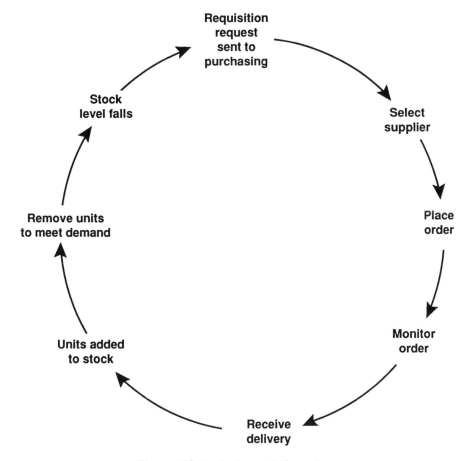

Figure 6.10 Purchasing cycle for an item

- *Selection of supplier.* The purchasing department must then identify the best supplier. If no suppliers are currently used for the item, new ones must be located and evaluated. If more than one supplier is available either the best is selected, or (particularly for larger, one-off purchases of plant or equipment) potential suppliers are asked to tender for the work.
- *Place order.* Large frequent orders may use blanket orders which are renegotiated, say, annually. These are routine orders where deliveries are requested on a regular basis. Smaller orders may be placed individually.
- *Monitoring orders.* Routine follow-up on orders, particularly large orders or those with long delivery periods, allows purchasing to foresee delays and either take steps to overcome these, or make plans to minimise their effects. Likewise, any changes in requirements must be passed on to suppliers.
- *Receiving orders.* Incoming orders are checked for quality and quantity. Then

purchasing, accounting and the operating department that placed the order are notified. If the goods are not in good condition they have to be returned to the supplier.

An interesting point concerns the amount of work done in each of these areas in a typical purchasing department. Intuitively we might suggest that the most important functions are getting details of requirements and discussing these with suppliers. In practice up to 80% of a purchasing department's time is spent in chasing late deliveries. The implication is that an organisation which can ensure reliable suppliers frees a lot of effort for more productive activities.

In Summary

Purchasing is the function which organises the supply of items to be stocked. This requires a series of activities which can often be described by the purchasing cycle.

SELF-ASSESSMENT QUESTIONS

6.11 What alternatives can be used to value current stock?
6.12 Does a LIFO system generally undervalue stock or overvalue it?
6.13 What is the connection between inventory control and logistics?
6.14 What functions are usually considered part of logistics?
6.15 What might be a reasonable objective for designing a warehouse layout?
6.16 What is the difference between warehousing and inventory control?
6.17 What is the overall purpose of purchasing?
6.18 What are the stages in the purchasing cycle?

6.4   ABC ANALYSIS OF INVENTORIES

We have seen that efficient inventory control needs a considerable effort. Most control systems are computerised, but they still need manual effort to input data, check values, update supplier details, confirm orders, make subjective judgements, monitor operations, and so on. For some items, especially cheap ones, this effort is not worthwhile. Very few organisations, for example, include routine stationery in their computerised stock system. At the other end of the scale are very expensive items which require special care above the routine calculations. A useful piece of information would be the amount of effort worth putting into the control of any item. An ABC analysis is one way of categorising items to get this information.

ABC analysis is sometimes called Pareto analysis or the "rule of 80/20". This originated with the observation by Pareto, who was a nineteenth-century Italian sociologist, that 20% of the population owned 80% of the wealth. This observation is widely applicable, and in inventory control terms it means that 80% of inventory items need 20% of the attention, while the remaining 20% of items need 80% of the attention. In particular, ABC analyses define:

- **A** items as expensive and needing special care
- **B** items as ordinary ones needing standard care
- **C** items as cheap and needing little care

Typically an organisation might use an automated system to deal with all **B** items. **A** items are more important, and although the computer system might make some suggestions, final decisions are made by managers after a thorough review of circumstances. **C** items may be included in the automatic system, but most are very cheap and can be left out, with control left to ad hoc procedures.

The procedure for an ABC analysis starts by taking each item and multiplying the number of units used in a year by the unit cost. This gives the total annual use of items in terms of value. Usually, a few expensive items account for a lot of use, while many cheap ones account for little use. If we list the items in order of decreasing annual use by value, **A** items are at the top of the list and **C** items are at the bottom. See Table 6.3 for what we might typically find. Plotting the cumulative percentage of annual use against the cumulative percentage of items gives a graph of the type shown in Figure 6.11.

Worked Example 6.4

A small store consists of ten categories of item with the following costs and annual demands:

Item:	X1	Y7	W4	X2	X3	Y9	W5	Z3	Z4	X4
Unit Cost (£):	3	2	3	8	2	10	1	5	20	4
Weekly demand (100s):	2	25	1	30	10	10	5	2	1	3

Do an ABC analysis of these items. How might stocks of each category be controlled?

Solution

Although the demand figures are in hundreds of units per week, we only want comparisons and need not multiply each by 5200 to give annual figures. Then the use of X1 in terms of value is $3 * 2 = 6$. Repeating this calculation for the other items and sorting them into order of decreasing annual use by value gives Table 6.4. The boundaries between categories are sometimes unclear, and fairly arbitrary decisions are needed. In this case X2 is clearly an **A** item. The line between **B** and **C** items is probably drawn so that Y9 and Y7 are **B** and all other items are **C**.

Table 6.3

Category	Percentage of items	Cumulative percentage of of items	Percentage use by value	Cumulative percentage of use by value
A	10	10	70	70
B	20	30	20	90
C	70	100	10	100

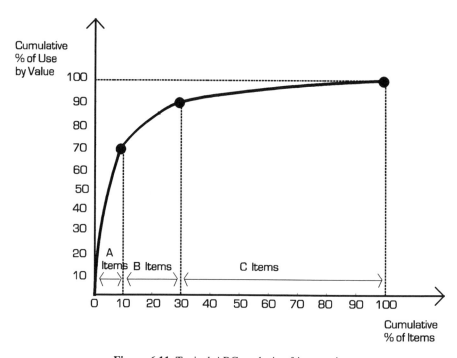

Figure 6.11 Typical ABC analysis of inventories

Table 6.4

Item	X2	Y9	Y7	X3	Z4	X4	Z3	X1	W5	W4
Cumulative percentage of items	10	20	30	40	50	60	70	80	90	100
Annual use	240	100	50	20	20	12	10	6	5	3
Cumulative use	240	340	390	410	430	442	452	458	463	466
Cumulative percentage annual use	52	73	84	88	92	95	97	98	99	100
Category	←A→		← - B - →		← - - - - - - - C - - - - - →					

Item X2 accounts for 52% of annual use, and stocks of this should be carefully controlled with management input to decisions. **B** items account for 36% of use, and these can be controlled automatically. **C** items account for only 12% of annual use and might be left to ad hoc procedures.

Having classified inventory items in this way, one suggestion would be to concentrate solely on **A** items (or possibly **A** and **B** items) and no longer stock **C** items. In practice this is generally not feasible. An organisation may need a stock of all items, including those which are not frequently used, to ensure its continued operation. An obvious example of this is a spare part which may be cheap and infrequently used, so it is classified as **C**. At the same time the part may be needed to repair a production machine, so a shortage could be very expensive and the part should be given more attention than its usage suggests.

Similarly, **C** items may be held in stock because they:

- are more important than their classification suggests
- allow continued sales of an old item
- are associated with sales of some **A** items
- give high profits
- are new items
- are expected by customers
- and so on

If the three categories are not descriptive enough additional ones can be added. A fourth category is sometimes used, where **D** items are used so infrequently they are "dead" and are being considered for withdrawal.

In Summary

ABC analyses allow items to be categorised according to importance so that available effort can be shared out appropriately. The most important, **A**, items should be given most careful control.

SELF-ASSESSMENT QUESTIONS

6.19 What is the purpose of doing an ABC analysis of inventories?

6.20 Which items can best be dealt with by routine, automated control procedures?

6.5 SIMULATION OF INVENTORY SYSTEMS

Because of its links with other functions, any changes to an inventory control system can affect the performance of other areas, and hence the performance of the organisation as a whole. Before changes are made, therefore, management need a thorough assessment of their effects. Experiments could be made on the actual system, but these would be disruptive or expensive. Suppose, for example, a proposal is made to move from a fixed order quantity system to a periodic review system. The organisation would need to assess the effect of this change on all operations, and it might try to introduce the system for some items, or for a trial period. Both of these alternatives would be disruptive and difficult to organise, and would have high costs.

An alternative for assessing the effects of changes would use quantitative models. Unfortunately, the complex and dynamic nature of stocks can lead to very complex analytical models which need a number of simplifying assumptions. Even then, analytical models may not be able to cope with all the complications of the real system. A better approach is to use simulation.

Simulation is based on a dynamic representation of a situation; it duplicates the continuous operation of a system over some time. The models of inventory systems described in Chapters 2 to 4 look at the system at a specific point of time. They describe a situation at a specific time, collect data relevant to that time and draw conclusions. Simulation on the other hand follows the workings of the system over some extended time period. A simple analogy has an ordinary model providing a snapshot of the system, while simulation makes a movie.

The first step in building a simulation model is to describe in detail the way the system functions. The best way of doing this is through a flow diagram which represents the sequence of activities. Although the inventory system and interactions with other functions will be unique to a particular system, we can give some guidelines for the development of a simulation model.

As a starting point we could look again at the purchasing cycle in Figure 6.10. Then we can add a few details and represent the result as the flow diagram in Figure 6.12. This model shows an inventory system which is triggered by demand for an item. This demand is noted and used to update statistics on forecasts, reorder quantity, reorder level, and so on. The demand is then met from stock, and if the item is below its reorder level an order is placed. The cycle ends with the system waiting for the next customer to arrive. This schematic is the first step in describing a larger model. It does not, for example, mention shortages, lead times, back-orders, or any interactions with other functions.

The original diagram can be expanded in many ways to suit individual circumstances. We can illustrate the start of one expansion by noting that the process is cyclical, so we can look at what happens during each discrete time period (perhaps every day). Then we might get the expanded model shown in Figure 6.13. The total customer demand in a period is noted, but is not yet satisfied. Firstly, the demand history is updated, forecasts compared with actual demand, errors noted and any necessary adjustment made to the forecasting methods or parameters. A check on orders received in the period is made and these are added to stock levels. Then checks are made for back-orders. These are satisfied if possible, but if there are still shortages expediting and emergency orders are considered. An emergency

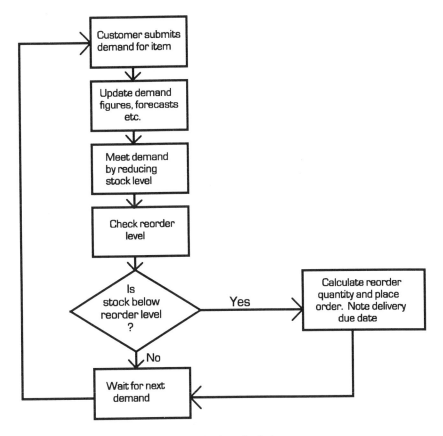

Figure 6.12 Schematic for a basic inventory system

order might be placed with higher costs for, say, air-freighting, and administration charges, but shorter lead time. When back-orders have been satisfied the model moves on to new demand. If there is enough stock, these demands are satisfied, but otherwise expediting and emergency orders are considered. After this, statistics for performance are updated, including recalculation of order quantity, reorder level and service level. Then a check is made to see if the final stock level is below the reorder level. If it is, an order is placed and the model moves on to the next period.

This is clearly one view of part of an inventory system and is at an early stage of development. The next stage might add quality checks on goods received with a proportion of unsatisfactory units returned to the supplier. In effect, the basic model could be expanded in many ways until it accurately describes the real system. By this stage, the amount of computation needed to run the simulation will be so great that it must be done on a computer. The next stage, then, is to transform the flow chart into a computer program. When this program is run it

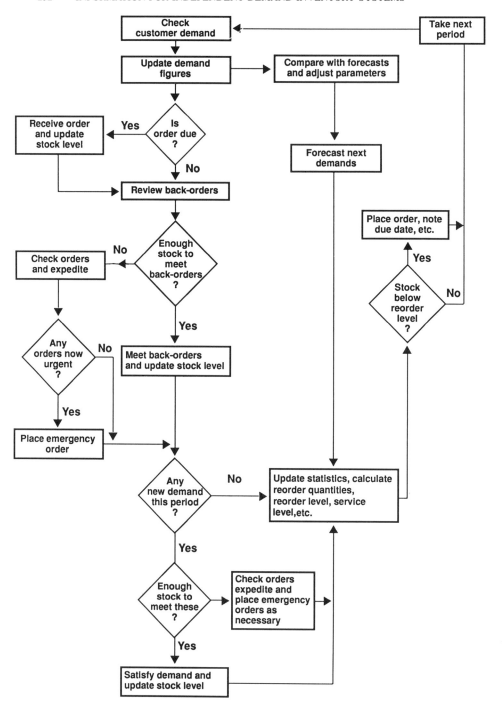

Figure 6.13 Adding some details to the simulation model

duplicates the actual operation of the system. It has the advantages, however, of allowing experimentation without affecting the actual system, getting results very quickly (several years of actual operation can be simulated in a few seconds), and presenting a range of results for analysis.

One simulation run will imitate the working of the system over the chosen time period. Repeating this run a large number of times will give varying results to show how the system would behave in different circumstances.

Many programs, both specialised and general, are available for simulating inventory systems. The output from one very simple simulation run is shown in Figure 6.14.

In the last section we saw how the effort needed to control stocks of some items was not really worthwhile. C items could often be omitted from the formal control procedures and left to ad hoc procedures. Similarly, we could build increasingly complex quantitative models of inventory systems, but there will come a point where the effort is not worthwhile and the benefits gained from increasing sophistication are less than the additional cost. In these circumstances simulation can provide a very useful tool for comparing alternative approaches. The results from optimal policies found by rigorous analyses can, for example, be compared with the results found from simpler, less demanding analyses. If there is little difference in the results, the simpler analyses might prove more useful. Then the general approach to independent demand inventory systems shown in Table 6.5 can be suggested.

In Summary

Simulation allows a dynamic representation of real systems. This has proved particularly useful for inventory systems where relationships can be too complex for analytical models.

SELF-ASSESSMENT QUESTIONS

6.21 What is meant by "simulation"?
6.22 Why is simulation useful for inventory systems?

SUMMARY OF CHAPTER

This chapter has described some of the information needed for an inventory control system. In particular it has:

- outlined the information flows in demand forecasting
- discussed the amount and type of information needed by an inventory control system

Table 6.5

Demand and lead time	Suggested approach
Known with certainty	Variations on deterministic quantitative models
With some uncertainty	Variations on probabilistic models with safety stocks or shortage costs
Complex variations and interactions	Simulate a range of approaches and select the best

```
            ****************************
                  SIMULATION SYSTEM
            ****************************


            INVENTORY CONTROL SIMULATION

               PROBLEM:   FIGURE 6.14
```

```
                    DATA ENTERED:

ORDER QUANTITY:                 AUTOMATIC
REORDER LEVEL:                  AUTOMATIC
FORECASTING METHOD:             EXPONENTIAL SMOOTHING
SYSTEM PARAMETERS:              USER DEFINED
UNIT COST:                      £20
REORDERING COST:                £75
HOLDING COST:                   £1
SHORTAGE COST:                  £50
BACK ORDERS:                    NONE
DEMAND HISTORY:                 USER DEFINED
DEMAND DISTRIBUTION:            UNIFORM
LOWEST DEMAND VALUE:            100
HIGHEST DEMAND VALUE:           500
LEAD TIME:                      VARIABLE
PERIOD:                         WEEK
NUMBER OF PERIODS:              10
RANDOM NUMBER SEQUENCE:         RANDOM
```

```
                  INITIAL VALUES:

OPENING STOCK:                  1,500
MEAN DEMAND:                    300
REORDER QUANTITY:               210
MEAN LEAD TIME:                 4 WEEKS
LEAD TIME DEMAND:               1,200
SAFETY STOCK:                   83
REORDER LEVEL:                  1,283
```

Figure 6.14 Output from an inventory control simulation

```
                    SIMULATION RESULTS:

Week    Opening Stock    Demand    Closing Stock    Shortage

 1          1,500          331          1,169
 2          1,169          372            797
        Order 1 placed for 210 units
 3            797          229            568
        Order 2 placed for 210 units
 4            568          205            363
        Order 3 placed for 210 units
 5            363          397              0           34
        Order 4 placed for 250 units
 6              0          227              0          227
        Order 5 placed for 260 units
 7              0          215              0          215
        Order 1 received at end of period for 210 units
 8            210          326              0          116
        Order 2 received at end of period for 210 units
        Order 6 placed for 280 units
 9            210          329              0          119
        Order 3 received at end of period for 210 units
        Order 7 placed for 290 units
10            210          336              0          126
        Order 4 received at end of period for 250 units
        Order 8 placed for 300 units
```

```
                    ANALYSIS OF RESULTS:

NUMBER OF PERIODS:    10 WEEKS
AVERAGE DEMAND:      296.7 UNITS
AVERAGE LEAD TIME:     5.0 WEEKS
AVERAGE STOCK:       396.2 UNITS    HOLDING COST:         76.19
NUMBER OF ORDERS:      8            REORDERING COST:     600.00
SHORTAGES:           837 UNITS      SHORTAGE COST:    41,850.00
                                                     _____
                                    VARIABLE COST:    42,526.19

DELIVERIES:          880 UNITS      FIXED COST:       17,600.00
                                                     _____
                                    TOTAL COST:       60,126.19


                    END OF SIMULATION
```

Figure 6.14 (continued)

- described the type of inputs needed to supply this information
- described the transactions in a typical inventory control system
- discussed the links between inventory control and other functions by reference to accounting, logistics, warehousing and purchasing
- described ABC analyses of inventories
- outlined the use of simulation in inventory systems

ADDITIONAL PROBLEMS

6.1 A store paid £10 a unit for items which it sold for £20. The last delivery of 100 units arrived when there were 100 units left in stock. The unit cost for this delivery had risen to £15, so the store immediately raised its price to £25. At the end of the financial year 70 units had been sold. Discuss the store's financial performance.

6.2 Company accounts note the transactions given in Table 6.6 for an item.

Table 6.6

Date	Purchases		Sales	
	Number	Unit cost	Number	Unit price
Jan 1—Opening stock	120	£21		
Jan			60	£32
Feb			50	£37
Mar	180	£26	20	£37
Apr			110	£39
May	90	£28		
Jun			80	£39
Jul	20	£28		

What is the value of stock held at the end of July? What is the gross profit from sales?

6.3 A furniture store wants to improve the control of its stocks, and is looking at the possibility of using a Pareto analysis. Records from eight types of furniture show the current sales and costs as follows:

Furniture:	3427	1822	5362	2777	1413	9719	5520	188
Sales:	25	150	30	80	10	40	1000	100
Cost (£):	1400	14	680	20	1020	150	20	30

Do a Pareto analysis on these items.

6.4 A store has 20 categories of items with the following costs and annual demands:

Item:	I0	I1	I2	I3	I4	I5	I6	I7	I8	I9
Unit cost (£):	40	20	40	100	20	100	10	40	200	10
Weekly demand:	5	100	40	30	30	10	20	10	5	100

Item	I10	I11	I12	I13	I14	I15	I16	I17	I18	I19
Unit cost (£)	50	30	65	150	40	180	25	80	100	5
Weekly demand:	10	120	50	30	40	15	25	20	5	120

Do an ABC analysis of these items. If resources are limited, which items should receive most attention?

REFERENCES FOR FURTHER READING

Banks, J. and Carson, J.S. (1984) *Discrete-Event Simulation*, Prentice Hall, Englewood Cliffs, NJ.

Bowersox, D.J., Closs, D.J. and Helferich, O.K. (1986) *Logistical Management*, Macmillan, New York.

Coyle, J.J., Bardi, E.J. and Langley, C.J. (1988) *The Management of Business Logistics* (4th edn), West Publishing, St Paul, MN.

Dauderis, H. (1990) *Financial Accounting*, Holt, Rinehart and Winston, Toronto.

Gordon, G. (1978) *System Simulation*, Prentice Hall, Englewood Cliffs, NJ.

Johnson, J.C. and Wood, D.F. (1990) *Contemporary Logistics* (4th edn), Macmillan, New York.

Law, A.M. and Kelton, W.D. (1982) *Simulation Modelling and Analysis*, McGraw-Hill, New York.

Payne, J.A. (1982) *Introduction to Simulation: Programming Techniques and Methods of Analysis*, McGraw-Hill, New York.

Stock, J.R. and Lambert, D.M. (1987) *Strategic Logistics Management* (2nd edn), Irwin, Homewood, IL.

Strassmann, P.A. (1985) *Information Payoff*, Free Press, New York.

Turban, E. (1988) *Decision Support and Expert Systems: Managerial Perspectives*, Macmillan, New York.

Watson, H.J. (1981) *Computer Simulation in Business*, John Wiley, New York.

SECTION III
DEPENDENT DEMAND
INVENTORY SYSTEMS

Section II discussed independent demand inventory systems. These have the characteristic that demands are assumed to be independent and are found from forecasts. Then quantitative models of the system can be used to set reorder quantities, reorder levels, and so on. Such systems work well for many situations but they do have disadvantages, particularly when dealing with batch production. This section, consisting of Chapters 7 to 9, deals with the alternative approach of dependent demand systems.

Dependent demand inventory systems have the characteristic that demand is found directly from production plans. Suppose, for example, that a production plan calls for 100 units of a product to be made in a particular week. We know that the materials needed to make these units must be in stock at the beginning of the week. Then we are linking the demand for materials directly to the production plan. Essentially, stocks are controlled by actual demand "pull" rather than historic demand "push".

Chapter 7 introduces the first approach of this type, which is material requirements planning (MRP). This uses the bill of materials together with a schedule of planned production to determine demand for materials. Once this demand is known, orders can be placed to ensure materials are delivered in time for their use. MRP is a rather formal process which relies on detailed plans being available some time before they are implemented. It also involves considerable amounts of data manipulation which can only realistically be tackled by a computer.

In recent years, considerable interest has been shown in an alternative approach to dependent demand systems, which is known as "just-in-time". The aim of just-in-time (JIT) systems is to minimise stocks of materials by having them arrive just as they are needed. Rather than use the formal approaches of materials requirement planning, JIT tries to simplify procedures and avoid reliance on computers. The principles of just-in-time inventories are discussed in Chapter 8.

Dependent demand inventory systems can only be used if a fairly rigorous planning process has been used. Chapter 9 describes some of the planning needed to support these systems.

7
MATERIAL REQUIREMENTS PLANNING

SYNOPSIS

Independent demand inventory systems are very widely used. There are, however, circumstances in which they do not perform well. They are not, for example, very good at controlling stocks of material needed to support batch production. The alternative dependent demand systems are better in these circumstances, and the most widely used method is material requirements planning.

Material requirements planning (MRP) is based on the idea that production plans for finished goods can be used to determine demand for materials needed to make these goods. The method was originally developed for manufacturing industry, but it is now used more widely. For convenience, we will stick to the original vocabulary which talks of stocks of material (parts and components) needed to support production.

MRP starts by taking the production plan described in a "master schedule". It then uses the "bill of materials" to transform this into detailed requirements for materials. This gives the gross requirements for components and parts needed to support the production plan. The timing and size of orders to satisfy these gross requirements can be found by referring to current stocks, outstanding orders, lead times, and other information.

When it can be used, MRP can bring a number of advantages. The close matching of material supply to known demand can, for example, significantly reduce stocks of raw materials. Conversely, the main disadvantages are the prerequisites before MRP can be used and the amount of data manipulation.

In its basic form, MRP may suggest small, frequent orders which are expensive to administer. Costs are reduced by combining several of these small orders into a single larger one. This kind of problem, with intermittent demand, is one of the most difficult inventory problems to tackle. Here a batching rule is described to give improved ordering policies.

The MRP approach can be extended in several ways. The most successful of these is manufacturing resource planning (MRP II).

OBJECTIVES

After reading this chapter and completing the exercises you should be able to:

- appreciate some weaknesses of independent demand inventory systems
- describe the approach of material requirements planning
- use MRP to timetable orders and operations
- discuss the benefits of using MRP
- discuss the disadvantages of MRP
- list requirements for the use of MRP and the outputs from a system
- use a batching rule for variable, discrete demand
- discuss ways in which MRP can be extended, including MRP II

7.1 LIMITATIONS OF INDEPENDENT DEMAND INVENTORY SYSTEMS

Independent demand inventory systems are very widely used. Since they were introduced in the 1920s they have proved a valuable and flexible tool for management. Nonetheless, there are some circumstances in which they do not perform well. The most obvious of these is in batch production.

In batch production, the output from a process is divided into discrete batches. After a batch of one item is made it is transferred to stocks of finished goods. This batch satisfies all customer demand for some time, so production facilities are transferred to other items. At some point in the future stocks of the item will run low, so another batch is made.

Production of an item determines demands for the raw materials needed to make it. Thus the demands for materials are not independent, but are related through the production plan. The basic assumption of independent demand inventory systems is that demands are independent, so we must question whether this approach is appropriate for dependent demands. The general answer is they can be used (and have been used successfully since the 1920s) but developments in recent years have led to more effective alternatives which are generally called "dependent demand inventory systems". These dependent demand systems recognise that some inventory control should not be treated in isolation from production plans. Moreover, the demand for a range of items can clearly be related through planned production.

In these circumstances we can list weaknesses of independent demand systems as follows.

- They assume that demand for all items is independent. In reality the demand for raw materials depends on the production of finished products (so demands for materials are linked through the demand for the finished product).
- They assume that demand is relatively stable, or can be accurately forecast.
- Dependent demand systems cannot be used for forward planning. The calculations for reorder level, reorder quantity and so on are all based on historic figures rather than future plans, even when these plans are known with some certainty.
- They forecast demand from historic values even when future demand can be found with certainty from production plans.
- They assume that stock should always be available, even during short periods when there is no expected demand.
- Reorder level calculations assume lead time demand follows a fixed distribution. In reality, the lead time can be varied by expediting procedures or stressing the urgency of an item.
- Even if a high service level is set for all materials, a product using many materials is unlikely to find all of them in stock at the same time. When a service level of 99% is used for materials, a product which is made from 100 materials has a probability of $0.99^{100} = 0.37$ of finding all of them in stock.
- Informal systems can affect operations, as they exert pressure to try and improve material flow and expedite items needed for an assembly.

These observations reinforce the view that independent demand systems do not work well in batch production. There can also be weaknesses in specific situations. The reorder cost, for example, may be very high and the economic order quantity suggests order sizes which are so large that units become obsolete before they are used.

We can conclude that independent demand inventory systems are very good at dealing with many situations, but alternative approaches would be better at dealing with batch production. The most important of the alternative dependent demand systems has developed since the 1960s and is called material requirements planning.

We should emphasise that independent demand systems are invaluable in most organisations. We are looking for alternative approaches to support them in specific circumstances. In particular, one suggestion has:

Stocks	Approach
Raw materials and work in progress	Dependent demand system
Finished goods	Independent demand system

This suggestion is, of course, a gross simplification. At present it would be fairer to say that independent demand systems are the most widely used, while dependent demand systems can be used in certain circumstances.

In Summary

Despite their widespread use, independent demand inventory systems have weaknesses when dealing with some situations. One of these situations is batch production. Material requirements planning has been developed as an alternative dependent demand system.

SELF-ASSESSMENT QUESTIONS

7.1 What is the essential difference between independent demand and dependent demand inventory systems?
7.2 Independent demand models cannot be used for batch production. Is this statement true?

7.2   APPROACH OF MATERIAL REQUIREMENTS PLANNING

7.2.1   Background

Organisations must plan their future operations. This planning is usually a complex process which involves a hierarchy of decisions. More details of the process are described in Chapter 9, but we will review the main points here (see Figure 7.1).

Planning starts with an organisation reviewing its long-range forecasts of aggregate demand and ensuring it has enough capacity to meet this. The overall capacity plans then allow more detailed aggregate plans which show production for families of products. These aggregate plans are, in turn, expanded to give a detailed master schedule, which shows a timetable for the production of each item. The master schedule can in turn be used to develop short-term schedules for equipment and operators. It can also be used to schedule the requirements of materials, and this is the function we are more interested in here.

Material requirements planning (MRP) is based on the master schedule. This shows a detailed timetable for production of each item, typically broken down by week. MRP uses this master schedule to plan material requirements. It starts by seeing what production is planned and uses this to calculate the materials needed. Then it develops a timetable for orders so the materials arrive in time for their use.

With MRP the stock of materials depends directly on the known demand. Then only enough stock is held to satisfy this demand. The alternative approach, used by independent demand systems, is to keep stocks of materials which are high enough to cover any likely demand. An analogy would be the way a chef plans the ingredients needed to cook a week's meals. The MRP approach would look at the menus for each day, use this to determine the ingredients needed, and then

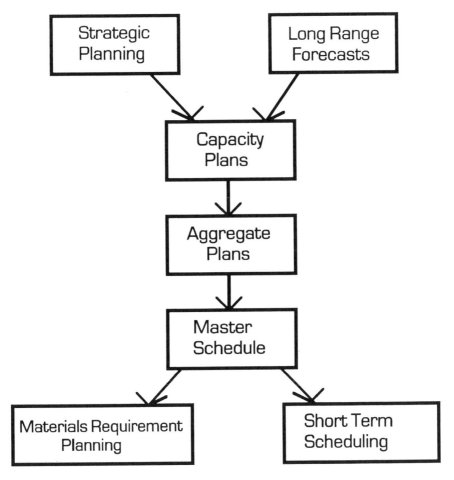

Figure 7.1 Summary of the planning process

ensure these are delivered in time for their use. The alternative independent demand system would see what ingredients were used in previous weeks and ensure that enough of everything is kept in stock to cover likely demand in the future.

The two approaches have different patterns of material stocks. With MRP stocks are generally low, but rise as deliveries are made just before production starts. Stock is then used during production and the amount held declines until it returns to a normal, low level. This pattern is shown in Figure 7.2(a). With independent demand systems stocks are not related to production plans, so higher levels must be maintained. These are reduced during production, but are replenished as soon as possible, to give the pattern shown in Figure 7.2(b).

MRP was originally developed for manufacturing industries. Although the approach is now used in many other industries we will, for convenience, stick

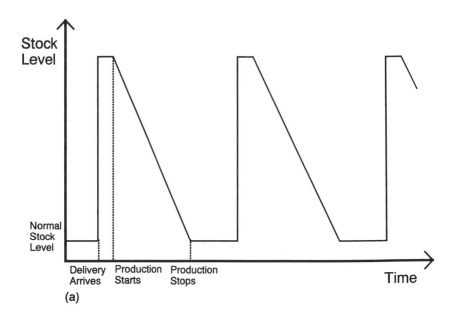

(a)

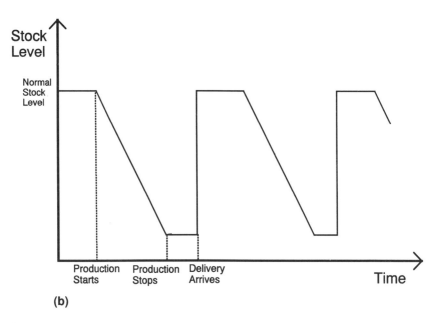

(b)

Figure 7.2 Comparison of stock levels. (a) Stock level of materials with MRP. (b) Stock level of materials with independent demand system

to the original vocabulary. This talks of materials (parts and components) being delivered to make products.

In Summary

Material requirements planning uses a master schedule to organise the delivery of materials. This allows stocks to be matched directly to production plans.

7.2.2   The MRP Process

MRP uses a master schedule to give an accurate assessment of demand for items needed by production. The first stage of the process is to "explode" the master schedule using a bill of materials. A bill of materials, or parts list, is an ordered list of all parts which are needed to make a particular product. Suppose, for example, a desk is made from a top and four legs. The bill of materials is shown in Figure 7.3. This diagram shows the levels of materials used, with Level 0 referring to final products and Level 1 to the parts. The numbers in brackets show the quantities needed to make each unit.

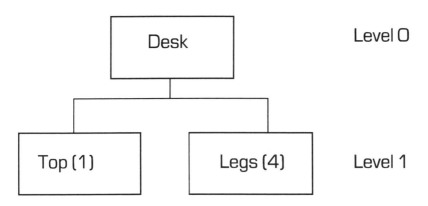

Figure 7.3 Bill of materials for a desk

Figure 7.3 shows a very simple bill of materials. They are usually much more complicated, involving many levels and materials. The bill of materials for a desk, for example, might show that each top is made from a wood kit and hardware. In turn, the wood kit consists of four oak planks, and so on. A partially completed diagram for this is shown in Figure 7.4.

We can continue looking at this example of a desk and use it to demonstrate the overall approach of MRP. Suppose, for example, the master schedule showed that six desks are to be made in the week beginning June 20th. We can use this information, together with the bill of materials, to calculate the quantities of materials needed. To make 6 desks we need 6 tops and 24 legs. In practice there may be some parts already in stock, so we have really used the master schedule and bill of materials to calculate gross requirements. If we subtract the current stocks

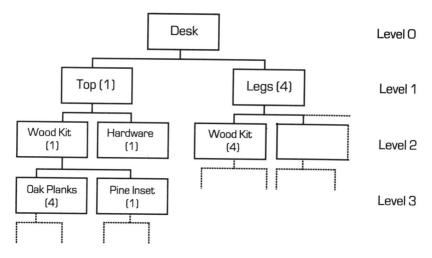

Figure 7.4 Partial bill of materials for a desk

from the gross stocks, we get a figure for net requirements. There might also be some orders for material which have already been placed and which will arrive in time to meet the net requirements. If we subtract these from the net requirements we find the amount of materials still to be ordered.

$$\begin{array}{l} \text{gross requirements} \\ \text{for materials} \end{array} = \begin{array}{l} \text{number of units} \\ \text{to be produced} \end{array} * \begin{array}{l} \text{materials required} \\ \text{for each unit} \end{array}$$

$$\begin{array}{l} \text{materials to be} \\ \text{ordered} \end{array} = \text{gross requirement} - \text{current stock} - \text{stock on order}$$

Finally, these orders may need some adjustment to allow for minimum order quantities, price discounts, and so on.

Now we have found the quantities to be ordered, and we know when they should arrive. The next step is to find the time when orders must be placed. We need information about lead times so that orders can be placed this lead time before materials are actually needed. The ordering of materials so they arrive when needed is sometimes called "time shifting" or "time phasing". Suppose, for example, that our desk has parts bought from suppliers with lead times of one week for tops and two weeks for legs. The parts are needed on June 20th, so the tops must be ordered on June 13th and the legs on June 6th. This gives a timetable:

- June 6th: order 24 legs
- June 13th: order 6 tops
- June 20th: start assembly of desks

This overall process is summarised in Figure 7.5.

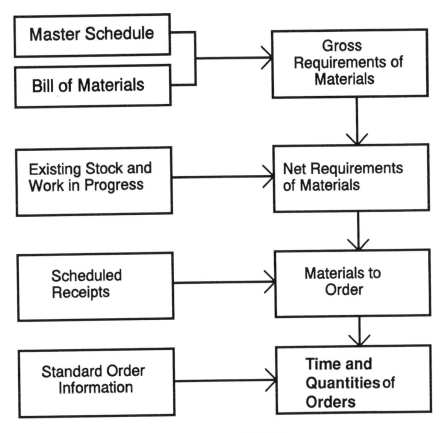

Figure 7.5 Summary of the MRP process

In detail, the MRP process is as follows.

(1) Use the master schedule to find the gross requirements of level 0 items.
(2) Subtract any stock on hand to give the net requirements for level 0 items, and schedule production to start so that these net requirements can be met.
(3) Use the bill of materials to translate this level of production starts into gross requirements for the next level of material.
(4) Take each of the materials in this level, and:
   • subtract the stock on hand and scheduled deliveries to find the quantities of materials to order
   • use the lead time and any other relevant information to find the time to place orders
   If there are more levels go to step (3), otherwise continue to step (5).
(5) Finalise the timetable of activities.

This procedure can be illustrated by a worked example.

Worked Example 7.1

A company assembles desks using bought-in parts of a top and four legs. These have lead times of one and two weeks respectively, and assembly takes a week. The company receives orders for 10 tables to be delivered in week 5 of a production period, and 20 tables in week 7. It has stocks of only 2 complete desks, 11 tops and 20 legs. When should it order parts?

Solution

The bill of materials for this problem has already been shown in Figure 7.3. The easiest way to arrange the calculations is in a table. This uses a standard format which is sometimes called an "MRP table". Now we can follow the procedure described above.

(1) Level 0 items are the finished products, so we start by looking at the production schedule for desks. This gives gross requirements, as shown in the first line of Table 7.1.
(2) Subtracting the stocks of finished desks from the gross requirements gives the net requirements. The assembly time for desks is one week, so assembly of the net requirements must be started one week earlier.

   The scheduled receipts are now added to show the number of units which become available in a week, which is the number started the lead time previously. This gives the assembly plan shown in Table 7.1.
(3) Now we use the "start assembly" line for Level 0 items (desks) to find the gross requirements for Level 1 items (tops and legs). This uses the bill of materials shown in Figure 7.3. In week 4 starts are made on 8 desks, which translates into gross requirements for 8 tops and 32 legs. Similarly, starts on 20 desks in week 6 translate into gross requirements for 20 tops and 80 legs.
(4) Subtracting stock on hand from these gross requirements gives the net requirements. To ensure the parts arrive on time they must be ordered the lead time in advance (i.e. one week for tops and two weeks for legs). These calculations are shown in Tables 7.2 and 7.3.
(5) There are no more levels of materials, so we can finalise the timetable of events as:

   - week 2: order 12 legs
   - week 4: order 80 legs and assemble 8 desks
   - week 5: order 17 tops
   - week 6: assemble 20 desks

This example has implicitly defined a number of relationships. For example:

Table 7.1

Level 0—Desks Week	1	2	3	4	5	6	7
Gross requirements					10		20
Opening stock	2	2	2	2	2		
Net requirements					8		20
Start assembly				8		20	
Scheduled receipts					8		20

Table 7.2

Level 1—Tops Week	1	2	3	4	5	6	7
Gross requirements				8		20	
Opening stock	11	11	11	11	3	3	
Net requirements						17	
Place order					17		
Scheduled receipts						17	

Table 7.3

Level 1—Legs Week	1	2	3	4	5	6	7
Gross requirements				32		80	
Opening stock	20	20	20	20			
Net requirements				12		80	
Place order		12		80			
Scheduled receipts				12		80	

$$\begin{array}{c} \text{scheduled receipts} \\ \text{in period } N \end{array} = \begin{array}{c} \text{production started or orders} \\ \text{placed in period } N - LT \end{array}$$

where LT is the lead time. Similarly the requirements are given by:

$$\begin{array}{c} \text{net requirements} \\ \text{in period } N \end{array} = \begin{array}{c} \text{gross} \\ \text{requirements} \\ \text{in period } N \end{array} - \begin{array}{c} \text{scheduled} \\ \text{receipts} \end{array} - \begin{array}{c} \text{free opening} \\ \text{stock} \end{array}$$

Here "free opening stock" is the amount of stock which is available for use. If, for example, the opening stock is 50 units, but the company always keeps a safety stock of 10 units, the free stock is 40 units.

$$\text{free opening stock} = \text{opening stock} - \text{safety stock}$$

Sometimes the MRP calculations are easier if the safety stock is excluded from all calculations so that only free stock is shown in MRP tables. We will not use this convention but will report all stock on hand.

Perhaps the most important relationship is:

$$\text{opening stock in period } N + 1 = \text{opening stock in period } N + \text{scheduled receipts in period } N - \text{gross requirements in period } N$$

In the MRP illustrations above, orders have been placed so that "scheduled receipts" are exactly the same as the "net requirement". This need not be the case. If, for example, suppliers have a minimum order size, the scheduled receipts may be considerably higher than the net requirements. We can illustrate this in the following slightly longer example.

Worked Example 7.2

A master schedule shows 20 units of product A to be made in week 7 of a cycle, 30 units in week 8 and 20 units in week 10. There are currently 6 units of the product in stock, but the company always keeps 3 units in reserve to cover emergency orders. Each unit of the product takes one week to assemble from 1 unit of part B and 3 units of part C. Each unit of part B is made in one week from 2 units of material D and 3 units of material E. Part C is assembled in two weeks from 1 unit of component F and 2 units of component G. Lead times (in weeks) and current stocks of materials are shown in Table 7.4.

Table 7.4

Material	Lead time	Current stock
D	2	80
E	3	110
F	1	100
G	2	100

There are currently stocks of 50 units of B and 50 units of C, and the company keeps minimum stocks of 50 units of D, 100 of E and 50 of F. The minimum order size for E is 200 units, while F and G can only be ordered in discrete batches of 100 units. An order placed with a subcontractor for 80 units of C is expected to arrive in period 3. Develop a timetable of activities for the company.

Solution

The bill of materials for the product is shown in Figure 7.6, where the lead times are added under each box. The analysis then starts at level 0, with assembly of product A (see Table 7.5). The company keeps a minimum stock of 3 in reserve, so this must be remembered when calculating net requirements.

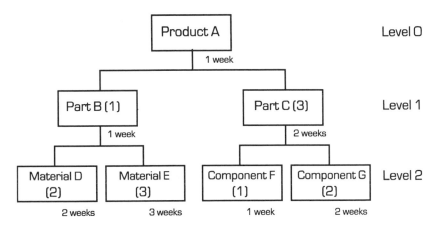

Figure 7.6 Bill of materials for Worked Example 7.2

Table 7.5

Level 0—Product A Week	1	2	3	4	5	6	7	8	9	10
Gross requirements							20	30		20
Opening stock	6	6	6	6	6	6	6	3	3	3
Net requirements							17	30		20
Start assembly						17	30		20	
Scheduled receipts							17	30		20

This completes the schedule for product A, and we can now move to level 1 materials and expand the assembly plan for A into gross requirements for components B and C (see Tables 7.6 and 7.7). The 17 units of A assembled in week 6 is expanded into gross requirements of 17 units of part B and 51 units of part C. The 30 units of A assembled in week 7 is expanded into gross requirements of 30 units of part B and 90 units of part C, and so on. Some

Table 7.6

| Level 1—Part B | | | | | | | | | | |
Week	1	2	3	4	5	6	7	8	9	10
Gross requirements						17	30		20	
Opening stock	50	50	50	50	50	50	33			
Net requirements							3		20	
Start making						3		20		
Scheduled receipts							3		20	

Table 7.7

| Level 1—Part C | | | | | | | | | | |
Week	1	2	3	4	5	6 ·	7	8	9	10
Gross requirements						51	90		60	
Opening stock	50	50	50	130	130	130	79			
Net requirements							11		60	
Start making					11		60			
Scheduled receipts			80				11		60	

of the gross requirements for B and C can be met from opening stocks, but the shortfall is shown as net requirements. We must also remember the planned delivery of 80 units of part C in week 3.

This schedule for level 1 parts can now be expanded to give the gross requirements for level 2 materials and components (see Tables 7.8 and 7.9). The gross requirements for materials D and E are found from the assembly

Table 7.8

| Level 2—Material D | | | | | | | | | | |
Week	1	2	3	4	5	6	7	8	9	10
Gross requirements						6		40		
Opening stock	80	80	80	80	80	74	74	74	50	50
Net requirements								16		
Place order						16				
Scheduled receipts								16		

Table 7.9

| Level 2—Material E | | | | | | | | | | |
Week	1	2	3	4	5	6	7	8	9	10
Gross requirements						9		60		
Opening stock	110	110	110	110	110	110	101	101	241	241
Net requirements								59		
Place order					200					
Scheduled receipts								200		

plans for part B. Three units of B are started in week 6 and this expands into gross requirements for 6 units of D and 9 units of E, and so on. One complication here is the minimum order size of 200 units of E. In week 8 there is a gross requirement of 60 for material E, 1 of which can be met from free stock (keeping the reserve stock of 100). The net requirement is 59, but 200 have to be ordered with the spare 141 added to stock.

Finally, the gross requirements for components F and G can be found from the assembly plan for part C (see Tables 7.10 and 7.11). Eleven units of C are started in week 5 so this expands into gross requirements of 11 units of F, 22 units of G, and so on. Orders for these must be in discrete batches of 100 units, so they are rounded to the nearest hundred above net requirements.

Table 7.10

Level 2—Part F Week	1	2	3	4	5	6	7	8	9	10
Gross requirements					11		60			
Opening stock	100	100	100	100	100	89	89	129	129	129
Net requirements							21			
Place order						100				
Scheduled receipts							100			

Table 7.11

Level 2—Part G Week	1	2	3	4	5	6	7	8	9	10
Gross requirements					22		120			
Opening stock	100	100	100	100	100	78	78	58	58	58
Net requirements							42			
Place order					100					
Scheduled receipts							100			

The timetable of activities now becomes:

week 3: 80 unit of C arrive from subcontractor
week 5: start 11 units of C
        order 200 units of E
        order 100 units of G
week 6: assemble 17 units of A
        start 3 units of B
        order 16 units of D
        order 100 units of F
week 7: assemble 30 units of A
        finish 3 units of B

> finish 11 units of C
> start 60 units of C
> 100 units of F arrive
> 100 units of G arrive
> week 8: start 20 units of B
> 16 units of D arrive
> 200 units of E arrive
> week 9: assemble 20 units of A
> finish 20 units of B
> finish 60 units of C

In Summary

Material requirements planning uses a bill of materials to explode a master schedule and give the gross requirements for materials needed to support production. Information about current stocks, orders outstanding, and so on are then used to find order quantities. Lead times are use to time phase these orders so that materials arrive in time for use.

SELF-ASSESSMENT QUESTIONS

7.3 MRP is only relevant for production systems. Is this statement true or false?

7.4 How is the net requirement for material found in MRP?

7.5 What information is needed by MRP systems?

7.3 BENEFITS AND DISADVANTAGES OF MRP

7.3.1 Benefits of MRP

Independent demand systems often do not perform well with batch production. They rely on projective forecasts to find likely demand for materials and then hold stocks which are high enough to cover them. With batch processing this can lead to excessively high stocks. A related problem is the unavoidable errors in forecasts, particularly when dealing with the lumpy demand found in batch production. Safety stock is held to cover these errors, and this raises stock levels yet further. MRP avoids these high stock levels and associated high inventory costs by relating the supply of materials directly to demand. The result is significantly reduced stocks and associated costs. Typically, organisations which move from an independent demand system to MRP report reductions in stock of 20–30%.

Among the direct benefits of MRP are:

- reduced stock levels (with consequent savings in capital, space, warehousing, etc.)
- higher stock turnover

- increased customer service with fewer delays caused by shortages of materials
- more reliable and faster quoted delivery times
- improved utilisation of facilities as materials are always available when needed
- less time spent on expediting and emergency orders

As well as these direct benefits there are a number of indirect ones, such as improved planning. MRP is based on an accurate master schedule, so there is an incentive to produce and maintain reliable plans. There is also an incentive to stick to plans, rather than tinkering with them to get short-term gains. It is often suggested that high stock levels allow more flexibility in the system so that plans can be changed at short notice. Supporters of MRP would reply that the need to modify plans is often a symptom of poor initial planning, or lack of control in sticking to an agreed plan.

MRP can give early warning of potential problems and shortages. If necessary, expediting procedures can be used to speed up deliveries, or production plans can be changed. This improves the wider performance of an organisation, and gives better equipment utilisation, productivity, customer service, response to market conditions, and so on.

Often, the problems identified by MRP have previously been hidden. The detailed analysis of material movement might, for example, identify a supplier whose lead time is unreliable. Independent demand systems can hide this and avoid potential problems by keeping higher safety stock. The problem is then hidden, but costs are increased. It would be better to recognise the problem and take steps to solve it, either by changing the supplier or discussing ways of improving its reliability. This theme of solving rather than hiding problems is discussed again in Chapter 8.

One of the stated advantages of MRP is that stocks are related directly to demand, so there is no need for safety stocks. In practice, there is a school of thought which says that safety stocks are still needed. With MRP they serve the same purpose as in independent demand systems, in that they allow for unexpected variations in demand and lead time. Uncertainty in lead time is the same as in independent demand systems, but there should be less uncertainty in demand, which is only introduced by short-term changes to production plans. The opposing school of thought says that plans should be changed infrequently and uncertainty should, therefore, be minimal. Any small changes can be allowed for by adjusting the quoted lead time to customers, expediting deliveries, or adjusting production priorities. Then safety stocks are an unnecessary waste of money. This latter view is becoming dominant, and is certainly closer to the underlying objectives and principles of MRP.

In Summary

The main advantage of MRP is its ability to relate demand for materials directly to the master schedule. This can bring a number of advantages, ranging from reduced costs to better planning.

7.3.2   Disadvantages of MRP

Although MRP can bring considerable benefits, it can also have disadvantages. The first of these relates to the information needed before MRP can be used. The MRP process starts with a detailed master schedule which must be produced some time in advance. Then MRP cannot be used if:

- there is no master schedule
- the master schedule is inaccurate
- plans are frequently changed
- plans are not made far enough in advance

Other requirements which must be met before MRP can be used include:

- a parts list or bill of materials which can translate the master schedule into a list of requirements for materials
- information about current stocks, orders outstanding, supplier reliability, etc.
- lead times and other information which is needed to allow deliveries of materials to arrive in time for use

Even when these requirements are met, the complexity of MRP systems can cause difficulties. The worked examples above describe very simple situations, yet the amount of data manipulation soon becomes tedious. With real problems, and items made up of hundreds or thousands of parts, the processing can only be done with a computer. MRP is not a new idea, but its use has only been practicable since cheap computing became available in the early 1970s. Since then many standard systems have been developed. The elements of a computerised MRP system are summarised in Figure 7.7.

We have already described the inputs to such a system, but there are several possible outputs. Some of these are needed directly by purchasing and production, while others are more general management reports. Typical outputs include:

- *Timetable of orders* and other operations.
- *Changes to previous plans*. As the master schedule is revised, or any other changes are made, MRP schedules are updated. The consequent changes in material requirements and previous orders are reported, including changes to order quantities, cancelled orders or changes of time.
- *Exceptions*. Sometimes the system may note serious discrepancies which cannot be dealt with automatically. Typically, these include errors, late orders, overdue deliveries, excessive scrap, requests for non-existent parts, and so on.
- *Performance reports*. These show how well the system is operating and might include measures for investment in stocks, inventory turnover, number of shortages, and so on. These reports may help managers make a number of planning and other tactical decisions.

Inputs

Outputs

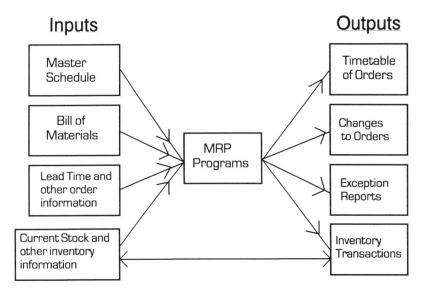

Figure 7.7 Inputs and outputs of a computerised MRP system

- *Inventory transactions.* All of these are both recorded, so that the system maintains accurate records of current stock positions, and reported, as a check on progress.

The amount of information needed to run an MRP system and the number of reports which can be produced have led many organisations to look on MRP as a computerised information system. They suggest that MRP's role in planning is really a by-product of its primary role as an information system. Other organisations suggest that this restricts the scope of MRP and diverts attention away from its main role of planning. Perhaps the most sensible view is that MRP is both an information system and a method of planning. Although developed as a tool for helping control stocks, it has certainly expanded beyond this original scope.

MRP is now widely used, and standard software is readily available. This should, however, be used with caution. There are many examples of MRP systems failing to live up to expectations or bringing their full benefits. Perhaps the main reason for this is the belief that a system can simply be bought and switched on. The introduction of MRP needs considerable changes to an organisation and these require commitment from all areas. Even if this commitment exists, it should not be assumed that MRP is simply an additional tool for planning. It is an integral part of the planning process and requires new procedures in many areas.

The prerequisites and substantial data manipulation are the main disadvantages with MRP, but there are others. It might, for example, reduce flexibility in responding to changes. Independent demand systems typically hold large stocks of all materials, and these allow production plans to be changed at short notice. With MRP the only materials in stock are those which are needed for the specified master schedule. If plans are suddenly changed the necessary materials will not be available, so the response to market changes may be slower.

In practice, flexibility may be improved by regular updating of the MRP schedule. Organisations typically update their schedule weekly. This updating can be done in two ways:

- Have a complete MRP run every period (typically every week). This is called "regenerative MRP" and has the advantage of regularly taking into account all new information. Conversely, it has the disadvantage of needing a lot of processing.
- Update the schedules when there are changes. This is called "net change MRP". Whenever a change is made to the schedule a limited MRP run is done to show the effects of these changes. This updating can be done more frequently (typically daily). The advantage of this is a reduction in processing by only recalculating and reporting changes from previous periods. Conversely, it has the disadvantage of allowing frequent changes which can make the system appear unstable or nervous.

One view of MRP suggests that the regular updating of plans means the system is not inflexible, but can be very responsive to changes. Whichever view is taken, there is agreement that MRP is a very formal system. This formality can be a disadvantage, as organisations sometimes concentrate so much on the process that they believe meeting schedules is of paramount importance: no decisions can be made outside the system. In practice, many organisations have informal systems working alongside the formal ones to ensure things get done. MRP does not encourage these informal systems, and while the formal system should be good enough for all proper operations, this may be a disadvantage.

Another disadvantage comes with the assumptions that materials are made in the "bottom-up" order described by the bill of materials. In other words high-level materials are made before lower-level ones, and so on. In practice many organisations make parts in an order which is very different from the engineering bill of materials. This is particularly relevant when MRP schedules are used to plan operations in, say, a job shop. The schedule may give inefficient work loads which could be improved by taking a longer-term view of production.

One final disadvantage is that the order pattern may give small frequent orders. These are inconvenient and it might be preferable to combine several orders into larger batches. A procedure for this is described in the following section.

Overall, we can say that MRP has been found to give considerable benefits and there are many illustrations of companies which have made substantial savings. To produce these savings, the companies have had to invest a lot of time and effort in developing a useful system.

In Summary

The main disadvantages with MRP are the conditions which must be met before MRP can be used and the amount of data manipulation.

SELF-ASSESSMENT QUESTIONS

7.6 What is the main advantage of MRP?
7.7 What is the main disadvantage of MRP?
7.8 What are the typical outputs from an MRP system?
7.9 Would it be possible to develop a manual MRP system?

7.4 BATCHING OF DISCRETE VARIABLE DEMAND

7.4.1 Intermittent Demand

So far we have assumed that in MRP an order is placed exactly to cover the net requirement. This could suggest a series of frequent, small orders which may be inconvenient and incur high administration and delivery costs. MRP schedules are frequently updated every week, so this "lot-for-lot" ordering would give weekly orders. It might be preferable to combine several of these small orders into a few larger batches. A batching rule for this is described in the following section.

Another aspect of these small, frequent orders, is that demand may appear sporadic or intermittent. When items are made in batches, demand for materials varies widely over time. In particular, demand for a material may be high during one production phase, and then zero during other production phases. A typical demand pattern for consecutive periods might then be:

    0 0 0 10 0 0 0 0 0 25 0 0 0 0 0 0 0 0 5 0

This kind of demand is often found with MRP, but it also occurs in other circumstances, such as spare parts for equipment. Independent demand inventory systems work best when demand is more or less stable, so they perform particularly badly in these conditions. Their main problem is finding a reasonable forecast. One approach is to consider separately:

• expected number of periods between demands
• expected size of a demand

Both of these can be forecast using exponential smoothing. Suppose there is a demand, $D(t)$ in period t which is $N(t)$ periods since the last demand. We can use exponential smoothing to calculate:

- expected time between demands: $ET(t + 1) = \alpha * N(t) + (1 - \alpha) * ET(t)$
- expected size of demand: $ED(t + 1) = \alpha * D(t) + (1 - \alpha) * ED(t)$

These equations need not be updated for those periods when there is no demand.

The probability of a demand in any period is $1/[ET(t + 1)]$, so we can forecast demand from:

$$F(t + 1) = \frac{ED(t + 1)}{ET(t + 1)}$$

This approach to forecasting sporadic demand gives better results than, say, exponential smoothing, but its reliability is still uncertain in practice.

In section 4.3.3 we looked at a problem with spare parts where the shortage cost was balanced against the holding cost. In particular we calculated an optimal value for A, the amount of stock of a spare part which minimises total costs. We could now suggest a similar analysis based on a service level. In particular:

service level $= 1 - $ Prob(shortage)
$\qquad\qquad\quad = 1 - $ [Prob(there is a demand) $*$ Prob(demand $> A$)]

where:
Prob(there is a demand) $= 1/ET(t + 1)$
Prob(demand $> A$) can be found from the distribution of demand

Again, we should say that this kind of problem is notoriously difficult to tackle with an independent demand system and the results are often unreliable. The main problem is clearly the forecasting intermittent demand. This forecasting is not needed in dependent demand systems and is another point in their favour.

In Summary

MRP schedules may give intermittent demands. These occur quite frequently and are very difficult to deal with using independent demand systems.

7.4.2   Developing a Batching Rule

MRP schedules show the demand for an item every period. We have seen how frequent ordering of small quantities can lead to high costs, so would prefer some means of increasing order size and reducing overall costs. In practice there are several approaches for this.

- *Lot-for-lot ordering*. This is the approach we have already described, and it has the drawbacks of giving small, frequent orders.
- *Fixed order quantity*. This is similar to the economic order quantity in that

an order of fixed size is always placed (which may be the calculated EOQ). The drawback is that it does not match supply directly to known demand, and hence reduces one of the main advantages of MRP.

- *Period order quantity*. This places regular orders for the quantities needed in the next period. Although it is simple to administer, this method does not attempt to minimise costs.
- *Dynamic lot sizing*. This determines the pattern of orders which minimises overall costs, but constant changes in both order quantities and timing are difficult to administer.

Because of its aim of minimising costs, dynamic lot sizing is often the best approach, despite the difficulty of administration. In this section we will describe dynamic lot sizing in terms of a simple batching rule. Although we are describing this analysis in relation to MRP, it can be used in any circumstances where demand is variable, but known in advance.

We found with independent demand systems that small, frequent orders give higher administration and delivery charges, while large, infrequent orders give higher holding costs. The situation with dependent demand inventories is exactly the same, and again we look for a compromise order quantity which balances these two competing costs. One way of approaching this is to assume there is some optimal number of periods' demand which should be combined into a single batch. If orders are placed more frequently than this, the administration and delivery charges will be high and give high overall costs; if orders are placed less frequently, stock levels will be high and again give high overall costs. Thus, we assume a cost curve with a distinct minimum, as shown in Figure 7.8.

In this analysis we will assume that demand for an item is variable and discrete. In other words the demand varies from one period to the next, and it occurs at discrete points in time (typically once a week). All the costs of placing and receiving an order are combined into the reorder cost, RC, while all costs associated with holding a unit of stock for a unit of time are combined into the holding cost, HC.

If enough stock is bought to cover all orders for the next N periods, we can calculate an average cost per period. The object is to find the optimal value of N which minimises this average cost.

Consider one order for an item, where enough is bought to satisfy demand for the next N periods. The variable demand in period i is $D(i)$, so that an order to cover all demand in the next N periods will be for:

$$A = \sum_{i=1}^{N} D(i)$$

units. We will assume that this arrives in stock at one time, so the highest actual stock level is A. We will also assume that the item is used steadily for production and the stock will return to zero when production has finished. The average stock level can be approximated by $A/2$ and the cost of holding this is $(A/2) * N * HC$ (see Figure 7.9). Then the variable cost of stocking the item over the N periods is the sum of:

- reorder cost component = RC
- holding cost component = average stock level $(A/2)*$ time held $(N)*$ holding cost (HC)

$$= \frac{HC * N * \sum_{i=1}^{N} D(i)}{2}$$

Adding these two components and dividing by N gives the average variable cost per period, $VC(N)$, of:

$$VC(N) = \frac{RC}{N} + \frac{HC * \sum_{i=1}^{N} D(i)}{2}$$

If we consider short stock cycles at the left-hand side of the graph in Figure 7.8, $VC(N)$ will be high because of reorder costs. Then increasing N will follow the graph downward until costs just begin to rise, at which point the optimal value has been found. This procedure can be formalised as follows.

- First calculate the cost of buying for a single period and compare this with the cost of buying for two periods. If it is cheaper to buy for two periods than for one we are going down the left-hand side of the graph in Figure 7.8 and the cost is reducing as the value of N is increasing.
- Next compare the cost of buying for two periods with the cost of buying for three periods. If it is cheaper to buy for three periods we are still on the declining part of the graph and have not yet reached the point of minimum cost.
- Continue this procedure, comparing the cost of buying for N periods with the cost of buying for $N+1$ periods, until at some point it becomes cheaper to buy for N periods than for $N+1$ periods. At this point we have reached the bottom of the graph and found the point of minimal cost. Any further increases in N would increase costs as we climb up the right-hand side of the graph.

We need a way of comparing the variable cost for a cycle of $N + 1$ periods with those for a cycle of N periods. If we substitute $N + 1$ for N in the variable cost equation above we get:

$$VC(N + 1) = \frac{RC}{N + 1} + \frac{HC * \sum_{i=1}^{N+1} D(i)}{2}$$

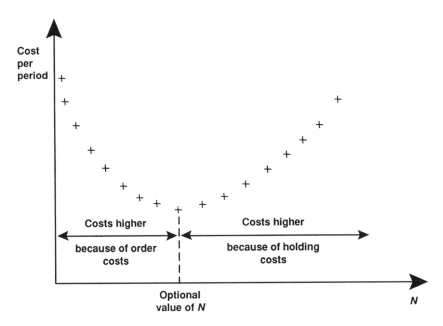

Figure 7.8 Variation of costs with number of periods, N, combined into a single order

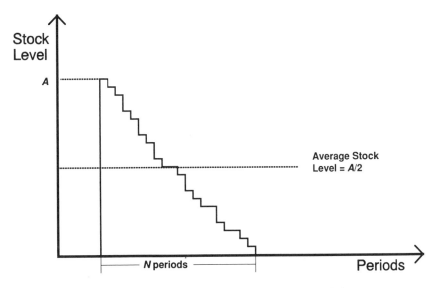

Figure 7.9 Stock level for an order covering N periods

Now we want to find the point at which $VC(N+1)$ becomes larger than $VC(N)$ so:

$$VC(N+1) > VC(N)$$

$$\frac{RC}{N+1} + \frac{HC * \sum\limits_{i=1}^{N+1} D(i)}{2} > \frac{RC}{N} + \frac{HC * \sum\limits_{i=1}^{N} D(i)}{2}$$

After some manipulation this can be simplified to:

$$N * (N+1) * D(N+1) > \frac{2 * RC}{HC}$$

Now we can use this inequality in an iterative procedure to find the optimal value of N. This starts by setting N equal to 1 and comparing the cost of ordering for one period with the cost of ordering for two periods. If the inequality is invalid it is cheaper to order for two periods than for one, so we are moving down the left-hand side of the costs in Figure 7.8. Then we set N equal to 2 and compare the costs of ordering for two and three periods. If the inequality is still invalid, the costs are reducing and we are still coming down the left-hand side of the curve. Then we keep on increasing N, until eventually the inequality will become valid. This means that we are at the bottom of the cost curve and an optimal value for N has been found. The process then stops. A flow diagram of this procedure is shown in Figure 7.10.

This solution procedure is best illustrated in a worked example.

Worked Example 7.3

The total cost of placing an order for an item and having it delivered is estimated to be £120. The holding cost for each unit of the item is £5 a week. An MRP analysis for the next 11 weeks gives demand for the item as follows.

Week:	1	2	3	4	5	6	7	8	9	10	11
Demand:	2	4	6	9	9	6	3	4	4	6	9

Find an ordering policy which gives reasonable costs for the item. What is the cost of this policy?

Solution

We know that:

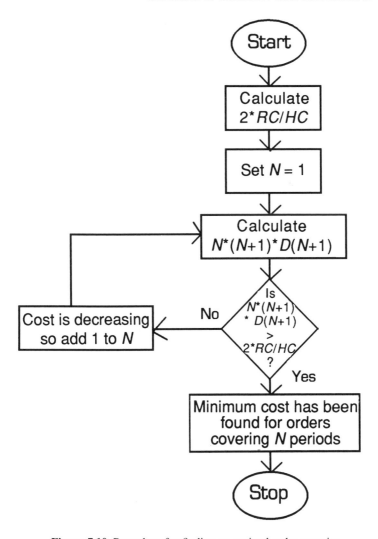

Figure 7.10 Procedure for finding an optimal order quantity

RC = £120 an order
HC = £5 a unit a week

Then following the procedure shown in Figure 7.10, we calculate:

$$2 * RC / HC = 2 * 120/5 = 48$$

Then, taking $N = 1$, $N + 1 = 2$ and $D(2) = 4$ we calculate:

$$N * (N + 1) * D(N + 1) = 1 * 2 * 4 = 8$$

As this is less than 48 the inequality is *invalid* and we have not reached the minimum.

Next take $N = 2$, $N + 1 = 3$ and $D(3) = 6$ we calculate:

$$N * (N + 1) * D(N + 1) = 2 * 3 * 6 = 36$$

This is less than 48 so the inequality is still *invalid* and we have not reached the minimum.

Next take $N = 3$, $N + 1 = 4$ and $D(4) = 9$ we calculate:

$$N * (N + 1) * D(N + 1) = 3 * 4 * 9 = 108$$

This is more than 48 so the inequality is *valid* and we have found the minimum cost with $N = 3$.

The first order is due to arrive at the beginning of week 1. This order should be large enough to cover demand in the first three weeks, which is $2 + 4 + 6 = 12$ units. Now, adding standard information about lead time and supplier conditions would tell us precisely when to place the order.

It is easier to do these calculations in a table, as shown in Table 7.12. (It is also worth mentioning that this analysis can be done very effectively on a spreadsheet.) Unfortunately, this result is only valid for the particular demand pattern in the first few weeks. It is not a general result and we have to repeat the calculation for every other stock cycle (see Table 7.13). The only thing to remember when repeating the calculations is that every time a new stock cycle

Table 7.12

Week, i	1	2	3	4
Demand, $D(i)$	2	4	6	9
N	1	2	3	
$N * (N + 1) * D(N+1)$	8	36	108	
Delivery	12			

Table 7.13

Week, i	1	2	3	4	5	6	7	8	9	10	11
Demand, $D(i)$	2	4	6	9	9	6	3	4	4	6	9
N	1	2	3	1	2	3	4	1	2	3	1
$N * (N + 1) * D(N + 1)$	8	36	108	18	36	36	80	8	36	108	
Delivery	12				27				14		

is started the value of N returns to 1 and the demand figures are updated accordingly. A good ordering policy would ensure 12 units arrive by week 1, 27 by week 4 and 14 by week 8. To ensure these deliveries arrive on time orders must be placed at least the lead time in advance.

We can find the cost of this policy by looking at each stock cycle in turn. Each cycle has one order which has a cost of $RC = 120$. The holding costs depend on the order quantity and cycle length. The first cycle has 12 units bought, so we can approximate the average stock as $12/2 = 6$ units. This has holding costs of 6 units for 3 weeks at a cost of £5 a unit a week. Then, the costs over the 10 weeks covered by the three cycles are as shown in Table 7.14.

Table 7.14

Cycle	Reorder cost	Holding cost	Total cost
1	120	$(12/2)*3*5 = 90$	210
2	120	$(27/2)*4*5 = 270$	390
3	120	$(14/2)*3*5 = 105$	225

The total variable cost over 10 weeks is £825, to give an average of £82.50 a week.

There are several alternative batching rules, but the one described usually gives good results. It does not guarantee optimal ones because of the assumptions made (such as fixed and known costs, fixed demand which occurs at discrete points, an optimal solution which occurs as soon as costs begin to rise, the approximation for average stock level, and so on). We can overcome one of these problems by adding a further calculation to the analysis. If costs are higher for $N+1$ period than for N, it is possible that they may decrease again for $N + 2$ periods. We should ensure that the cost of ordering for N period is also less than the cost of ordering for $N + 2$ periods. Using exactly the same argument as before we can find that:

$$VC(N+2) \geq VC(N)$$

which leads to:

$$N * (N+2) * [D(N+1) + D(N+2)] \geq \frac{4*RC}{HC}$$

This adds a test to the procedure described above. When a turning point is found and we know it is cheaper to order for N periods than for $N + 1$, we simply see if it is also cheaper to order for $N + 2$ periods. If the inequality above is valid, we stop the process and accept the solution: if the inequality is invalid the process is continued until another turning point is found.

In Summary

Without modification, MRP would suggest small frequent orders. Costs can be reduced by combining several of these into a single larger order. A batching rule, which gives low costs, has been described for this.

SELF-ASSESSMENT QUESTIONS

7.10 Why do independent demand systems generally perform badly with intermittent demand?

7.11 The expected time between demands for a spare part is 5 weeks, with expected demand size of 10 units. If the demand size is Normally distributed with standard deviation of 3 units, what stock level would give a 95% service level?

7.12 It is always preferable to combine small orders into larger ones. Is this statement true or false?

7.13 What is a batching rule?

7.14 Why does the batching rule described only give a good rather than an optimal solution?

7.5 EXTENSIONS TO MRP

MRP systems of any size must be computerised, and they must have direct links with other systems (inventory records, supplier information, engineering designs, and so on). This means that MRP only really became feasible in the early 1970s. Since then it has been widely adopted in manufacturing industries. Typically, manufacturers who adopt MRP report stock reductions of 20–30% and gain a number of other benefits. Because of this proven success, it is not surprising that extensions have been found to the basic system, or that areas of application have been expanded.

The first of the extensions were fairly small and gave enhanced procedures for dealing with variable supply, supplier reliability, wastage, defective quality, variable demand, variable lead times, and so on. Several different batching rules were also developed for different circumstances. These extensions were often quite small, and were made to take advantage of increasingly sophisticated computer systems. More fundamental changes were, however, soon considered.

For some time MRP was limited to manufacturing. Although it is more difficult to use in service industries, there are places where it has proved effective. The main problem is that services combine simultaneous production and consumption with widely varying demand. Nonetheless, some service organisations produce a detailed master schedule which can be used for MRP. Universities and colleges, for example, have used MRP to plan requirements for classrooms based on known student demands. Similarly, health services have based requirements for surgical facilities on known schedules for patient treatment.

These applications point to an expanding role for MRP, in that they use the MRP process to plan more than material requirements. This theme is formalised in manufacturing resource planning, or MRP II.

MRP II recognised that the MRP approach of exploding a master schedule to determine material requirements could be expanded to show requirements for other resources. Ordering and purchasing are included in MRP, but why not extend the analyses to dispatching, distribution, production processes and even to marketing and finance? A master schedule could, for example, be used to show the amount of machinery and equipment needed in each period. This in turn could be used to determine manning levels, and so on. Eventually the master schedule could be used as the basis for planning most resources used in an operation. This was the intention of MRP II.

MRP II aims to provide an integrated system, with all parts linked back to a master schedule. Several computer systems have been developed for this, including:

- COPICS (Communications Oriented Production Information and Control System) by IBM, which was later enhanced in MAPICS (Manufacturing Accounting and Production Information Control System)
- Factory Management System by Hewlett-Packard
- Production Control System by Burroughs
- MAC-PAC by Arthur Anderson
- and many other packages

We have already suggested that MRP requires a considerable effort to implement successfully, and MRP II needs an even bigger commitment. Perhaps not surprisingly, most organisations have found such complete integration to be impracticable, or at least not worth the effort. Nonetheless, they adopted some parts of the system, often using different names.

- *Closed loop MRP* includes a feedback of information to ensure the proposed MRP schedule is feasible and presents no major problems. If difficulties are identified, plans can be adjusted before they are implemented.
- *Capacity requirements planning* is similar to closed loop MRP. It feeds back information about capacities needed by all operations to ensure there is enough to meet the production specified in the master schedule.
- *Resource requirements planning* is sometimes used to mean the same as MRP II, and sometimes used in a wider sense to include all planning decisions.
- *Distribution requirements planning* (DRP) considers the movement of products through the distribution system. Then demands placed by customers will translate into gross requirements at local warehouses. These in turn will set the gross requirements at regional warehouses, which will set the gross requirements at national warehouses, and so on.
- *Distribution resource planning* (DRP II) expands the scope of DRP in the

same way that MRP II expands the scope of MRP. Thus it schedules transport, drivers, warehouse space and other logistics functions.

- *Manufacturing resource productivity* (MRP III) uses some elements of just-in-time systems (described in Chapter 8) to enhance the planning done with MRP II.

All such systems rely heavily on computing. The installation and maintenance of working systems can be very complicated and expensive. This has encouraged some dependent demand systems to adopt a radically different approach. We will describe these in Chapter 9.

In Summary

There have been continual improvements to MRP systems since they were introduced in the early 1970s. Some improvements have extended the functions considered by MRP to give manufacturing resource planning (MRP II) and other systems.

SELF-ASSESSMENT QUESTIONS

7.15 What is MRP II?

7.16 MRP II relies on substantial computer resources. Is this statement true or false?

SUMMARY OF CHAPTER

This chapter has discussed some aspects of dependent demand inventory systems. In particular it has:

- described some weaknesses of independent demand systems, particularly when dealing with batch production
- described the alternative approach of dependent demand systems
- shown how materials requirement planning (MRP) explodes production plans to give demand for materials
- used time phasing of orders to build a timetable of activities
- discussed the prerequisites for MRP and the expected outputs
- discussed the benefits and disadvantages of MRP
- mentioned difficulties with intermittent demand
- described a batching rule for discrete, variable demand
- outlined some extensions to MRP, including MRP II.

ADDITIONAL PROBLEMS

7.1 A company assembles dining-room tables using bought-in parts of four legs and a top. These have lead times of two and three weeks respectively, and assembly takes a week. The company receives orders for 40 tables to be delivered in week 5 of a production period and 80 tables in week 7. There are current stocks of 4 complete tables, 80 legs and 44 tops. When should parts be ordered?

7.2 A master schedule shows 90 units of a product to be made in week 12 of a cycle, 120 units in week 13 and 80 units in week 16. There are currently 20 units of the product in stock, but the company always keeps 10 units in reserve to cover emergency orders. Each unit of the product takes two weeks to assemble from 2 units of part B and 3 units of part C. Each unit of part B is made in one week from 1 unit of material D and 3 units of material E. Part C is assembled in 2 weeks from 2 units of component F. Lead times for D, E and F are 1, 2 and 3 weeks respectively. Current stocks are 100 units of B, 200 of C, 80 of D, 300 of E and 200 of F. The company keeps minimum stocks of 40 units of D, 200 of E and 100 of F. The minimum order size for E is 500 units, while F can only be ordered in discrete batches of 100 units. An order placed with a subcontractor for 200 units of C is expected to arrive in period 8. Develop a timetable of activities for the company.

7.3 A company makes three sizes of filing cabinet with 2, 3 and 4 drawers. Each cabinet consists of a case, drawers and a lock. Each case is made from drawer slides (two for each drawer) and a formed case (which is itself made from a sheet of steel). Each drawer is made from two roller supports, a handle and a formed drawer (which is made from a sheet of steel). The lead times, in weeks, are:

cabinet	1	lock	1	sheet steel	3
case	1	formed case	1	formed drawer	2
drawer	3	drawer slide	3	roller support	3
handle	2				

There are currently stocks of 30 complete drawers and 80 roller supports, and a delivery of 300 roller supports is expected in period 1. The master schedule for the next 10 weeks is as given in Table 7.15.

Table 7.15

Week	1	2	3	4	5	6	7	8	9	10
2-drawer cabinets		50			100			100		100
3-drawer cabinets				60	120		80		120	
4-drawer cabinets			50		150		110			110

Devise a plan for ordering and production.

7.4 It costs £1.50 to store a unit of an item for one month. The total cost of placing an order for the item, including delivery, is £950. An MRP analysis has found the following demands for the item.

Month:	1	2	3	4	5	6	7	8	9	10	11	12	13
Demand:	50	25	30	30	50	60	40	30	20	30	40	50	70

Find a good ordering policy for the item. What is the cost of this policy?

REFERENCES FOR FURTHER READING

APICS (1971) Special Report: Materials Requirement Planning by Computer, American Production and Inventory Control Society, Falls Church, VA.

Hall, R. (1987) *Attaining Manufacturing Excellence*, Dow Jones–Irwin, Homewood, IL.

Love, S. (1979) *Inventory Control*, McGraw-Hill, New York.

Martin, A.J. (1983) *DRP: Distribution Resource Planning*, Prentice Hall, Englewood Cliffs, NJ.

New, C. (1974) *Requirements Planning*, Gower Press, London.

Orlicky, J. (1975) *Material Requirements Planning*, McGraw-Hill, New York.

Smolik, D.P. (1983) *Material Requirements of Manufacturing*, Van Nostrand Reinhold, New York.

Tomkins, J.A. and White, J.A. (1984) *Facilities Planning*, John Wiley, New York.

Vollmann, T.E., Berry, W.L. and Whybark, D.C. (1988) *Manufacturing Planning and Control Systems* (2nd edn), Irwin, Homewood, IL.

Wight, O.W. (1974) *Production and Inventory Management in the Computer Age*, Cahners Publishing, Boston, MA.

Wight, O.W. (1982) *The Executive's Guide to Successful MRP II*, Oliver Wight Publications, Williston, VT.

8

JUST-IN-TIME SYSTEMS

SYNOPSIS

Dependent demand inventory systems find the future demand for an item directly from a master schedule. Chapter 7 described how material requirements planning (MRP) controlled the stocks of materials needed to support production. This was based on an integrated computer system to control all aspects of production and inventory. In this chapter we will look at an alternative, simpler dependent demand system which is known as "just-in-time" (JIT).

The distinctive feature of just-in-time systems is the organisation of operations so that they occur just as they are needed. Stocks of materials, for example, arrive just as they are needed in production. This approach was pioneered in Japan where it is widely used in large-scale assembly. JIT may be a contributory factor in Japan's economic success, and this has encouraged considerable interest in the method.

The JIT view of stock is that it is a waste of resources whose main purpose is to hide the problems which occur in a process. A more satisfactory approach would be to identify and solve the problems, rather than hide them. The implication is that stocks should be eliminated or at least minimised. JIT has a number of prerequisites which limits its use, mainly to high-volume continuous processes. Even when it can be used, there are a number of factors to consider. One of these is the need for a simple control system to coordinate the movement of materials. Kanban provides this using a system of cards. Another problem with installing JIT is the difficulty of getting suppliers to adapt. Perhaps the most important factor, though, is the need for perfectly reliable quality. This has encouraged the development of total quality and quality at source.

When a successful JIT system is installed it can bring substantial benefits. There are, however, relatively few processes which are suited to JIT. Even when the right kind of process is used, JIT can only be implemented after a fundamental review of operations within an organisation. JIT is a simple idea, but implementing it is far from easy. One common belief is that JIT can be installed quickly, whereas it is really an iterative process which makes continuous improvements over a long period.

OBJECTIVES

After reading this chapter and completing the exercises you should be able to:

- discuss the approach of just-in-time systems
- appreciate the view of stock as a waste of resources which should be eliminated
- list the prerequisites before JIT can be used
- describe Kanban systems for controlling JIT
- appreciate the need for total quality and how quality assurance programmes achieve this
- discuss the relationships that JIT requires with suppliers
- discuss some effects of JIT systems on employees
- list the benefits and disadvantages of JIT
- make some comparisons with other methods of inventory control.

8.1   PRINCIPLES OF JUST-IN-TIME SYSTEMS

8.1.1   Background

In the past few years there has been considerable interest in just-in-time or JIT. This is an approach to manufacturing which can almost revolutionise the performance of an organisation. Consequently, almost every major company has shown interest in JIT and explored its potential. The main problem is that, like MRP, JIT can only be used in specific circumstances. Even when it can be used, there are many conditions to its use and the benefits often come after considerable effort.

Just-in-time methods were developed in Japan, primarily by Toyota. In essence, JIT refers to a system of production in which all operations occur just at the time they are needed. This means, for example, that if materials are needed for production, they are not bought some time in advance and kept in stock, but are delivered directly to the production process just as they are needed. The result is that stocks of materials are virtually eliminated.

In one sense this is not a new idea. In the 1920s iron ore arriving at Ford plants in Detroit was turned into steel within a day and into finished cars a few days later. This was seen as an efficient way of using resources and reducing stocks of work in progress. Unfortunately, most organisations did not follow this lead, and there has been a consistent belief that substantial stocks of work in progress are needed to ensure smooth operations. These large stocks mean that customer demand can be met, production continued without interruption, problems with breakdowns overcome, and so on.

This view that stocks are needed to provide a buffer between uncertain and variable supply and demand held from the 1920s to the 1980s. The proof of the system was that everybody seemed satisfied with the situation, so organisations were willing to pay the necessary price. Their inventory control was based on the question, "How can the buffer stock be provided at minimum cost?". During the past few years, however, some organisations changed their view and started asking another question, "How can the need for a buffer be eliminated?". The answer to this has laid the foundations of just-in-time.

The simplest view of JIT regards it as a way of reducing stock levels. It is, however, much more than this. Its supporters described as "a way of eliminating waste", or, "a way of enforced problem solving". It starts with a desire to eliminate all waste from an organisation. Stock holdings are seen as having no useful purpose and are, therefore, a waste of resources which should be eliminated. Then JIT looks for ways of operating without stocks. It identifies the problems which arise if there are no stocks, and looks for ways of overcoming these.

The reason that so much attention has been given to JIT is undoubtedly the success of Japanese manufacturing. Since the 1950s, Japan has been continuously increasing its share of world trade, and is now the dominant manufacturing economy. Some major Japanese companies use JIT, and if this has played even a small part in the success of Japanese industry it should be considered elsewhere.

The approach is known by different names, including "zero inventory", "stockless production", "Toyota system", "Japanese manufacturing", "world class manufacturing" and "continuous flow manufacturing".

In Summary

Just-in-time systems organise operations so that they occur just as they are needed. This approach was developed in Japan and may contribute to the success of her manufacturing industry.

8.1.2   Overall Approach of JIT

We will start describing JIT by looking at its effect on stocks. The main purpose of stock is to allow for short-term mismatches between supply and demand. Independent demand inventory systems allow for this mismatch by ensuring stocks are high enough to cover most expected demand. In some circumstances, however, notably the lumpy demand met in batch production, independent demand systems lead to excessively high stocks. MRP overcomes this problem by using the master schedule to match the supply of materials more closely to demand. The more closely supply can be matched to demand, the smaller are the stocks needed to cover any differences. It follows, then, that if the mismatch can be completely eliminated, so can stocks.

This is the basis of just-in-time systems. Their aim is to coordinate the flow of materials so that supply exactly matches demand. In essence, all materials are timed to arrive just as they are needed (see Figure 8.1).

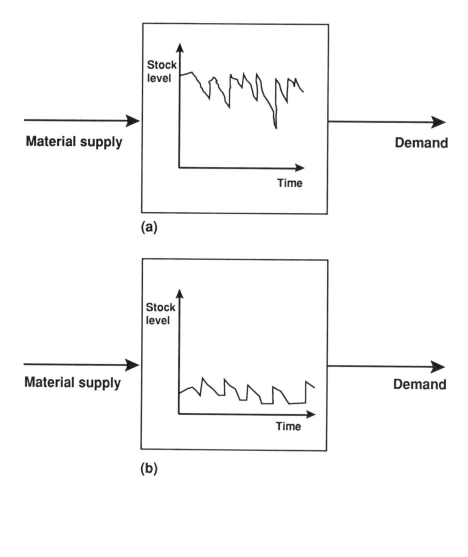

Figure 8.1 Comparison of stock levels with different control systems. (a) Independent demand system has high stocks to cover mismatch between supply and demand. (b) MRP system has lower stocks as the mismatch is reduced. (c) JIT has no stocks as the mismatch is eliminated

> The aim of just-in-time is to coordinate activities so they occur just as they are needed. By matching the supply of materials exactly to demand, stocks can be eliminated.

An analogy for this is someone buying fuel for their lawnmower. If the lawnmower has a petrol engine there is a mismatch between fuel supply (petrol bought from a garage) and demand (when the lawn is being mowed), so stocks of fuel have to be kept in a petrol tank and spare can. If the lawnmower has an electric motor the supply of electricity is exactly matched to demand and no stocks are needed. The petrol engine uses an independent demand system, while the electric motor uses a JIT system. At one level JIT can be viewed as a system for controlling stocks, but it has a much wider impact than this. JIT really involves a change in the way an organisation views its operations. The basis of this view is that all wastage of resources should be eliminated. In particular, stock holdings are seen as a resource which serves no useful purpose. They should, therefore, be eliminated or at least minimised.

JIT now seems a simple idea, and we can summarise its main argument as follows.

> - Stocks are held in an organisation to cover short-term variation and uncertainty in supply and demand.
> - JIT systems assume these stocks serve no useful purpose. They only exist because poor coordination does not match the supply of materials to demand.
> - As long as stocks are held, organisations will continue to be poorly organised and many associated problems will be hidden.
> - The proper thing for an organisation to do is improve its performance, find the reasons why there are differences between supply and demand, and then take whatever action is necessary to overcome them.

JIT believes that stock is only held for negative reasons. In other words it is used to allow for poor coordination and management. The implication is that an organisation has a series of problems which hinder the smooth flow of materials. These problems include long equipment set-up times, unbalanced operations, constrained capacity, machine breakdowns, defective materials, interrupted operations, and so on. Stock is held to avoid the effects of these problems and effectively hide them from sight. A much more constructive approach would be to identify the hidden problems and solve them. This approach leads to a number of changes in viewpoint, which we can illustrate by the following examples.

- Organisations have traditionally specified acceptable levels of quality for their products. This usually defines some arbitrary figure like "3 defective units or less in a batch of 100 means product quality is acceptable". JIT recognises that all defects have costs and it is cheaper to prevent these from ever happening than to correct them later. In other words, it aims for perfect quality with no defects.
- Suppliers and customers are seen as competing, so that one can only benefit at the expense of the other. JIT recognises that customers and suppliers are partners with a common objective and they should work closely together to achieve this.
- Sometimes there is an entirely unprofitable friction between "managers" and "workers". JIT recognises that this is a meaningless distinction as the welfare of all employees depends on the success of the organisation. All employees are, therefore, treated with respect.
- When a production machine breaks down the usual practice is either to continue operations and build up a stock of work in progress before the broken machine, or to transfer production to another product. JIT is based on continuous, uninterrupted production which does not allow this kind of flexibility. It recognises there is a problem with the reliability of a machine, the reasons for the breakdown are identified, and actions taken to ensure these do not occur again.

Now JIT can be seen not just as a means of minimising stocks, but as a whole way of viewing operations. Its overall aim is to minimise waste by identifying and solving all problems which occur in a process. It achieves this by organising operations so that they occur at just the time they are needed.

There is one other key element in JIT. It also regards effort put into administrations as an overhead which is largely wasted. Then it tries to simplify operations and systems so that the effort needed to control them is minimised. JIT systems are largely manual with little paperwork or decisions made away from the shop floor. This is in marked contrast to MRP systems which are computerised, expensive to control, and centred around decisions made by planners who are some distance from the shop floor.

This aim of simplicity means that the methods used by JIT are all practical and based largely on common sense. Thus plant layouts are simplified, routine maintenance of equipment is scheduled to avoid breakdowns, everyone is trained in quality control to reduce the number of defects, simpler designs are used to reduce processing time, set-up procedures are changed to reduce their time, reorder costs are reduced to allow smaller deliveries, suppliers are encouraged to make more frequent deliveries, and so on. These changes have major effects on operations, so they cannot be introduced in one go, but evolve with small continuous improvements over a long period. Toyota, for example, is reputed to have made continuous improvements in some of its operations over a period of 25 years. Now that other organisations can use Toyota's experience, they may be able to reduce this time to, say, ten years.

We can now see one reason why there is misunderstanding about JIT. It is based on simple ideas. However, there is an apparent contradiction in that the simple ideas are very difficult to implement. Getting materials to arrive just as they are needed is a simple idea, but is very difficult to achieve. Similarly, avoiding disruptions by ensuring perfect quality is a simple idea, but again is very difficult to achieve. Perhaps the key element in achieving them is the time scale. As we said above, JIT generally evolves over time so that stock is reduced and quality improved in a series of small steps.

In Summary

A fundamental idea in just-in-time systems is the elimination of waste. Stocks are seen as a waste of resources which should be eliminated. A key element in this approach is the identification of problems and their solution, often in small steps over a long time.

8.1.3   Key Elements in JIT Systems

When it is working properly, JIT can bring considerable benefits to an organisation. The elimination, or at least minimisation, of stock can alone bring substantial savings, but this is only one of the benefits (which are discussed in more detail later). Encouraged by the potential savings, many organisations have considered the introduction of JIT. Unfortunately, this is not easy and JIT can only be used in particular types of organisation. We noted that MRP was only really effective in batch manufacturing industries. JIT is even more specialised and can only really be used in large-scale assembly. At present, the most successful users of JIT are car-assembly plants which make large numbers of identical products in a continuous process. We can say, then, that the operations within an organisation must have several characteristics before JIT can be considered.

- Every time that production is changed from one item to another there are delays, disruptions and costs. JIT suggests that these changes waste resources and should be eliminated. The implication is that JIT needs a stable environment where production of an item remains at a fixed level for some time. Standard products are emphasised with few variations offered.
- This kind of stable environment allows costs to be reduced by using specialised automation. The fixed costs of this can be recovered with high production volumes. The implication is that JIT systems work best with high-volume assembly line operations.
- The specified production level must allow a smooth and continuous flow of products through the process. Each part of the process must be fully utilised

and not leave resources under-used. In other words, careful planning is needed to ensure the assembly line is balanced.

- Deliveries of materials are made at just the time they are needed. Suppliers must, therefore, be able to adapt to this kind of operation. It would be impracticable to bring each individual unit from suppliers, so the next best thing is to use very small batches (avoiding the higher stocks given by larger batches).
- If small batches are used, reorder costs must be reduced as much as possible or the frequent deliveries would be prohibitively expensive. This is a key part of the JIT process. Other inventory control systems assume the reorder cost is fixed, while JIT looks at the problem of supplying small batches and finds ways of reducing the associated costs.
- Lead times (or set-up times) must be short or the delay in responding to a request for materials is too long. Again, traditional inventory control systems assume that lead times are fixed, while JIT sees long lead times as a problem which must be solved. This inevitably involves working closely with suppliers.
- Materials only arrive just as they are needed. If any are defective, there are no stocks to provide cover and production is disrupted. Suppliers must, therefore, be totally reliable and provide materials which are free from defects.
- If something goes wrong and there is a disruption, the workforce must be able to find out what happened, take the action necessary to correct it, and ensure that it does not happen again. This needs a skilled and flexible workforce which is committed to the success of the organisation.

If we continued arguing in this way we could draw up a list of the key elements in a JIT system. They include:

- a stable environment
- standard products with few variations
- continuous production at fixed levels
- automated, high-volume operations
- a balanced process which uses resources fully
- reliable production equipment
- minimum stocks
- small batches of materials
- short lead times for materials
- low set-up and delivery costs
- efficient materials handling
- reliable suppliers
- consistently high quality of materials
- flexible workforce
- fair treatment and rewards for employees
- ability to solve any problems
- an efficient method of control
- and so on.

Although it is a simple idea, it is clear that the introduction of JIT has a widespread effect in an organisation. Everything is changed, from the way that goods are ordered to the role of people on the shop floor. It is, therefore, a step which needs total commitment from all the workforce at all levels. The result is a completely different view of operations.

In Summary

Not every organisation can use JIT. There are several conditions which must be met before JIT becomes possible, and these usually limit its use to certain types of large-scale production. When implemented properly, JIT brings fundamental changes to an organisation.

SELF-ASSESSMENT QUESTIONS

8.1 How are the basic questions asked by JIT systems fundamentally different from those asked by other inventory control systems?

8.2 JIT is a system for controlling stocks. Is this statement:
(a) true?
(b) false?
(c) partly true?

8.3 What are the main characteristic of a JIT system?

8.4 How does JIT view stocks?

8.5 What type of process is JIT most suited to?

8.6 JIT principles cannot be used for small service operations. Is this statement true or false?

8.2 ACHIEVING JUST-IN-TIME OPERATIONS

Just-in-time systems try to eliminate all wastage within an organisation. Their aim is to meet production targets using the minimum amount of materials, with the minimum amount of equipment, the smallest number of operators, and so on. Their way of doing this is to ensure all operations are done at just the time they are needed.

Now, having described these foundations of JIT systems, we can look in more detail at how their objectives are achieved. Having said, for example, that JIT systems organise materials to arrive just as they are needed, we must suggest ways in which this can be arranged.

8.2.1 Kanban—Control of JIT Systems

The principles of JIT may appear attractive, but it can only be used if there is some practical way of implementing and controlling the system. In other words, there must be some means of ensuring that materials do actually arrive just as they are needed. We have also said that this method of control should be simple, and preferably manual. One way of doing this is based on Kanbans. This method was developed by Toyota and is sometimes called the Toyota or Japanese production system.

"Kanban" is the Japanese for visible record, or card. The basis of the system is that materials are moved in containers, with movements controlled by Kanbans which are attached to the containers. The Kanbans are typically plastic cards which describe the materials in the container, the quantity, the source and destination of movements, and any other relevant information.

The use of Kanbans is based on a "pull" from later stages in a process demanding materials. This "pull" approach of JIT can be contrasted with the "push" of materials in other systems. An analogy compares the flow of materials through a process to a piece of string. If the string is pulled, it moves smoothly and without problems; if the string is pushed, it lies in a heap and gets tangled.

Traditionally, each work station in a process is assigned a timetable of work which it must finish 'in a specified period. Finished items are then "pushed" through to form a stock of work in progress in front of the next work station. This ignores what the next station is actually doing. It might be working on something completely different or be waiting for a different item to arrive. At best, the second work station must finish its current job before it can start working on the new material just passed to it. The result is delays and increased stock of work in progress. If there are serious imbalances or disruptions to production these stocks become substantial.

JIT uses a "pull" system, where a work station continues its operations until it needs more materials, at which point it sends a request to the preceding work station. When it receives this request, the preceding work station starts producing the materials. In practice, there must be some lead time, so requests for materials are passed backwards the lead time before they are actually needed. In principle, this eliminates stocks of work in progress. In practice, however, materials are delivered in small batches rather than continuous amounts. This means that some stock of work in progress is still kept, but this is very little compared with alternative "push" systems (see Figure 8.2). It would, though, be more accurate to say that JIT minimises stocks of work in progress rather than eliminates them.

Kanban systems provide a mechanism for coordinating the flow of materials for JIT pull operations. They use simple cards to arrange the movement and production of materials. There are several ways in which Kanbans can be used, with the simplest system as follows (see Figure 8.3).

- All material is stored and moved in standard containers. A container can only be moved when it has a Kanban attached to it.
- When a work station needs more materials (i.e. when its stock of materials falls to some predetermined reorder level) a Kanban is attached to an empty

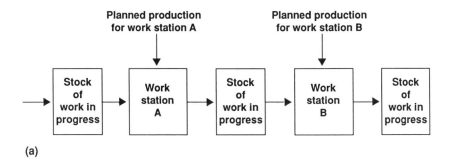

(a)

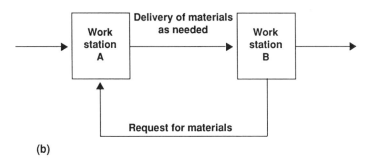

(b)

Figure 8.2 Comparison of "push" and "pull" control systems. (a) Traditional "push" system where plans are used to control operations at each work station. (b) JIT "pull" system where requests from following work stations are used for control

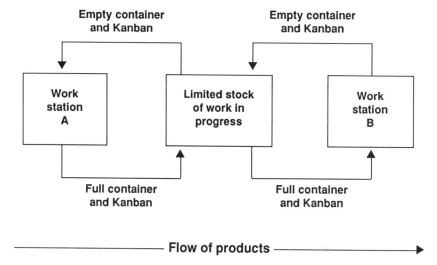

Figure 8.3 A single Kanban system with two work stations

container and this is taken to the preceding work station. The Kanban is then attached to a full container, which is returned to the work station.

- The empty container is a signal for the preceding work station to start work on this material, and it produces just enough to refill the container.

This single Kanban system has obvious similarities with a fixed order quantity independent demand system. However, there are a number of distinct features.

- The main point is that the message is passed *backwards* to the preceding work station to start production, and it only makes enough to fill a container.
- Standard containers are used which hold a specific quantity. This is usually quite small, and is typically 10% of a day's requirements.
- The size of each container is the smallest reasonable batch which can be produced and there are usually only one or two full containers at any point.
- A specific number of containers and/or Kanbans is used.
- The stock of work in progress can be controlled by limiting the size of containers and the number of Kanbans.
- Materials can only be moved in containers, and containers can only be moved when they have a Kanban attached. This gives a rigid means of controlling the amount of materials produced and time they are moved.
- While it is simple to administer, this system ensures stocks of work in progress cannot accumulate.

One obvious problem is that operations must be perfectly balanced, with the output from each work station exactly matching the requirements of following stations. If there is any imbalance some equipment will remain idle until it is called on to start production. This reduces utilisation and increases costs. In practice, this problem is met in all operations and is by no means unique to JIT systems. However, with its emphasis on solving problems, JIT would consider any imbalance to be unacceptable and would find ways of eliminating it.

Although the single-card Kanban is simple and easy to implement, a slightly more complex system is usually recommended. This uses two distinct types of card:

- a production Kanban
- a movement Kanban

Control is then achieved by the following procedure.

- When a work station needs more materials a movement Kanban is put on an empty container. This gives permission to take the container to an area where work in progress is kept.
- A full container is then found, which will have a production Kanban attached.
- The production Kanban is removed and put on an empty container. This gives

permission for the preceding work station to produce enough to replace the container of materials.

- A movement Kanban is put on the full container, giving permission to take it back to the work station.

This process is summarised in Figure 8.4.

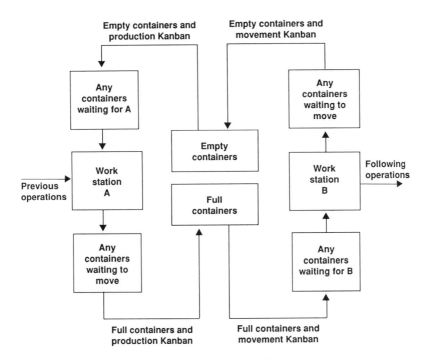

Figure 8.4 A two-card Kanban system with two work stations

There are, of course, many variations on these schemes. Some systems use different Kanbans for emergency requests, high-priority needs, materials requested from suppliers, signals for batch processes to start, and so on. Whatever the differences in detail, each system has the essential characteristic that it allows a signal between one stage in a process and the previous stage to show when it is time to start producing an item.

Although the system illustrated has a stock of work in progress, this stock is small and may be very short-term. When a full container is removed, it is usually the only container in stock, and is not replaced until the previous work station produces the item. Similarly, the description of moving to the store of work in progress is misleading. JIT operations almost always use a product layout, which is typified by assembly lines. Then the small stocks of work in progress are kept as part of the line, and there is no actual movement.

Each container in use has a Kanban attached to it. Therefore, the number of Kanbans effectively sets the amount of work in progress. Suppose, for example, there is only one production Kanban. Then the stock of work in progress is limited to at most one container of items. Conversely, if there is a large number of Kanbans, then there may be quite high stocks. JIT will clearly aim to set the number of Kanbans to the minimum which allows continued smooth production.

Suppose demand for an item is D per unit of time. Each container holds C units of an item (and as a guideline the value of C should be below 10% of expected daily demand). Each container spends:

- a time TP in a production part of a cycle (waiting, being filled and moving to the store of work in progress)
- a time TD in a demand part of a cycle (waiting, being emptied and moving to the store of work in progress)

Then the total cycle length is $TP + TD$ and the number of Kanbans to maintain smooth operations is:

$$\text{number of Kanbans} = \frac{\text{demand in the cycle}}{\text{size of each container}}$$

$$K = \frac{D * (TP + TD)}{C}$$

where: K = number of Kanbans
D = average demand per unit time
TP = time in production part of cycle
TD = time in demand part of cycle
C = capacity of each container

Any number of Kanbans used above this adds an element of safety. Thus, when a new JIT system is installed, some flexibility may be kept by having a fairly large number of Kanbans. Over time, however, JIT will look for continuous improvements, so that when the system is working properly there will be fewer Kanbans. As a guide, the maximum element of safety should be less than 10% so that:

$$K < \frac{D * (TP + TD) * (1 + SF)}{C}$$

where SF is a safety factor of less than 0.1. Then the maximum stock of work in progress is held in K containers, each with capacity C, so:

$$\text{maximum stock level} = K * C = D * (TP + TD) * (1 + SF)$$

We can see from this equation that the only way in which *no* stock can be held is to have either the demand, D, equal to zero or the cycle time $(TP + TD)$. Hence, as we said before, JIT minimises stocks of work in progress but does not eliminate them.

Worked Example 8.1

Demand for an item is 100 units an hour. The item is moved in containers which hold 10 units. Each container spends an average of 15 minutes in the production part of a cycle, and 30 minutes in the demand part.

- How many Kanbans should be used to control stocks of the item without any safety factor?
- What is the resulting stock of work in progress?
- A scheme has been proposed which reduces the time in the demand part of the cycle to 20 minutes. If a safety factor of 10% is added during initial operations, how many Kanbans are needed?

Solution

The figures given, in consistent units, are:

D = 100 units an hour
TP = 0.25 hours
TD = 0.5 hours
C = 10 units

With no margin for safety the number of Kanbans needed is:

$$K = \frac{D * (TP + TD)}{C}$$
$$= \frac{100 * (0.25 + 0.5)}{10}$$
$$= 7.5 \text{ which must be rounded to 8 Kanbans}$$

This gives a stock of work in progress of:

$$K * C = 8 * 10 = 80 \text{ units of the item}$$

Reducing TD to 20 minutes, and adding a 10% safety margin gives:

$$K = \frac{D * (TP + TD) * SF}{C}$$

$$= \frac{100 * (0.25 + 0.33) * 1.1}{10}$$

$$= 6.38 \text{ or } 7 \text{ Kanbans}$$

This gives a stock of work in progress of:

$$K * C = 7 * 10 = 70 \text{ units}$$

One further element in the control of JIT systems comes into play when things go wrong. Associated with JIT, there is often a system called Andon. This is the mechanism which allows operators more control over a process when problems occur. It essentially has three signals, often coloured lights, above each work station:

- a green signal shows that the station is working as planned
- an amber signal shows the work station is falling a bit behind
- a red signal shows a serious problems

These allow everyone to see where problems are growing, and to look for ways of solving them before they get too serious.

This discussion of Kanban shows how material flow can be organised within a process. It might be suggested that using a similar system with external suppliers would be more difficult. JIT, does not, however, see this as a problem, as discussed in the following section.

In Summary

JIT requires a simple means of controlling the supply of materials in a process. Kanban is one way of doing this, using cards to signal the pull of demand from later work stations to earlier ones.

8.2.2   Relations with Suppliers

Traditionally there has been some friction between suppliers and customers. Because one pays money directly to the other, there is a common belief that one can only benefit at the expense of the other. Suppliers are often rigid in their conditions and, as there is little customer loyalty, they try to make as much profit as possible from each sale. Customers on the other hand shop around to make sure they get the best deal, and remind suppliers of the competition; they are only concerned with their own objectives and will, when convenient to them, change specifications and conditions at short notice. The result is uncertainty among suppliers about items being ordered, the size of likely orders, the time when orders will be placed, the possibility of repeat orders, and so on.

JIT recognises that customers and suppliers have the same objective, which is a mutually beneficial trading arrangement. The primary requirement, then, is for an organisation to find a single supplier who can best meet their conditions. These conditions are quite demanding and include items of perfectly reliable quality, with small frequent deliveries and at reasonable cost. In return for meeting these conditions, organisations with JIT use single-sourcing. This means they buy each item exclusively from one supplier and agree long-term contracts to ensure stability. At one point, after Toyota had introduced JIT, they were using 250 suppliers, while General Motors, who had not yet introduced JIT, were using around 4000.

JIT recognises the importance of stability to suppliers. It knows that they are geared to work with present operations and any changes will inevitably cause disruption. Moreover, their own suppliers are in turn affected by changes, and so on down the supply chain. A small change in the finished product may have considerable effects on earlier suppliers. JIT considers such changes to be inefficient, so it relies on a product which remains largely unchanged throughout long production runs.

The stability allowed by long production runs gives considerable benefits to suppliers. They can specialise in one type of item, and may reduce their product range and number of customers. This leads many suppliers to JIT operations to become "focused factories". A focused factory is a small plant which concentrates almost entirely on making one product, but aims to make this very well and very efficiently. Because they are small, focused factories are easier to manage than large, general-purpose factories. Moreover, they can use specialised equipment, which means that production is very efficient.

The alternative to focused factories is general-purpose ones which adjust their operations to make the parts which are needed at the moment. These have general, non-specialised equipment which needs adjusting and setting up for each new item, and the layout of equipment will be inefficient. Typically, 90% of an item's production time in such factories is spent waiting or being moved. General-purpose factories are also larger and more complicated, so they are more difficult to manage, more expensive to run and less efficient.

JIT aims for closer cooperation between a customer and its suppliers. This cooperation can be used to help suppliers adapt to the requirements of JIT, and even install JIT in their own operations. It also allows suppliers to make suggestions for improvements to customers, without the fear that their future profits will be reduced. Ideally, suppliers become a part of an extended JIT system. Suppose Work Station A in Figure 8.3 or 8.4 is a supplier, then we can see how it can become part of the JIT system (see Figure 8.5). Whenever the customer needs some material it sends a vehicle with containers and Kanbans to the supplier. The vehicle delivers empty containers and exchanges them for full ones from the supplier's stock of finished goods. The Kanbans are then transferred to the full containers, which are delivered to the customer. The supplier now has empty containers, which give a signal that

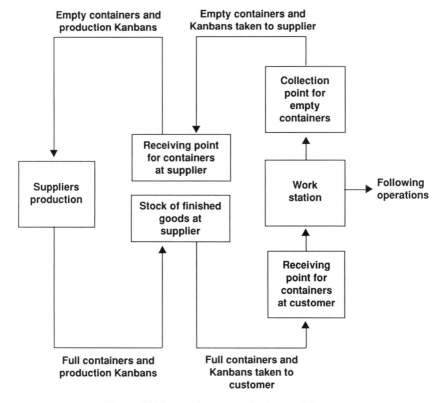

Figure 8.5 Integrating a supplier into a JIT system

it is time to replace the contents. As before, many variations on this basic scheme are possible.

Despite the close relationships with suppliers, most will, in practice, have to maintain a number of customers with different types of operation. This means that some compromise is needed on both sides to avoid any possible disagreements.

In Summary

JIT encourages close contacts between customers and suppliers. It sees them as partners who must cooperate to obtain mutual benefits. This often leads to the development of specialised suppliers and focused factories.

SELF-ASSESSMENT QUESTIONS

8.7   What is the purpose of Kanban?

8.8   How is the amount of work in progress limited using Kanban?

8.9   What is the JIT view of the relationship between customers and suppliers?

8.10 Why would JIT systems expect to be supplied by focused factories?

8.2.3   Jidoka—Quality at Source

An important requirement of JIT is that materials must be delivered with perfect quality. When materials are only delivered as they are needed any defect will disrupt the process. There are two ways of avoiding this.

- Firstly, the organisation could accept the possibility of defects and check the quality of all items as they arrive. This is, however, wasteful and it destroys many of the benefits JIT is aiming for.
- The alternative is to ensure that all items arriving are of perfect quality. This is clearly the better alternative and is the one adopted by JIT.

Traditionally manufacturers have accepted a certain proportion of deliveries as defective. Typically, suppliers would quote a maximum percentage of defective units in their supplies. A high-quality product might have less than 1% of units unsatisfactory, while a lower-quality product might have over 3% defective. Sometimes, suppliers would compensate for defects by giving an amount of "overage" as an implicit statement that they could not guarantee quality. Until recently everyone seemed to accept this situation. It was implicitly agreed that production was not perfect and quality control methods could not detect all the defective units made. Therefore some defects were inevitable and customers would have to accept this. The number of defects might be improved by better production or quality checks, but this would inevitably increase costs.

The problem with this approach is that even low defective rates are not good enough for JIT operations. This situation has been met for some time by organisations which must ensure their products are of perfect quality. In the late 1950s, for example, the Martin Corporation was building Pershing missiles and was looking for ways of completely eliminating defects from their production. Similarly, manufacturers of artificial heart valves tried to ensure their products were uniformly perfect. Adding more inspections has only a limited effect, and confirmed the well-known saying, "You cannot inspect quality into a product". The solution is to use an approach to quality assurance which is fundamentally different from the statistical testing of finished products which has become universally accepted. The details of the solution were, however, largely to come from Japan.

One simple observation points the way to an improved means of quality assurance. This notes that the longer a unit stays in a process, the more money is spent on it. If a fault is introduced to a unit but the unit continues through its process, all subsequent work on it is wasted. This suggests that the cheapest way of ensuring quality is to detect any faults as soon as they occur, rather than doing more work on a defective unit and then finding the fault at a later inspection. JIT took this one step further, and suggested that even more money could be saved by finding out why faults occurred, and then taking whatever steps to prevent them ever happening. It transferred the effort in quality assurance away from detecting faults, and towards ensuring faults do not develop in the first place. This is the basis of "quality at source". The principles have become known by a number of names including total quality control (TQC), Jidoka, 100% quality assurance, quality engineering, and so on.

The cost of quality assurance can be divided into four categories:

- *Prevention*, which includes all the work aimed at ensuring faults do not occur in an item.
- *Appraisal*, which is the cost of inspections and checks to find any faults which do occur, or to confirm there are no faults.
- *Internal failure*, which is the cost of finding a defect in a unit while it is still in the plant.
- *External failure*, which is the cost of shipping a defective unit to a customer and then having to correct it.

Quality at source works on the principle that an increase in the cost of prevention and appraisal is more than covered by a reduction in the cost of internal and external failures (see Figure 8.6).

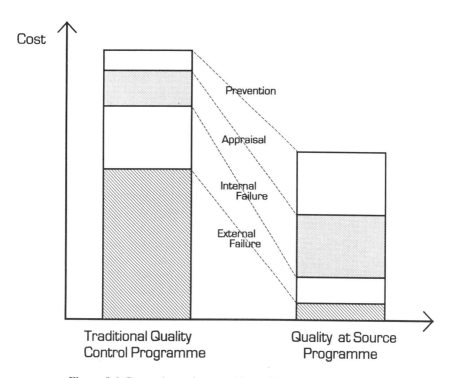

Figure 8.6 Comparison of costs with quality assurance programme

Traditionally, organisations have used a separate quality control department to inspect the work of production departments. Quality at source moves away from this separation of duties, and towards a general quality assurance programme which is integrated with other functions in the organisation. In particular, production departments are made responsible for their own quality. This transfer of responsibility does not simply mean that different people do the same inspections. It is part of a wider programme which involves a different attitude to quality.

Quality at source starts with each person in the production process being responsible for passing on only goods which are of perfect quality to following operations. This is sometimes described as "job enlargement" as each person is now responsible for both his or her previous job and an inherent quality assurance function. As part of this change people should now be rewarded for achieving high quality when they have previously been rewarded for high volumes, often with little regard to quality. This is a key point for management. Traditionally organisations have tried to improve productivity, which was viewed simply as a ratio of output to inputs (units produced per employee, for example). Now the suggestion is that any measure of productivity should include an element of quality to record how good the production has been.

One consequence of quality at source, which is also inherent in JIT, is that any faults are seen as symptoms of something going wrong. Then everyone involved in production has authority to stop the process and investigate a fault. The reason for the fault is found, and suggestions made for ensuring the same fault does not occur again. This compares with traditional practices which only stop production as a last resort, by which time the causes of a problem may have become severe.

The main factors which are needed for successful quality at source are listed below. Many of these ideas are not new, but have been promoted by various people (including Deming (1988)) for the past 40 years or so.

- Top management must be committed to achieving high quality.
- The organisation must adopt a long-term approach to improving quality.
- It must persist despite short-term problems.
- Managers must clearly state their quality objectives and what must be done to achieve them.
- Do not accept the view that there must inevitably be some defects.
- Do not accept the cheapest materials, but insist on their being of high quality.
- Do not emphasise output at the expense of quality.
- Use statistical methods to identify sources of poor quality.
- Encourage discussion of ways to improve quality (including suggestion boxes and quality circles).
- Be open to suggestions for improvement.
- Make sure everyone is properly trained to do his or her job.
- Improve supervision.
- Do not use arbitrary numerical targets.
- Encourage a "do it right first time" approach.

Worked Example 8.2

Two years ago a company introduced a new quality assurance programme. The expenditure (in thousands of pounds) on quality assurance over the past four years have been as given in Table 8.1.

Table 8.1

Year	1	2	3	4
Sales	2846	2785	3103	3543
Prevention	12	13	45	42
Appraisal	25	30	93	90
Internal failure	106	110	35	33
External failure	125	136	54	27

Has the quality assurance programme been successful?

Solution

A quick look at the costs of quality assurance show that the costs have reduced from £268 000 in year 1 to £192 000 in year 4 despite an increase of 24% in sales. This suggests the quality assurance programme has been a financial success. It may also be a reason for increasing sales.

A more objective judgement can be made by calculating the cost of quality as a proportion of sales. Table 8.2 shows the cost of quality assurance per thousand pounds of sales. The quality assurance cost per thousand pounds of sales has almost halved over the four years, while its main thrust has moved towards prevention and appraisal.

Table 8.2

Year	1	2	3	4
Prevention	4.22	4.67	14.50	11.85
Appraisal	8.78	10.77	29.97	25.40
Internal failure	37.25	39.50	11.28	9.31
External failure	43.92	48.83	17.40	7.62
Total	94.17	103.77	73.15	54.18

In Summary

JIT systems demand materials of perfect quality. In recent years organisations have become increasingly aware of the importance of quality. In particular, there has been a realisation that improving quality can reduce costs. Programmes like "quality at source" aim at preventing defective units from being made rather than detecting defects which are already there.

8.2.4 Respect for Employees

We have mentioned several times the kind of relationship JIT expects with employees. Quality at source, for example, expects employees to be responsible for their own quality. At the same time JIT gives each employee the authority to stop a process if they see a fault, everyone is expected to suggest ways of improving operations, and so on. It is worth mentioning this relationship again.

Japanese companies generally offer their employees a job for life. In return an employee is expected to stay with the same organisation for his or her entire working life. This is one aspect of a wider feature in Japanese industry, that companies consider their employees as their most important resource, and the most important part of their operations.

The respect for employees is particularly relevant to JIT, where it has a number of consequences. There has traditionally been some friction between "managers" and "workers" in an organisation. This comes about as managers are judged and rewarded for the performance of the organisation and this performance is often measured by profit. Conversely, workers are not rewarded for performance, but their wages are seen as a drain on profits. JIT suggests that all employees are concerned with the success of an organisation, and they should, therefore, all be treated equally. One aspect of this is that, by ensuring they all have a share in profits, employees are all rewarded for the organisation's performance.

Another aspect of this respect for employees is the approach to improving a process. In many organisations, management look for improvements while they work in isolation away from the details of the process, or they employ consultants who have little knowledge of the operations. JIT suggests that the best people to suggest improvements are those who actually work on the process. Thus JIT inevitably has suggestion boxes, with rewards for people offering good ideas. A more formal approach for getting suggestions is to use quality circles. A quality circle is an informal group of people who are involved in a particular operation. They meet once or twice a month to discuss ways in which their operation can be improved.

JIT's use of automation can also be seen as evidence of the respect for employees, although this is more debatable. One view suggests that JIT encourages automation because it is more reliable and cheaper for the high-volume processes used. Another view is that some jobs are so boring, repetitive and unsatisfying that they should not be done by humans if there is any alternative. Robots and computer-controlled machines can do most of the tedious work in assembly lines, and this should be automated as a matter of principle.

In return for their respect, organisations using JIT demand more from their employees. When, for example, operators are given authority to stop a process, it is assumed they will then actively try and solve the problem which led to the stoppage. Again, the job enhancement implicit in quality at source requires everyone to be responsible for the quality of his or her own work. In essence, there is a devolution of responsibility from managers working at a distance, to people working on the shop floor. There is also an explicit requirement of flexibility to do a variety of jobs, willingness to adapt to new practices, possession of relevant skills and knowledge, active participation in the running of the organisation, interest in its continuing success, and so on.

One problem with JIT which is only recently getting attention is the increased stress it can put on the workforce. There is some evidence that employees who work on JIT assembly lines are subject to higher levels of stress than those who work on traditional lines. More work is needed in this area, but even a suggestion of dissatisfaction in the workforces runs contrary to JIT principles.

In Summary

JIT requires employees to be treated with respect. In return, it needs a workforce that is dedicated to the success of their organisation.

SELF-ASSESSMENT QUESTIONS

8.11 What is the basis of quality at source?
8.12 Higher quality can only be achieved at higher price. Is this statement true or false?
8.13 How might the costs of quality assurance be categorised?
8.14 Because JIT relies on automated processes, it puts less emphasis on the skills of individuals. Is this statement
      (a) true?
      (b) false?
      (c) partly true?

8.3   BENEFITS AND DISADVANTAGES OF JIT

When viewed as a means of inventory control, the major advantage of just-in-time is its dramatic reduction of stocks of raw materials and work in progress. Some companies have reported reductions of more than 75% of these stocks. This leads directly to a number of other advantages, such as reductions in space needed, lower warehousing costs, less investment in stocks, and so on. Other benefits of JIT come from the reorganisation necessary to get a working system. Several of these have already been mentioned, including:

- reduced lead times
- shorter time needed to make a product
- increased productivity
- increased equipment utilisation
- simplified planning and scheduling

- reduced paperwork
- improved quality of materials and products
- reduction in scrap and wastage
- improved morale in the workforce
- improved relations with suppliers
- emphasis on solving problems in production
- and so on

Some of these benefits can only be bought at a high price. Ensuring high-quality products with few interruptions by breakdowns, for example, implicitly means that better equipment must be used. Similarly, reduction in set-up times is usually achieved by using more sophisticated equipment. This equipment must respond quickly to changing demands, so there must be enough capacity. The result is that JIT can only work if organisations buy better and higher-capacity equipment. Many smaller companies have found the cost of this investment prohibitively expensive, particularly if the costs of training all employees is added. Although the long-term rewards may be high, the short-term costs of JIT can be too high for many organisations to consider.

In addition to the benefits there are, of course, some disadvantages with JIT. We have just mentioned that it may be expensive to implement and may involve many years of slow progress. Its inflexibility is another weakness. It is difficult to change product design, mix or demand levels, so it does not work well when, for example, there are irregularly used parts or specially ordered materials. Seasonal variations in demand also cause problems with seasonal variations. There are usually four ways of overcoming these.

- Stocks of finished goods may be built up when demand is low and used when demand is high. This option is, of course, contrary to JIT principles.
- Production can be changed to match demand. Again these changes are contrary to JIT principles.
- Demand can be smoothed out by pricing policies. In particular, discounts or other offers can be given during periods of low demand.
- The delivery time promised to customers can be adjusted. Customers can be asked to wait longer for deliveries when demand is high, with the backlog being cleared when demand falls.

None of these options is entirely satisfactory, but JIT systems must be made flexible enough to deal with some variation in demand.

Some of the benefits of JIT may also be seen as disadvantages. Having frequent set-ups and small batches, for example, is essential for JIT, but unless care is taken this can lead to high reorder costs. Similarly, JIT requires decisions to be made on the shop floor. This devolved decision making, with responsibility given to lower levels in the workforce, may be considered an advantage or a disadvantage depending on viewpoint.

Some specific problem areas identified by JIT users include:

- initial investment needed and cost of implementing programmes
- time needed to generate improvements (compared with repayment period of capital)
- reliance on perfect quality of materials from suppliers
- problems with maintaining product quality
- inability of suppliers to adapt to JIT methods
- need for stable production
- changing customer schedules
- variable demand from customers
- demand for a variety of options with products
- slowness of reaction to changes in products
- difficulty of reducing set-up times
- lack of commitment within the organisation
- lack of cooperation and trust between employees
- problems with linking to existing information systems
- need to change layout of facilities
- increased stress in workforce

Perhaps one disadvantage of JIT is its deceptive simplicity. This has led many organisations to try and introduce it without any understanding of its underlying principles. Some companies have tried to add some elements of JIT into an existing operation. In extreme cases of misunderstanding a note has been circulated simply stating, "The company is adopting JIT principles by eliminating stocks of work in progress over the next two months, so please change your practices accordingly". It must be emphasised that JIT, in its full sense, is an approach which needs a complete change of attitudes and operations within an organisation. Its successful introduction is likely to take several years of careful planning and controlled implementation.

JIT can bring substantial benefits to an organisation which is involved in large-scale manufacturing. Perhaps the best examples of its use are found in car-assembly plants. Before these benefits can be gained, however, there are considerable problems to overcome. Ultimately, the largest of these is the adoption of practices which are radically different from existing ones.

In Summary

Just-in-time systems can bring considerable advantages. Some of these come directly from the procedures used, while others are indirect results of the reorganisation. A successful system requires careful planning and implementation.

8.4   COMPARISONS WITH OTHER INVENTORY CONTROL SYSTEMS

At first sight JIT seems radically different from the other inventory control systems we have described.

- Independent demand systems, and to a lesser extent MRP, work within an existing organisation, while JIT says that major changes are needed before a system can be introduced.
- Most independent demand inventory systems use computers, while MRP is only feasible if considerable computing resources are available. JIT, on the other hand, simplifies operations to eliminate computers from day-to-day operations.
- Quantitative models assume that some values, such as lead time and reorder cost, are fixed, while JIT assumes these can be altered.

Despite these differences JIT systems have several points in common with other inventory control systems. Systems based on the economic order quantity, for example, monitor stock level and place an order of fixed size whenever this declines to the reorder level. If this procedure is compared with a Kanban system, there are clear similarities. Kanban also monitors stock continuously and when it declines to a predefined level gives a signal for replenishment with a fixed quantity. The major difference is that Kanban systems assume each withdrawal reduces stock to its reorder level, so that replenishments occur after each withdrawal.

There are also similarities between JIT and MRP systems. They are, for example, both dependent demand systems, where demand for materials is found directly from production schedules. There are, however, a number of contrasts.

- JIT is a manual system, while MRP relies on computers
- JIT is purely a "pull" system while MRP allows a "push" system on the shop floor
- JIT emphasises physical operations, while MRP is largely an information system
- JIT allows the actual process (using Kanbans) to control work, while MRP uses predefined schedules
- JIT puts overall control of the process on the shop floor, while MRP gives control to managers who maintain schedules
- JIT works with a minimum amount of data records, while MRP tries to capture all possible data
- JIT reduces the amount of clerical effort, while MRP increases it
- JIT requires a constant rate of production, while MRP can work with varying production
- JIT makes a priority of reducing set-up cost, while MRP considers these to be fixed

- JIT can be easily understood by everyone using it, while MRP is more difficult to understand
- MRP uses order quantity calculations to determine batch sizes, while JIT does not
- MRP typically carries some days' stock of materials, while JIT typically carries some hours' stock

It is fair to say that we have described three fundamentally different approaches to inventory control:

- quantitative models used in independent demand systems
- materials requirements planning
- just-in-time systems

Although there are similarities between the three, there are important differences. The choice of best in any particular circumstances must be a decision for management (see Table 8.3). Clearly the most important factor is that independent demand systems are widely applicable, while both MRP and JIT systems can only be used in specific circumstances. In particular, MRP is most frequently used in batch production, while JIT is used in the continuous production of high-volume manufacturing. When used for other purposes these approaches can be very inefficient.

Table 8.3

Approach	Typical use
Independent demand systems	
deterministic models	finished goods, etc. where there is little uncertainty
probabilistic models	finished goods, etc. where there is some uncertainty
Dependent demand systems	
material requirements planning	raw materials for batch production
just-in-time	raw materials and work in progress for high-volume production

In Summary

Although they have some points in common, independent demand systems, MRP and JIT are essentially different approaches to inventory control. The choice of best depends on specific circumstances, particularly the type of process being used.

SELF-ASSESSMENT QUESTIONS

8.15 JIT systems eliminate stocks of work in progress. Is this statement true or false?

8.16 Would it be a good idea to introduce JIT in part of a process to see how it works?

8.17 What are the two most important factors in choosing the best inventory control system to use?

SUMMARY OF CHAPTER

This chapter has described some aspects of just-in-time systems. These organise the operations of an organisation so that they occur just as they are needed. In particular, the chapter:

- described how just-in-time systems developed in Japan as a way of eliminating waste
- discussed the view of JIT systems that stocks are a waste of resources which should be eliminated
- discussed the requirements in an organisation before JIT can be used
- described some key elements of JIT systems
- described Kanban systems for controlling JIT
- outlined the role of suppliers in JIT
- discussed the need for total quality and quality at source programmes
- listed the benefits and disadvantages of JIT systems
- outlined the similarities and differences between inventory control systems

ADDITIONAL PROBLEMS

8.1 The output from an assembly line is 1600 units in an eight-hour shift. The item is moved in containers, each of which holds 50 units. Each container spends an average of 30 minutes in the production part of a cycle, and 20 minutes in the demand part. How many Kanbans should be used for the item? What is the resulting stock of work in progress? A scheme has been proposed which reduced the time in the demand part of the cycle to 15 minutes. How many Kanbans should be used now? What is the margin of safety in each case?

8.2 Two years ago a company introduced a new quality assurance programme. The costs (in thousands of pounds) over the past four years have been as given in Table 8.4.

Table 8.4

Year	1	2	3	4
Sales	2019	1905	2374	2770
Prevention	15.4	15.7	52.3	57.9
Appraisal	18.6	19.3	89.5	73.6
Internal failure	113.5	121.8	42.6	38.5
External failure	106.3	127.4	45.7	34.6

Has the quality assurance programme been successful?

REFERENCES FOR FURTHER READING

Crosby, P.B. (1979) *Quality is Free*, McGraw-Hill, New York.
Crosby, P.B. (1984) *Quality without Tears*, McGraw-Hill, New York.
Deming, W.E. (1988) *Out of the Crisis*, Cambridge University Press, Cambridge.
Fucini, J. and Fucini, S. (1990) *Working for the Japanese*, Free Press, New York.
Goldratt, E. and Cox, J. (1986) *The Goal*, North River Press, New York.
Hall, R. (1983) *Zero Inventories*, Dow Jones–Irwin, Homewood, IL.
Hall, R. (1987) *Attaining Manufacturing Excellence*, Dow Jones–Irwin, Homewood, IL.
Ishikawa, K. (1985) *What is Total Quality Control? The Japanese Way*, Prentice Hall, Englewood Cliffs, NJ.
Lee, S.M. and Schwendiman, G. (Eds) (1983) *Management by Japanese Systems*, Praeger, New York.
Monden, Y. (1983) *Toyota Production System: Practical Approach to Production Management*, Industrial Engineering and Management Press, Atlanta, GA.
Ohno, T. and Mito, S. (1988) *Just-in-Time for Today and Tomorrow*, Productivity Press, Cambridge.
Schonberger, R.J. (1982) *Japanese Productivity Techniques: Nine Hidden Lessons in Simplicity*, Free Press, New York.
Schonberger, R.J. (1986) *World Class Manufacturing*, Collier Macmillan, London.
Shingo, S. (1985) *A Revolution in Manufacturing*, Productivity Press, Cambridge.
Townsend, P.L. and Gebhardt, J.E. (1986) *Commit to Quality*, John Wiley, New York.

9
PLANNING FOR DEPENDENT DEMAND INVENTORY SYSTEMS

SYNOPSIS

Dependent demand inventory systems use planned production to determine the demand for materials. This is unmistakable in MRP and, although less obvious, is also true of JIT. As the plans directly affect stocks, it is relevant to ask how these plans are made. In this chapter we will look at the planning needed to support a dependent demand inventory system.

Decisions are made at several levels in an organisation.

- Strategic decisions have an effect in the long-term and set the overall direction of an organisation.
- Tactical decisions are medium-term.
- Operational decisions are short-term.

The fundamental issue for an organisation concerns its mission, which describes its overall beliefs and aims. This mission leads to other strategic decisions about the organisation as a whole, and these define the corporate strategy. When the corporate strategy is in place, a series of strategic decisions can be made about different functions within the organisation. One of the key issues here concerns capacity.

The strategic decisions set the scene for lower levels of planning. They are expanded into tactical plans, which we will discuss these in terms of aggregate plans and master schedules. Aggregate planning translates the forecast demand and capacity plans into production schedules for families of products for, typically, each of the next few months. The next stage of planning is to expand aggregate plans into master schedules. These show a timetable for production of individual items, typically by week. Generating and evaluating tactical plans can be difficult and can need several iterations before a satisfactory result is found.

The final step in planning is to use the master schedule to generate short-term schedules. These give detailed plans for individual jobs, equipment and other resources, typically by day. We have already seen how another outcome from the master schedule can be an MRP schedule which is used to generate orders for materials.

The chapter ends with some comments on how plans can be maintained and controlled.

OBJECTIVES

After reading this chapter and completing the exercises you should be able to:

- appreciate the different levels of decision making in an organisation
- discuss an organisation's mission and relate this to corporate strategy
- appreciate capacity planning at different levels
- describe the planning process in terms of capacity plans, aggregate plan, master schedule and short-term schedules
- appreciate the purpose of aggregate planning
- outline methods for designing aggregate plans
- understand the role of master schedules and how they are designed
- understand the role of short-term plans and how they are designed
- discuss the control of schedules

9.1   HIERARCHY OF DECISIONS IN ORGANISATIONS

Dependent demand inventory systems use planned production to determine the demand for materials. This is seen most clearly in material requirements planning, where demand is found directly from a master schedule. With just-in-time systems the link is less clear, but stocks of materials are still linked directly to production plans, via the control system. In this chapter we will see how the production plans are designed.

Some decisions are very important to an organisation, with consequences felt for many years in the future; others are minor, with consequences felt over days or even hours. A standard classification reflects this importance by describing decisions as strategic, tactical or operational.

- Strategic decisions are made by senior management; they are long-term, use many resources and involve high risk.
- Tactical decisions are made by middle management; they are medium-term, use fewer resources and involve less risk.
- Operational decisions are made by junior or supervisory management; they are short-term, use few resources and involve low risk.

A decision by a manufacturer to build a new factory three or four years in the future is strategic; a decision to introduce a new product next year is tactical; a decision about the number of units to make tomorrow is operational. It is difficult to be specific about the timescale or costs of each type of decision as this depends on the organisation in which it is made. In electricity generation, for example, a strategic decision might concern the building of new power stations, look twenty years or more into the future and involve the expenditure of hundreds of millions of pounds. A strategic decision for a small restaurant might look one or two years into the future and involve expenditure of a few thousand pounds. The important point is that all organisations make decisions at different levels (see Figure 9.1).

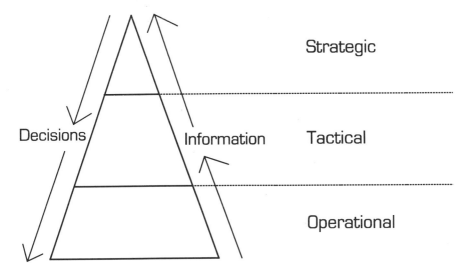

Figure 9.1 Levels of decision making in an organisation

The strategic decisions made by senior managers set an organisation on its course. They are the beginning of a planning process which filters down through the entire organisation. In essence, strategic decisions provide the environment in which lower-level decisions are made; they are passed down to middle management and provide the constraints and objectives for more detailed tactical decisions. These tactical decisions, in turn, are passed down to provide the constraints and objectives for the very detailed operational decisions made by junior managers.

All decisions should be based on accurate information. This means that the dominant flows in an organisation are decisions passing downwards through the management hierarchy, and information about actual performance passing upwards. This exchange of information and decisions should allow consistent and achievable objectives to be set for each part of the organisation.

Decisions specifically about stock occur at all levels. A strategic issue, for example, would be the choice between building warehouses for finished goods, or shipping direct to customers from production facilities. A tactical issue would be planned investment in stock during the next few months. An operational decision would say how much of an item to order this week.

In Summary

Decisions within an organisation occur at different levels. Strategic decisions are made by senior management, involve more resources, more risk and long time scale. They set the objectives and constraints for lower-level tactical and operational decisions.

SELF-ASSESSMENT QUESTIONS

9.1 What are the different levels of decision made in an organisation?
9.2 How are the objectives and constraints set for tactical decisions?

9.2 STRATEGIC DECISIONS

9.2.1 Corporate Strategy and the Mission

Most organisations have some overriding statement of their purpose which, either explicitly or implicitly, defines their overall mission. Thus, a manufacturer might define its mission as "making high quality products for a wide market, while ensuring a satisfactory profit"; a university might define its mission around "education, research and training". These statements say something about the fundamental beliefs and aims of an organisation, and look for answers to questions like, "What is our purpose?", "What business are we in?" and "What are our overall objectives?".

The mission sets the context for all other decisions within an organisation. Once it is defined, a series of other strategic decisions can be made about the organisation as a whole. These include questions about:

- the structure of the organisation
- geographical area of operation
- relations with other organisations
- how it treats customers
- level of technology used
- financial objectives
- marketing objectives
- competitive strategy
- and so on

The competitive strategy is particularly important as it searches for a favourable position in the industry. Such favourable positions can be found by cost leadership (providing the same products cheaper) or product differentiation (providing different products).

When taken together, these strategic decisions affecting the whole organisation form the "corporate strategy". This sets the overall direction in which an organisation will move for some years in the future.

In Summary

The mission of an organisation defines its fundamental views and aims. This sets the context in which other strategic decisions are made. The set of strategic decisions which affect the whole organisation form the corporate strategy.

9.2.2   Capacity Planning

One decision which is usually part of the corporate strategy concerns overall capacity. Capacity measures the maximum amount which can be produced in a given period. The capacity of a restaurant, for example, might be 500 meals a day, while the capacity of an oil well is 20 000 barrels a week. All production must be sold to customers, so the capacity should be designed to match long-term forecasts of demand. This match between capacity and demand should be as close as possible.

- If there is spare capacity, resources are not being used as efficiently as possible. The excess capacity might be reduced by closing facilities, laying off staff, cutting the number of shifts worked, selling equipment, and so on.
- Conversely, if there is a shortage of capacity, some demand is not being met. Then capacity might be increased by building more facilities, recruiting more staff, changing the process to use higher technology, increasing capital investment, and so on.

Capacity planning aims to overcome any mismatch between supply and demand, so the stages involved are:

Stages in capacity planning
(1) Examine long-term forecast demand and translate this into a capacity requirement.
(2) Find the capacity available in present facilities.
(3) Identify mismatches between the capacity requirement and projected availability.
(4) Generate alternative plans for overcoming any mismatch.
(5) Evaluate alternative plans and select the best.

Capacity planning is primarily a strategic function. The main determinants of capacity (such as building size and process used) need strategic decisions.

However, when these strategic decisions have been made there is scope for short-term adjustments. This might involve rescheduling maintenance periods, working overtime, using subcontractors, using an appointment system, and so on. The capacity of a manufacturing process, for example, might be increased by building another factory (a strategic decision). While this factory is being built, capacity might be increased by leasing additional space (a tactical decision). While the leased space is being prepared, overtime may be worked at week-ends (an operational decision).

Worked Example 9.1

Long-term demand forecasts for an item suggest 1000 units a week could be sold. Current facilities have only enough capacity to supply 800 units of the item a week. Overtime might be worked, with fixed costs of £1000 a week and variable cost of £10 a unit. Alternatively, a subcontractor can be used to supply the item with a unit cost of £18. Present facilities might also be extended, and then each unit could be made for £13. Unfortunately, the extension will take a year to install. What is the best policy for the item?

Solution

Following the procedure described above, we have:

(1) Capacity requirement = 1000 units a week.
(2) Capacity available = 800 units a week.
(3) Mismatch = shortage of 200 units a week.
(4) The alternatives for overcoming this mismatch are working overtime, using a subcontractor or extending facilities.
(5) These alternatives have costs of:
   - work overtime: $1000 + 200 * 10 = £3000$ a week
   - use a subcontractor: $200 * 18 = £3600$ a week
   - extend facilities: $200 * 13 = £2600$ a week

The best choice is to extend facilities, provided the item can be sold for more than £13 a unit. As this extension will take a year to complete, overtime should be worked until it is available, provided the item can be sold for more than $3000/200 = £15$ a unit.

In practice, the generation and evaluation of alternative plans is quite complicated. There is usually a range of competing objectives, non-quantifiable factors, soft constraints, and many other complications. A more realistic view of planning would replace the single procedure described by an iterative one which keeps modifying proposed plans until a satisfactory result is found. This procedure is illustrated in Figure 9.2. The diagram also shows that the planning process does not end, but is

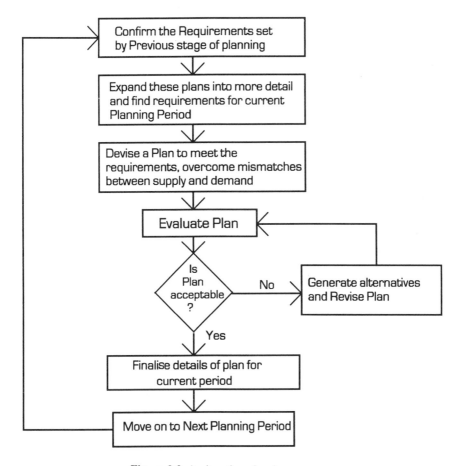

Figure 9.2 An iterative planning process

continuous. As plans for each period are finalised and implemented, planning starts for the next period.

Although we have described this process in terms of capacity planning, it is more general than this. The approach of devising a plan, evaluating it and then making modifications to find improvements, forms the basis of most planning. Evaluation takes into account a number of factors, particularly the constraints and objectives supplied by the previous stage in planning.

In Summary

Capacity planning is an important area for decision making. It is essentially a strategic function, but there are tactical and operational aspects. A general planning procedure finds the mismatch between supply and demand, devises plans to overcome this, evaluates these plans and selects the best. In practice, this usually requires an iterative procedure.

SELF-ASSESSMENT QUESTIONS

9.3 What is the difference between an organisation's mission and its corporate strategy?

9.4 Capacity planning is a purely strategic function. Is this statement true or false?

9.3 TACTICAL DECISIONS

9.3.1 Introduction

When strategic capacity plans have been made, the next stage in planning is to expand them into tactical and operational plans. Unfortunately, there is some disagreement about the terms used to describe the various stages in this hierarchy of plans. We will describe the distinct steps as follows.

- *Aggregate plans*, which show the overall production planned for families of products, typically by month.
- *Master schedules*, which show a detailed timetable of production for individual products, typically by week.
- *Short-term schedules*, which show the detailed timetable of resources and jobs, typically by day.

The first two of these are tactical, while the third is operational. With these definitions, we can describe the sequence of decisions in a manufacturing context as follows (see Figure 9.3).

- An organisation's mission gives an overall statement of beliefs.
- This mission is translated into overall strategic decisions about what to make, where to make it, how to make it, and so on. These define the corporate strategy.
- Part of corporate strategy includes a major decision about capacity plans which match available capacity to long-term forecast demand. Typically, capacity plans set the overall output of each facility by year.
- Capacity plans are expanded into medium-term aggregate plans which, typically, show monthly production of families of products in each facility over the next year or so.
- The aggregate plan is expanded to give the master schedule, which shows a timetable for production of individual products by week.
- The master schedule is expanded to give short-term schedules which show daily timetables for machines, operators and other equipment assigned to each product.

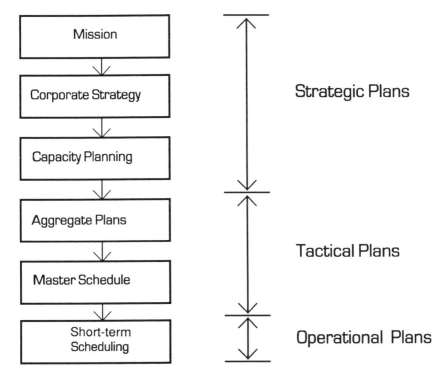

Figure 9.3 Hierarchy of plans

In Summary

Capacity plans are expanded to allow tactical decisions. These can be described in terms of aggregate plans (showing monthly production of families of products) and master schedules (showing weekly production of each product).

9.3.2 Aggregate Planning

Aggregate plans and master schedules bridge the gap between long-term strategic plans and operational details. These tactical decisions start with aggregate planning, which takes the results from capacity plans and adds more details. This typically gives a set of production plans for each family of products, for each of the next few months. Aggregate plans are only concerned with families of products and do not look at individual items. A furniture manufacturer, for example, may produce many different types, styles and sizes of tables and chairs. The aggregate plan will only show the total production of tables and the total production of chairs.

Important questions in the design of aggregate plans include:

- Should production be kept at a constant level or change with demand?
- Should stocks be used to meet changing demand (producing for stock during periods of low demand and using stocks during periods of high demand)?

- Should subcontractors be used for peak demands?
- Should the size of the workforce change with demand?
- How can work patterns be changed to meet changing demand?
- Should prices be changed?
- Are shortages allowed (perhaps with late delivery or back orders)?
- Can demand be smoothed?

One of the key questions here concerns the amount of variation allowed in the aggregate plan. We have seen that JIT systems insist on completely stable production. This has distinct advantages, including:

- planning is easier
- flow of products is smoother
- there are fewer problems with changes
- experience with a product reduces problems
- throughput can be faster
- quality is more reliable
- and so on

A reasonable objective of aggregate planning, then, is to devise medium-term schedules for families of products which:

- allow all demands to be met
- keep production stable
- keep within the constraints of the capacity plan
- meet any other specific objectives and constraints

In Summary

Aggregate planning expands strategic plans into medium-term schedules for families of products. These schedules allow demand to be met with available capacity, while maintaining stable production and satisfying any other specific constraints and objectives.

9.3.3 Role of Stocks in Aggregate Plans

There are four ways in which organisations can deal with varying demand:

- adjust the supply (by working overtime, etc.)
- adjust the demand (by changing prices, using incentives, etc.)
- altering the lead time offered to customers
- use stocks of finished goods

Changing the supply can be disruptive and, as we suggested above, is often not desirable. Changing the demand may be difficult, especially in the short term.

Competition will usually limit the ability to make customers wait for deliveries. This means that the most frequently used option for dealing with variable demand is to use stocks of finished goods.

Stocks have an important role in aggregate planning. Most importantly, stocks of finished goods provide a buffer, so that production during a period need not exactly match forecast demand in the period. Then demand in a period can be met from three internal sources:

- stocks already held at the beginning of the period
- production during the period
- future production with late delivery

If we define $S(T)$ as the stock level at the end of period T, $P(T)$ as the production in period T and $D(T)$ as the demand. Then:

$$\begin{array}{ll} \text{stock at end} & \text{stock at} & \text{production} & \text{demand met} \\ \text{of this} & = \text{end of last} + & \text{during} & - & \text{during} \\ \text{period} & \text{period} & \text{this period} & \text{this period} \end{array}$$

$$S(T) = S(T-1) + P(T) - D(T)$$

This assumes there are no back-orders; but these can be added to give:

$$S(T) = S(T-1) + P(T) - D(T) - B(T-1) + B(T)$$

where $B(T)$ is the number of units back-ordered in period T which are met from production in period $T + 1$.

When aggregate plans are designed for a particular period they must, therefore, not just calculate planned production, but must also take into account existing stock levels, possible back-orders, and a number of other features. The mix adopted should minimise overall costs, maximise overall profit, or optimise some other measure of performance.

Worked Example 9.2

Demand for a product over the next seven months has been forecast as follows.

Month:	1	2	3	4	5	6	7
Demand:	30	50	50	60	80	80	50

A minimum of 20 units are kept in stock, and no back-orders are permitted. There are currently 70 units in stock and production is in batches of 100, with a very short lead time. Devise a production plan which satisfies the demand.

Solution

Average monthly demand is 57 units, but production must be in batches of 100 units. This means that production must be somewhat lumpy, and that stocks are used to cover this variation. Ideally, ways of reducing the batch size would be found so that supply could be matched more closely to demand.

There must be at least 20 units left in stock, so a batch of 100 is made whenever stock at the beginning of a month minus demand in the month gives a closing stock of less than 20 units.

At the beginning of the first month there are 70 units in stock and demand during the month is 30 units. Thus no production is needed and the stock at the end of the month is 70 − 30 = 40 units. This stock of 40 is available at the beginning of the next month, when demand is 50. A batch of 100 units must be made to meet this, and stock at the end of the month is 40 + 100 − 50 = 90 units.

Continuing this procedure for subsequent months gives the results shown in Table 9.1. The production plan shown is only one alternative. Many others are possible, and they should each be evaluated before a final choice is made.

Table 9.1

Month	1	2	3	4	5	6	7	8
Opening stock	70	40	90	40	80	100	20	70
demand	30	50	50	60	80	80	50	
Production	0	100	0	100	100	0	100	
closing stock	40	90	40	80	100	20	70	

The procedure illustrated in Worked Example 9.2 has obvious similarities with material requirements planning. Then, in the same way that MRP is extended to MRP II, we can use this procedure for planning other resources. If, for example, we replace stock levels by employees we can start manpower planning.

$$\begin{array}{c} \text{number} \\ \text{employed} \\ \text{in current} \\ \text{month} \end{array} = \begin{array}{c} \text{number} \\ \text{employed} \\ \text{last} \\ \text{month} \end{array} - \begin{array}{c} \text{dismissals and} \\ \text{resignations} \\ \text{at end of last} \\ \text{month} \end{array} + \begin{array}{c} \text{new hires} \\ \text{at beginning} \\ \text{of current} \\ \text{month} \end{array}$$

Similarly we could find the availability of any other resource in a particular period.

In Summary

Production during a period need not exactly match demand. Stocks of finished goods can be used as a buffer which allows stable production despite varying demand. This approach can be extended to other resources.

SELF-ASSESSMENT QUESTIONS

9.5 Aggregate plans give schedules of production for each item. Is this statement true or false?

9.6 What period is used in a typical aggregate plan?

9.7 What are the main inputs for aggregate planning?

9.8 What is the main output from aggregate planning?

9.9 The only way of keeping production stable when demand varies is to keep stocks of finished goods. Is this statement:
(a) true?
(b) false?
(c) partly true?

9.3.4 Methods of Aggregate Planning

The plan designed in Worked Example 9.2 was found intuitively. By looking at the constraints and objectives a reasonable plan can usually can be found, particularly by a skilled planner using tools like computer spreadsheets. Intuitive methods are the most widely used, but there are more formal alternatives, including graphical methods and mathematical programming.

Intuitive Methods

Aggregate plans are not usually designed from scratch, but will be variations on previous plans; next month's production will probably be similar to last month's. The simplest approach to aggregate planning, then, is to use an experienced planner to review the current situation and, in the light of experiences with similar plans, produce updated ones.

Unfortunately, intuitive methods can give results which are of variable and uncertain quality; they may take a long time to produce, may include bias, and so on. The benefits of the approach are that it is convenient and easy to use, the process is well understood, and planners give credible results which are trusted by the organisation.

Graphical Methods

The most popular graphical approach to aggregate planning is based on a graph of cumulative demand over time (see Figure 9.4). Then an aggregate plan is drawn as a line of cumulative supply. The objective is to get the cumulative supply line nearly straight (implying constant production) and as close as possible to the cumulative demand line. The difference between the two lines shows the level of mismatch:

- if at any point the cumulative demand line is below the cumulative supply line, there has been excess production which is accumulated as stock

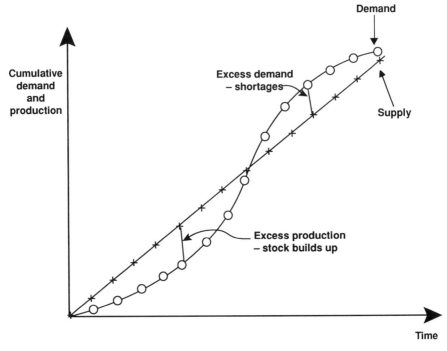

Figure 9.4 Graphical method of aggregate planning

- if the cumulative demand line is above the cumulative supply line there has been insufficient production and some demand has not been met

Graphical approaches have the advantage that they are easy to use and understand. Conversely, their limitations are that optimal solutions are not guaranteed, sometimes very poor solutions are found, and the planning may take some time.

Mathematical Programming

Both intuitive and graphical methods rely, at least to some extent, on the skills of a planner. This is usually reasonable, as planning is a complex process which involves many subjective factors. Nonetheless, a more formal approach sometimes gives better results. A suitable mathematical model of the process could increase the quality and reliability of the plans, but would also reduce the subjective input. Several mathematical models have been proposed, usually based on linear programming. We can illustrate this approach by the following example.

Worked Example 9.3

The most important factors for a company's aggregate plan are inventory levels, changes in production rate and availability of operators. There are costs for:

- supplying a unit of product
- holding stocks
- every unit of unmet demand
- amount of overtime used
- amount of undertime used (i.e. normal working time which is not used)
- increasing production rate
- decreasing production rate

The objective is to minimise total costs. Formulate this problem as a linear programme.

Solution

We can start by defining the costs involved. Let:

VC = variable cost of supplying a unit
HC = cost of holding a unit of stock for a unit time
LC = cost per unit of unmet and (therefore lost) demand
OC = additional cost per unit made with overtime
UC = cost per unit of undertime
CI = cost of increasing the production rate
CR = cost of reducing the production rate

There are two other constants:

DT = demand in period T
NCT = normal capacity in period T

Then we can define the variables:

$P(T)$ = production in period T
$SH(T)$ = stock held at the end of period T
$UD(T)$ = unmet demand in period T
$OT(T)$ = units produced on overtime in period T
$UT(T)$ = units of undertime in period T
$IP(T)$ = increase in production rate during period T
$RP(T)$ = reduction in production rate during period T

The objective is to minimise total cost:

$$\text{Minimise} \sum_{T} [VC * P(T) + HC * SH(T) + LC * UD(T) + OC * OT(T)$$

$$+ UC * UT(T) + CI * IP(T) + CR * RP(T)]$$

This is subject to a number of constraints which hold for each time period. Supply and demand must be balanced:

$$SH(T) = SH(T-1) + P(T) - D(T) + UD(T)$$

Deviation from normal capacity is either overtime or undertime:

$$P(T) - NC(T) = OT(T) - UT(T)$$

Changes in production rates balance production in each period:

$$P(T) - P(T-1) = IP(T) - RP(T)$$

Techniques like linear programming have the advantage of finding an optimal solution, in that total costs will be minimised or some other objective achieved. They also have the disadvantages of being complex, being expensive, not being easy to understand, needing a lot of reliable data, being time-consuming, and needing appropriate expertise, and the mathematical formulations may not describe accurately the real situation.

This means that the use of mathematical programming for aggregate planning is limited to problems where a small deviation from an optimal solution may increase costs considerably. Intuitive and graphical methods can be done quickly and cheaply, but their results are less reliable. The choice of best approach depends on the balance between the costs and benefits of more sophisticated methods. In oil companies, for example, small deviations from optimal plans give much higher costs, so aggregate planning is almost always done by linear programming. In most other organisations slight deviations from optimal plans add comparatively little extra cost and aggregate planning uses graphical or intuitive methods.

In Summary

There are several methods of designing aggregate plans. These range from informal intuitive methods to formal mathematical programming. The choice of the best method depends on the balance between the expected benefit and costs.

SELF-ASSESSMENT QUESTIONS

9.10 What are the benefits of intuitive methods of aggregate planning?

9.11 When using a graphical method for aggregate planning, what does it mean when the cumulative supply line is above the cumulative demand line?

9.12 What is the main benefit of using mathematical programming for aggregate planning?

9.13 When should mathematical programming be used for aggregate planning?

9.3.5   Producing a Master Schedule

The aggregate plan shows overall production by families of products. Once this plan has been finalised it is expanded into a master schedule. The master schedule "disaggregates" the aggregate plan and specifies the number of individual products to be made in, typically, each week. An aggregate plan may, for example, show 1000 motors being made next month, while the master schedule shows 100 outboard motors and 150 electric motors in week 1, 50 outboard motors and 200 electric motors in week 2, and so on. This is the first time that due dates are associated with individual products.

The constraints and objectives for the master schedule come from aggregate plans. In particular, the overall production in the master schedule must equal the production specified in the aggregate plan. There may, however, be some small differences to allow for short-term variations, incorrect forecasts, capacity constraints, changes in stock, and so on. Then, the overall objective of the master schedule is to devise a detailed timetable for individual products which allows the aggregate plan to be achieved as efficiently as possible.

The design of a master schedule starts by taking demand in a period as the larger of:

- production specified by the aggregate plan
- actual customer orders booked for the period

We know that forecasts are not totally accurate, so this gives the first opportunity to compare actual customer orders with forecast demand.

Some of this demand can be met from stock, so current stocks levels and production capacities are compared and a schedule designed to make up any differences. As suggested above, an iterative approach to planning is usually used. This is illustrated for a master schedule in Figure 9.5.

A variety of inputs may affect the master schedule, including promised delivery times, resources available, shortages, costs, raw materials available, and so on. A schedule is designed, assessed and iteratively improved until all requirements are satisfied. If this proves impossible and a feasible schedule cannot be found, either the aggregate plan or the availability of some resources must be changed.

In principle, the design of a master schedule is very similar to the design of an aggregate plan. It is essentially a matter of balancing supply and demand while keeping within known constraints. In some ways, however, the master schedule is more difficult as it deals with more detail, often down to individual customer orders. This usually means that master schedules are designed by intuitive methods based largely on the skills of experienced schedulers. This approach can generally give good results, particularly with a computer spreadsheet to calculate the consequences of a plan.

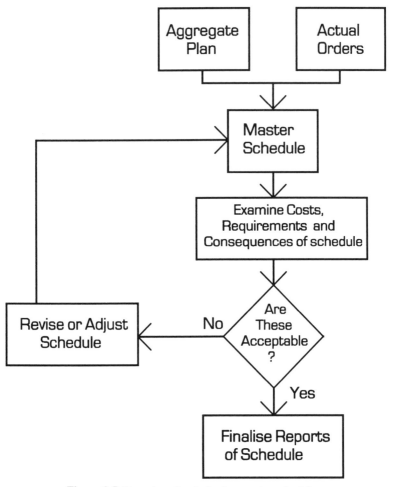

Figure 9.5 Procedure for designing master schedule

Worked Example 9.4

The aggregate plan for a factory specifies production of 2400 units and 2000 units respectively in the next two months. A master schedule is needed for two products, A and B. Current stocks are 140 units of A and 100 units of B, and the factory has a capacity of 600 units a week. Sales of A are usually twice as large as sales of B, and actual orders have been received for deliveries as shown in Table 9.2.

Table 9.2

Week	1	2	3	4	5	6
A	510	360	340	220	160	—
B	270	210	150	80	40	—

Design a master schedule for the next eight weeks.

Solution

The aggregate plan allows for a production of 2400 units in the first month, and the maximum capacity is 600 units a week. An obvious policy then is to aim for production of 600 units a week, two-thirds of which should be A. During the second month the aggregate plan calls for 2000 units, so an obvious policy is to make 500 units a week, two-thirds of which should again be A.

Then we can use the following approach to set the details of the plan:

- firstly meet all known orders
- then assign two-thirds of spare production to making product A and one-third to making product B

There are already orders of 780 units in week 1, so the first priority is to meet these. 140 units of A and 100 units of B can be met from stock, and the remaining orders (540) are met from production. This leaves 60 units of free production which is divided into 40 units of A and 20 units of B.

In week 2 the demand for 360 units of A and 210 units of B is met partly from stock (60 units) and partly from production (510 units). This leaves 90 units of free production which is divided into 60 units of A and 30 units of B.

Repeating this procedure for every period gives the results shown in Table 9.3.

The build-up of stock in later weeks shows that this production has not yet been allocated to customers and reflects stock levels if no more orders are received.

This is, of course, only one of many feasible solutions. It has the advantages of meeting the aggregate plan and keeping production at a stable level, but iterative improvements could now be made.

In Summary

The master schedule disaggregates the aggregate plan to give a detailed timetable of production for each product in a specified period (usually a week).

Table 9.3

Week	1	2	3	4	5	6	7	8
Product A								
Actual orders	510	360	340	220	160	—	—	—
Opening stock	140	40	60	133	333	533	866	1199
Production	410	380	413	420	360	333	333	333
Product B								
Actual orders	270	210	150	80	40	—	—	—
Opening stock	100	20	30	67	167	267	434	601
Production	190	220	187	180	140	167	167	167
Total Production	600	600	600	600	500	500	500	500
Aggregate plan	← - - - - -2400- - - - →				← - - - - -2000- - - - →			

SELF-ASSESSMENT QUESTIONS

9.14 What is the main purpose of a master schedule?

9.15 What constraints are set on a master schedule?

9.4 OPERATIONAL DECISIONS

The master schedule gives a timetable for production of finished items. There are now two further stages which can be done in planning.

- The first is to break this master schedule down into detailed timetables for jobs to be done on individual pieces of equipment. This is the role of short-term scheduling.
- The second is to use the master schedule to plan the arrival of materials, as described in MRP.

In essence, these two aspects of the same process, which is expanding the master schedule, give a detailed timetable of operations.

We have already discussed the approach of MRP, so will now outline an approach to scheduling equipment. This approach assumes production, described in a master schedule, is made in batches on separate pieces of equipment. Producing the timetable for this equipment is often called short-term or job-shop scheduling.

The object of short-term scheduling is to devise a timetable which allows batches of items to move as efficiently as possible through equipment. In this context the measure of efficiency might involve minimising the waiting time, minimising the total processing time, keeping inventories low, reducing the maximum lateness, achieving high utilisation of equipment, or some other specific objective. This kind of problem may seem easy, but in practice is notoriously difficult. Mathematical programming has been the most successful approach, but it can rarely be used for real problems of any size or complexity. Despite considerable efforts, the most effective way of designing short-term schedules is to use simple rules. These scheduling rules are heuristic procedures which have been found, through experience, to give generally good results.

Suppose a number of batches are waiting to be processed on a single machine, and the set-up time for each batch is fixed regardless of the batch which was processed before it. The total time for processing all batches cannot be changed, regardless of the order in which jobs are taken. Different schedules can, however, affect other measures, such as the average waiting time or the average number of batches waiting to be processed. Different scheduling rules could, therefore, be used to give schedules which achieve specified objectives. Some common rules are as follows.

(1) First-come-first-served. This is the most obvious scheduling rule and simply schedules batches in the order they arrive to be processed. It assumes no priority, no urgency, or any other measure of relative importance. The benefits of this rule are simplicity, ease of use and a clear equity. The drawbacks are that urgent or important jobs may be delayed while less urgent or important ones are being processed.

(2) Most urgent first. This rule assigns an importance, or urgency, to each batch and they are processed in order of decreasing urgency. A hospital emergency department, for example, will schedule patients in this order. Similarly, a manufacturer might calculate the times when current stocks of an item will run out and define the most urgent batch as the one which replenishes items which are due to run out first. The benefit of this rule is that more important batches are given higher priority. Unfortunately, those jobs which have low priority may get stuck at the end of a queue for a very long time.

(3) Shortest job first. A useful objective would be to minimise the average time spent in the system, where this time is defined as:

$$\text{time in the system} = \text{processing time} + \text{waiting time}$$

The average time in the system is minimised if batches are taken in order of increasing processing time. This allows any batch which can be done quickly to be processed and moved on through the system, while longer jobs are left until later. The disadvantage of this rule is that long jobs can spend a long time in the system.

(4) Earliest due date first. For this rule the queue of batches is examined and sorted into the order of required delivery date. Those which are expected first are then processed first. This has the benefit of minimising the maximum lateness of batches, but again some batches may have to wait a long time.

(5) Critical ratio. The critical ratio is the time remaining until a batch is needed divided by the time required to complete the batch. If this ratio is low, the time to complete the batch is short compared with the time available and the batch becomes urgent. If the ratio is high, there is plenty of time remaining and the batch is less urgent. This ratio changes as batches progress through the operations so that priority changes depend on progress of other jobs within the system.

This list illustrates a few scheduling rules, but there is a wide range of other rules for achieving different objectives. We could, for example, schedule batches in the order of least work remaining, or fewest operations remaining. We might look at the next process and consider combined times for two or three of these. We could look at the slack (which is the time remaining until the job is due minus the time remaining for processing). Each of these would be useful in particular circumstances, and the choice of best must be a matter of judgement.

Worked Example 9.5

Six batches of items are to be scheduled on a piece of equipment. Each batch replaces parts used in production, and fully occupies the equipment for the durations specified below. If the average demand for products and current stocks are as follows, what schedule would you suggest? Will stocks of any item run out?

Batch:	1	2	3	4	5	6
Duration (days):	9	5	2	4	1	4
Demand:	3	5	13	1	5	25
Current stock:	84	65	260	7	25	225

Solution

If items are made to replenish stocks, it implies there is a different priority for each batch. Then we can schedule batches in the order "most urgent first", where urgency is measured by the number of days of remaining stock (i.e. current stock divided by mean demand).

Batch:	1	2	3	4	5	6
Days' stock remaining:	28	13	20	7	5	9
Order of urgency:	6	4	5	2	1	3

Scheduling batches in order of urgency then gives the results shown in Table 9.4.

Table 9.4

Batch	Days' stock remaining	Duration	Start batch	Finish batch
5	5	1	0	1
4	7	4	1	5
6	9	4	5	9
2	13	5	9	14
3	20	2	14	16
1	28	9	16	25

All batches are finished before the items are due to run out of stock, except for product 2. Stocks of this will run out one day before the batch is finished. The easiest way to avoid this is to arrange for a delivery of part of batch 2 a day early.

In Summary

Short-term scheduling designs detailed timetables for individual equipment and resources. This is a deceptively difficult problem which is usually tackled by simple scheduling rules.

SELF-ASSESSMENT QUESTIONS

9.16 What is the objective of short-term scheduling?
9.17 What is a scheduling rule and why are they used?

9.5   CONTROL OF SCHEDULES

We have now described the scheduling process from mission statement down to short-term scheduling. In this we have moved from an overall statement of an organisation's purpose, to detailed timetables for individual pieces of equipment and resources. The last part of the planning process is to keep these schedules accurate and up-to-date.

The maintenance of schedules is in two parts.

- The first part records the progress of batches and feeds back information. Details of each batch's progress through operations are recorded, with efficiency, productivity, utilisation and other measures reported. This is the procedure when things are working smoothly and there are no problems beyond minor adjustments.
- The second part of maintenance occurs when there is a more serious change or disruption to the schedules. The schedules may then have to be completely revised.

The ability to do this maintenance relies on an effective control system. The inputs to such a system might include inventory records, bills of materials, routing through the machines, orders for batches to be done, due dates, priorities, and so on. The output might include the release of job orders for batches, dispatch of finished batches, scheduled receipts and status reports.

Then the main requirements of a control system can be summarised as:

- to schedule orders and batches in line with agreed plans
- to warn of problems with resources, delivery dates, etc.
- to ensure the materials, equipment and operators are available for each batch
- to assign batches to specific orders and set delivery times
- to check progress as batches move through the process
- to make small adjustments as necessary to plans
- to allow rescheduling if there is a major disruption to plans
- to give feedback on performance

Control systems can become complex and yet need decisions quickly. This is one area where expert systems have been suggested, but progress on their development is still disappointing. The argument for their use says that control systems usually require humans to access many computer files and programs, and then extract information needed to adjust plans. As they base their decisions on simple rules, this could be done by an expert system in a fraction of the time.

In Summary

Once schedules have been designed, there must be some control mechanism for comparing actual performance with plans, and making adjustments as necessary.

SUMMARY OF CHAPTER

This chapter described the planning needed to support a dependent demand inventory system. In particular it:

- described the different levels of decision making in an organisation
- outlined the purpose of an organisation's mission and related this to corporate strategy
- discussed capacity planning as a link between strategic and other levels of plans
- discussed tactical decisions in terms of aggregate planning and master scheduling
- discussed operational decisions in terms of short-term scheduling
- outlined the requirements for controlling plans

ADDITIONAL PROBLEMS

9.1 A coach operator plans its capacity in terms of "coach-days". It classifies its business according to "full day", which are long-distance journeys, or "half day" which are shorter runs. Forecasts show expected annual demands for the next two years to average 275 000 full day passengers and 750 000 half day passengers. The company has 41 coaches, each with an effective capacity of 40 passengers a day for 300 days a year. Breakdowns and other unexpected problems reduce availability to 90%. The company employs 86 drivers who work a nominal 220 days a year, but illness and other absences reduce their availability to 85%. If there is a shortage of coaches the company can buy extra ones for £110 000 or hire them for £100 a day. If there is a shortage of drivers they can recruit extra ones at a total cost of £20 000 a year, or hire them from an agency for £110 a day. How should the company approach its capacity planning?

9.2 The forecast monthly demand for a family of products is shown below. At the end of each month the performance is evaluated, and a notional holding cost of £30 is assigned to every unit held in stock. If there are shortages 20% of orders are lost with a cost of £300 a unit, and the rest are met by back-orders, with a cost of £75 a unit. Each time the production rate is changed it costs £22 500. Designed capacity of the system is 600 units a month, but utilisation seldom reaches 80%. Devise an aggregate plan for the products.

Month:	1	2	3	4	5	6	7	8	9	10
Aggregate demand:	460	420	390	450	540	375	240	150	100	210

9.3 A bicycle manufacturer produces two bicycles, a ladies' and a men's. The aggregate plan has 8000 bicycles to be made next month, and 6400 the month after. Current stocks are 500 men's and 300 ladies', and the factory has a capacity of 2200 bicycles a week. Men's bicycles usually account for 60% of sales, and actual orders have been received for the following deliveries:

Week:	1	2	3	4	5	6
Men's:	1400	1200	1000	700	300	—
Ladies':	2000	800	400	100	—	—

Design a master schedule for the eight weeks.

9.4 Eight batches of items are to be scheduled on a piece of equipment. Each batch fully occupies the equipment for the following number of hours.

Batches:	1	2	3	4	5	6	7	8
Duration (hours):	12	5	4	16	2	10	7	8
Due date (hours):	25	30	14	22	56	23	49	33

Use different rules to find alternative schedules for these batches.

REFERENCES FOR FURTHER READING

Berry, W.L., Vollmann, T.E. and Whybark, D.C. (1979) *Master Production Scheduling: Principles and Practice*, American Production and Inventory Control Society, Falls Church, VA.

Buffa, E.S. and Miller, J.G. (1979) *Production-Inventory Systems: Planning and Control*, (3rd edn), Irwin, Homewood, IL.

Chase, R.B. and Aquilano, N.J. (1989) *Production and Operations Management*, Irwin, Homewood, IL.

Freeland, J. and Landel, R. (1984) *Aggregate Production Planning: Text and Cases*, Reston Publishing, Reston, VA.

Glueck, W.F. and Jauch, L.R. (1984) *Business Policy and Strategic Planning*, McGraw-Hill, New York.

Krajewski, L.J. and Ritzman, L.P. (1990) *Operations Management* (2nd edn), Addison-Wesley, Reading, MA.

McLeavy, D.W. and Seetharama, L.N. (1985) *Production Planning and Inventory Control*, Allyn and Bacon, Boston, MA.

Salvendy, G. (Ed.) (1982) *Handbook of Industrial Engineering*, John Wiley, New York.

Vollman, T.E., Berry, W.L. and Whybark, D.C. (1988) *Manufacturing Planning and Control Systems* (2nd edn), Irwin, Homewood, IL.

APPENDIX I
PROBABILITIES FOR THE NORMAL DISTRIBUTION

Example $Z = \dfrac{X - \mu}{\sigma}$

$P[Z > 2] = 0.0228$

$P[Z > 1] = 0.1587$

Normal Derivative z	.00	.01	.02	.03	.04	.05	.06	.07	.08	.09
0.0	.5000	.4960	.4920	.4880	.4840	.4801	.4761	.4721	.4681	.4641
0.1	.4602	.4562	.4522	.4483	.4443	.4404	.4364	.4325	.4286	.4247
0.2	.4207	.4168	.4129	.4090	.4052	.4013	.3974	.3936	.3897	.3859
0.3	.3821	.3783	.3745	.3707	.3669	.3632	.3594	.3557	.3520	.3483
0.4	.3446	.3409	.3372	.3336	.3300	.3264	.3228	.3192	.3156	.3121
0.5	.3085	.3050	.3015	.2981	.2946	.2912	.2877	.2843	.2810	.2776
0.6	.2743	.2709	.2676	.2643	.2611	.2578	.2546	.2514	.2483	.2451
0.7	.2420	.2389	.2358	.2327	.2296	.2266	.2236	.2206	.2177	.2148
0.8	.2119	.2090	.2061	.2033	.2005	.1977	.1949	.1922	.1894	.1867
0.9	.1841	.1814	.1788	.1762	.1736	.1711	.1685	.1660	.1635	.1611
1.0	.1587	.1562	.1539	.1515	.1492	.1469	.1446	.1423	.1401	.1379
1.1	.1357	.1335	.1314	.1292	.1271	.1251	.1230	.1210	.1190	.1170
1.2	.1151	.1131	.1112	.1093	.1075	.1056	.1038	.1020	.1003	.0985
1.3	.0968	.0951	.0934	.0918	.0901	.0885	.0869	.0853	.0838	.0823
1.4	.0808	.0793	.0778	.0764	.0749	.0735	.0721	.0708	.0694	.0681
1.5	.0668	.0655	.0643	.0630	.0618	.0606	.0594	.0582	.0571	.0559
1.6	.0548	.0537	.0526	.0516	.0505	.0495	.0485	.0475	.0465	.0455
1.7	.0446	.0436	.0427	.0418	.0409	.0401	.0392	.0384	.0375	.0367
1.8	.0359	.0351	.0344	.0336	.0329	.0322	.0314	.0307	.0301	.0294
1.9	.0287	.0281	.0274	.0268	.0262	.0256	.0250	.0244	.0239	.0233
2.0	.0228	.0222	.0217	.0212	.0207	.0202	.0197	.0192	.0188	.0183
2.1	.0179	.0174	.0170	.0166	.0162	.0158	.0154	.0150	.0146	.0143
2.2	.0139	.0136	.0132	.0129	.0125	.0122	.0119	.0116	.0113	.0110
2.3	.0107	.0104	.0102	.0099	.0096	.0094	.0091	.0089	.0087	.0084
2.4	.0082	.0080	.0078	.0075	.0073	.0071	.0069	.0068	.0066	.0064
2.5	.0062	.0060	.0059	.0057	.0055	.0054	.0052	.0051	.0049	.0048
2.6	.0047	.0045	.0044	.0043	.0041	.0040	.0039	.0038	.0037	.0036
2.7	.0035	.0034	.0033	.0032	.0031	.0030	.0029	.0028	.0027	.0026
2.8	.0026	.0025	.0024	.0023	.0023	.0022	.0021	.0021	.0020	.0019
2.9	.0019	.0018	.0018	.0017	.0016	.0016	.0015	.0015	.0014	.0014
3.0	.0013	.0013	.0013	.0012	.0012	.0011	.0011	.0011	.0010	.0010

APPENDIX II
SOLUTIONS TO SELF-ASSESSMENT QUESTIONS

CHAPTER 1

1.1 An inventory is the list of items stored, while stocks are the actual units. (This distinction is becoming less clear.)

1.2 A single copy of *Everyperson's Encyclopaedia*.

1.3 To act as a buffer between variable and uncertain supply and demand.

1.4 There are several possible classifications, but a useful one has: raw materials, work in progress, finished goods, spare parts and consumables.

1.5 To achieve a specified level of customer service at minimum cost.

1.6 Because it has taken advantage of developments in computing.

1.7 What items to stock, when an order should be placed, how much should be ordered.

1.8 Periodic reviews, fixed order quantity and matching demand.

1.9 Because the average stock level is fixed when order quantities and times are set.

1.10 From forecasts based on historic demand.

1.11 Unit, reorder, holding and shortage cost.

1.12 A rough estimate for the value of food in a freezer is £200 and storage costs 25% of this a year. This gives a rough estimate of £1 a week.

1.13 Usually the time taken by the supplier. This can vary and sometimes one of the other delays (particularly delivery) takes most time.

1.14 A high one.

1.15 No.

1.16 False. There are other objectives, particularly related to customer service.

1.17 Because production falls before demand, so extra demand is met by reducing stocks and liquidating companies.

1.18 True.

1.19 Not much. If a company has stocks of 20% of output a rise of interest rate from 10% to 15% increases costs by 1% of output.

CHAPTER 2

2.1 The analysis finds an optimal order size (EOQ) which minimises the cost of holding stocks. This leads to other optimal values such as the cycle length and costs.

2.2   The main assumptions are: a single item is considered; demand is known and is constant and continuous; lead time is zero and replenishment is instantaneous; unit cost, reorder cost and holding cost are all known exactly and are fixed; no shortages are allowed. A number of other assumptions are also implicit in the analysis.

2.3   Unit cost, reorder cost, holding cost and shortage cost (which is not used in the analyses described in this chapter).

2.4   The economic order quantity is the order size which minimises total inventory costs, assuming the assumptions made in the classic analysis are valid.

2.5   (d): either greater than or less than the fixed costs. The variable cost is equal to $RC * D/Q + HC * Q/2$ while the fixed cost is $UC * D$. These are not related and the value of one is nqt affected by the value of the other.

2.6   (c): either increase or reduce total cost. If the assumptions of the classic analysis are valid, the total cost is minimised by placing orders with size equal to the economic order quantity. This might lead to small frequent orders (when holding costs are high) or large infrequent orders (when reorder costs are high).

2.7   (a): at the optimal order quantity the reorder cost component equals the holding cost component.

2.8   No. They mean that the calculated value for Q_0 may not be exactly optimal, but it gives a very good guideline which is useful in many circumstances. The use of EOQ calculations can significantly reduce stock holding costs.

2.9   (a): the economic order quantity defines the point of minimum variable (and hence total) cost per unit time. If orders of any other size are placed the variable cost will rise.

2.10   (b): the variable (and hence total) cost per unit time rises slowly around EOQ.

2.11   The total cost curve rises less steeply for order sizes larger than EOQ so it is generally better to over-estimate values.

2.12   No. Although accurate values will ensure the models give optimal solutions, managers may make a decision to adjust these to suit special circumstances.

2.13   Calculate the optimal value Q_0 and then find the integers Q' and $Q' - 1$ surrounding it. If $Q' * (Q' - 1)$ is less than Q_0^2 it is better to round-up, otherwise it is better to round-down.

2.14   The reorder level defines the amount of stock on hand when another order should be placed. It is equal to the lead time demand minus any previous orders which are still outstanding:

$$\text{reorder level} = \text{lead time demand} - \text{stock on order}$$

2.15   The stock cycle is 3 weeks long, so the lead time is between 2 and 3 stock cycles. When another order is placed there will still be 2 orders outstanding, so:

$$ROL = 7 * 10 - 2 * 30 = 10 \text{ units}$$

2.16   Yes, unless some alternative can be found to send a message that stock level has declined to the reorder level. One such alternative is the two-bin system.

CHAPTER 3

3.1   (e): all costs can vary with order quantity, depending on circumstances.

3.2   (a) 0 to 500; (b) more than 500.

3.3   A calculated economic order quantity which can actually be used (i.e. is on the valid total cost curve).

3.4 There will always be at least one valid minimum, but sometimes there are more (depending on the shape of the curves). All cost curves which do not have a valid minimum must have an invalid one.

3.5 (e): either at a valid minimum or at a cost break.

3.6 (c): at or to the right of the valid minimum.

3.7 (b): at or to the left of the valid minimum.

3.8 Because this analysis would be the same as the classic analysis, but with the saw-tooth stock level pattern reversed.

3.9 Zero. Production is not keeping up with demand and there are no stocks.

3.10 (c): either greater than or less than PT, depending on the relative values taken by variables.

3.11 (b): all things being equal, finite production rates lead to larger batches, lower stock levels and lower holding costs.

3.12 When there are no stocks of the item, but customers are willing to wait until the next delivery.

3.13 An obvious problem is defining a reasonable shortage cost. This is often a matter of subjective evaluation and agreement.

3.14 (c): either more or less expensive, depending on the relative values of costs.

3.15 When there are no remaining stocks of an item and customers are unwilling to wait for back-orders.

3.16 (b): some demand is left unsatisfied, so the amount entering stock (Q) is less than the demand $(D * T)$.

3.17 Any value of Z would be suitable, as costs exactly match gross revenue and the net revenue will always be zero.

3.18 Holding stock always involves costs, so if shortages are allowed the costs may be minimised by not holding any stock at all. A more reasonable approach to problems with shortages is to maximise net revenue.

3.19 The analysis would be identical except the objective would change:

- *from* minimise total cost per unit time $= UC * D + \dfrac{RC * D}{Q} + \dfrac{HC * Q}{2}$

- *to maximise net revenue per unit time* $= SP * D - UC * D - \dfrac{RC * D}{Q} - \dfrac{HC * Q}{2}$

This clearly gives the same results.

3.20 (b): the EOQ is inversely proportional to the square root of holding cost and usually, therefore, to unit cost. Higher unit cost will usually lead to smaller order size.

3.21 Because the extra units have to be stored and this may cost more than potential savings.

3.22 No. There are sometimes interactions in supply and storage which might be important.

3.23 By adding an additional cost for space used. This increases the effective holding cost, reduces the order quantity and hence reduces average stocks.

3.24 (c): the constraint will lower the average stock, and hence the order quantity.

CHAPTER 4

4.1 In any area of supply and demand, but notably in demand, costs, lead time and supplied quantities.

4.2 No. Deterministic models can give very useful results, particularly if the amount of uncertainty is small.

4.3 Variability means values change over time: the changes may be known with certainty or be uncertain. Uncertainty means that values occur at random from a known probability distribution. Ignorance means we do not know anything about the values in a system.

4.4 A model where an item is only held in stock for a single period, and any unsold units are scrapped at the end of the period.

4.5 These models are most useful for highly seasonal goods, such as Christmas fare, Easter eggs, winter clothes, and so on.

4.6 A profit is made on the first Q units, but the $(Q+1)$th unit has an expected cost which reduces the profit.

4.7 Any values may be difficult to find, but shortage costs are the most consistently difficult.

4.8 This is for convenience, and it reflects more accurately the way stores of spare parts operate.

4.9 Because its derivation does not include shortage costs.

4.10 The amount of accurate information needed and the amount of computation to get results.

4.11 An amount of stock which is held in reserve to cover unexpectedly high demand or late deliveries.

4.12 This can be defined in several way. We use "cycle service level" which is the probability there are no shortages in a stock cycle.

4.13 By holding more safety stock.

4.14 If demand is uncertain it may on occasions be very high, and the safety stock needed to cover this would be prohibitively large (in theory infinite).

4.15 Because any uncertainty outside the lead time can be allowed for by the size and timing of the next order. During the lead time, however, it is too late for such adjustments and no allowances can be made for unexpected variations.

4.16 Increase.

4.17 $ROL = LT * D + Z * \sigma * \sqrt{LT}$.

4.18 No. The safety stock depends on the variability of demand and not its absolute value.

4.19 The lead time is made up of several parts, including internal and external administration, transport, and so on. These will usually include some variability and uncertainty.

4.20 Size and variability of lead time demand, and desired service level.

4.21 False. Lead time demand is often Normally distributed, but it may follow any other distribution.

4.22 The best order quantity is generally the economic order quantity.

4.23 By finding the stock on hand and on order and subtracting this from the target stock level.

4.24 (b): (all other things being equal).

4.25 There are several possible reasons, including ease of administration, setting a routine for purchasing, ease of combining orders, and so on.

CHAPTER 5

5.1 All plans and decisions are effective at some point in the future. They need relevant information about prevailing circumstances, and this must be forecast.

5.2 Judgemental, causal and projective forecasting.

5.3 What is to be forecast, is quantitative data available, how far in the future are forecasts needed, what external factors are relevant, how much will the forecast cost, how much will errors cost, how much time is available, and so on.

5.4 Yes.

5.5 When there is no historic data on which to base a quantitative forecast.

5.6 Personal insight, panel consensus, Delphi method, historical analogy and market surveys.

5.7 Unreliability, conflicting views from experts, cost of data collection, lack of available expertise, and so on.

5.8 A series of observations at regular intervals.

5.9 Forecasting methods may identify the underlying pattern in demand, but they cannot deal with short-term, random noise. Errors are introduced by noise, incorrectly identifying the underlying pattern and unexpected changes in the demand.

5.10 Positive and negative errors cancel each other, so the mean error should have a value around zero unless there is bias.

5.11 By using alternative methods for a typical time series and calculating the errors. All other things being equal, the best method is the one with smallest errors.

5.12 Forecasting which looks for the reason for a particular demand. In essence, the value for one variable is forecast by looking at the value given to a related variable.

5.13 It finds the line of best fit (in the least squares sense) through a set of points.

5.14 The proportion of the total sum of squared error which is explained by the regression.

5.15 -1 to $+1$. The coefficient of determination is the square of the coefficient of correlation.

5.16 Because older data tends to swamp more recent (and more relevant) data.

5.17 Forecasts are based on the most recent data, while old data is ignored.

5.18 By using a lower value of N.

5.19 By calculating a moving average with N equal to the cycle length.

5.20 Because the weight given to data declines exponentially with the age of the data, and the method smoothes the effects of noise.

5.21 By using a higher value of α.

5.22 A measure used to monitor a forecast. When its value increases beyond some point, it is a signal that the forecast is performing badly and some remedial action is needed.

5.23 Because it cannot get the correct timing of seasons and lags behind trends.

5.24 t = time period, $F(t + 1)$ = forecast for time $t + 1$, $U(t)$ = smoothed underlying value for t, $T(t)$ = smoothed trend for t, $I(n)$ = smoothed seasonal index for period $t + 1$, which is the nth period of a cycle.

5.25 By using the method described but setting all the seasonal indices to 1.0.

CHAPTER 6

6.1 The procedures which ensure everybody in an organisation gets the information they need to function properly.

6.2 True.

6.3 For important or expensive items, when forecasts are giving large errors, when demand suddenly changes, when there has been no recent demand, and so on.

6.4 The number of transactions to be recorded, calculations to be performed and information to be processed.

6.5 In principle a system could work with current stocks, reorder levels, reorder quantities and goods on order. In practice much more information is needed.

6.6 (c): partly true. The quality of decisions depends on the skills of managers. Nonetheless, if they have insufficient information they cannot make good decisions. There comes a point, however, when enough useful information is presented and any more would be wasted.

6.7 Product, sales, current stock and goods on order.

6.8 The files show the true stock position all the time (with no errors caused by delayed updates).

6.9 There are many of these, including data validation, transaction recording, automatic purchasing, invoice clearing, and so on.

6.10 To all parts of the organisation (including management and computer systems) and to connected organisations (principally suppliers and customers).

6.11 Specific identification, average cost, first-in-first-out (FIFO) and last-in-first-out (LIFO).

6.12 It generally undervalues it.

6.13 Inventory control is often considered to be one of the functions of logistics.

6.14 Facilities location, transport, inventory control, warehousing and associated communications.

6.15 To maximise some measure of efficiency. Typically this might involve minimising movements between item locations and other areas.

6.16 Inventory control is a management function which makes decisions about stock, while warehousing physically stores and moves the stock.

6.17 To organise the supply of materials needed by an organisation.

6.18 Requisition request is received by purchasing, who select the supplier, place an order, monitor the order, receive delivery, add items to stock. Units are removed to meet demand and when stock falls to the reorder level a requisition is sent to purchasing.

6.19 To categorise items and see which ones should be given most attention.

6.20 B items.

6.21 Simulation uses a dynamic representation of a system to reproduce its operation over time.

6.22 Because it allows the effects of proposed changes to be examined quickly and in detail, without affecting the actual performance of the system.

CHAPTER 7

7.1 Independent demand systems forecast demand from historic figures, while dependent demand systems use production plans.

7.2 No. They are widely used, but in some circumstances do not perform as well as dependent demand systems.

7.3 False. MRP was initially developed for manufacturing systems, but it has since been applied in a variety of circumstances.

7.4 By subtracting free stock and scheduled receipts from gross requirements.

7.5 A master schedule, bill of materials, current stocks, lead times and any other relevant information.

7.6 The direct linking of supply to demand reduces stocks and gives a number of related benefits.

7.7 The requirements which limit its applicability, and the amount of data manipulation.

7.8 Timetables of orders, changes to orders, exception reports, performance reports and inventory transactions.

7.9 In principle, yes; but realistically the amount of data manipulation would make a manual system impracticable for any but the simplest products.

7.10 Because of the difficulty of finding reliable forecasts from historic data.

7.11 We know:

$$\text{service level} = 1 - \text{Prob(shortage)}$$
$$= 1 - [\text{Prob(there is a demand)} * \text{Prob(demand} > A)]$$

so: Prob(there is a demand) $*$ Prob(demand $> A$) $= 1 - 0.95 = 0.05$
but: Prob(there is a demand) $= 1/ET(t+1) = 1/5$
so we want: Prob(demand $> A$) $= 0.05/0.2 = 0.25$
From Normal tables this corresponds to $Z = 0.67$, so:

$$A = ED(t+1) + Z * \sigma = 10 + 0.67 * 3 = 12 \text{ units}$$

7.12 False. Larger orders give higher holding costs which may be more than the savings made from lower reorder costs.

7.13 A rule to suggest how many separate orders should be combined into a single larger order.

7.14 Because it uses approximations for the average stock level, assumes demands are discrete and occur at fixed points, assumes costs are fixed, and so on.

7.15 Manufacturing resources planning, which extends the MRP approach to a wide range of functions.

7.16 True. All procedures based on MRP rely heavily on computer systems.

CHAPTER 8

8.1 Traditionally inventory control systems have assumed that stocks are essential and have asked, "How can costs be minimised?". JIT assumes that stocks are not necessary and asks the question "How can the need for stock be removed?".

8.2 (c): partly true. JIT does control stocks, but this is only one of its functions.

8.3 Operations are organised so that they occur just as they are needed (materials are delivered just as they are to be used, and so on).

8.4 They are a waste of resources which should be eliminated; they hide problems which should be tackled and solved.

8.5 High-volume continuous processes, often using automated assembly lines.

8.6 False. Although JIT is not generally suited to small operations or services there are some operations where it may work. Some hamburger restaurants, for example, come close to JIT.

8.7 To control the flow of materials in a JIT system.

8.8 Each container in use has a Kanban, so the number of Kanbans sets the number of containers and hence the amount of work in progress. The size of each container is set as the smallest reasonable batch size.

8.9 They are long-term partners who cooperate and have a mutually beneficial trading arrangement.

8.10 Focused factories specialise in making one item very efficiently. They can use specialised equipment in the long production runs guaranteed by JIT systems.

8.11 Each person in a process is responsible for passing on only units of perfect quality.

8.12 False.

8.13 Prevention, appraisal, internal failure and external failure.

8.14 (c): partly true. JIT certainly encourages automation, but it is more concerned with individual skills than traditional automated processes.

8.15 False. JIT minimises stocks of work in progress but does not eliminate them.

8.16 JIT requires a fundamental change in attitudes, plans, operations and procedures. It is not the sort of thing which can be tried as a small experiment.

8.17 There may be some debate about this, but probably the type of stock being held and the process being used.

CHAPTER 9

9.1 Strategic, tactical and operational.

9.2 By the strategic decisions which provide the context for lower-level decisions.

9.3 The mission is a statement of the overall purpose of an organisation. This sets the framework for the corporate strategy which is the set of strategic decisions concerned with the entire organisation.

9.4   False. It is essentially strategic, but there are also tactical and operational issues.

9.5   False. Aggregate plans only deal with families of products.

9.6   A month.

9.7   Forecast demand, capacity plans, objectives for production plans, constraints on production for the next few months, and any other relevant information.

9.8   A schedule of production for each family of items, typically by month.

9.9   (c): demand and delivery dates can be varied to some extent, but stock must be kept for genuinely variable demand. Some of this may be work in progress rather than finished goods.

9.10   They are convenient and easy to use; the results may be good, and an experienced planner has credibility in the organisation; the process is well understood and trusted.

9.11   There has been excess production and stocks have built up.

9.12   An optimal solution can be found which does not rely on the skill of planners.

9.13   When small deviations from optimal solutions give significant increases in cost or some other penalty.

9.14   To disaggregate the aggregate plan and show a timetable for producing individual items.

9.15   These mainly come from the aggregate plan and include available capacity, actual customer orders, costs and any other specific constraints.

9.16   To produce timetables for individual pieces of equipment and other resources.

9.17   A heuristic rule which experience has found to give good results. They are used because scheduling problems are very difficult to solve by analytical means.

INDEX